Arnold Cohen

An Introduction to

JEWISH CIVIL LAW

FINKELSTEIN
MEMORIAL LIBRARY
SPRING VALLEY, N.Y.

FELDHEIM PUBLISHERS
Jerusalem □ New York

First published 1991
Second corrected edition 2000

Copyright © 1991 by Arnold Cohen

Phototypset at Targum Press

Library of Congress Cataloging-in-Publication Data

Cohen, Arnold J.
  Jewish civil law/Arnold J. Cohen
    p. 344 cm. 22.5
  Includes bibliographical references and index
  ISBN 0-87306-537-9
  1. Jewish law. I. Title.
LAW GENERAL Cohen 1990   90-3729
340.5'8—dc20   CIP

distributed by:
FELDHEIM PUBLISHERS
POB 35002, Jerusalem, Israel 91350
200 Airport Executive Park, Nanuet, N.Y. 10954

www.feldheim.com

Printed in Israel

To the memories of:

Ruthi, Reb Yeshiah Dovid, Rozi,
Reb Shmuel and his father Reb Yaakov,
and Harav Shohel, z"l.

Contents

Preface

SEVERAL YEARS AGO, I was asked to give a series of *shi-urim* to the top class of the Hasmonean High School, London, and, as the series developed, the School considered making Jewish Civil Law a graduation subject. To achieve this end it was necessary to prepare a concatenated textbook, and this is the work now being presented.

I would like to express my thanks to the Headmaster of the School, Rabbi Meir Roberg, and to the Head of Jewish Studies, Rabbi Dr. Leonard Bondi, for the support and encouragement they gave me. This is especially true of Rabbi Bondi, who steadily encouraged me both to continue teaching and to publish my notes in book form.

Therefore, the book itself, as such, was never pre-planned and indeed the lectures themselves changed as a result of topics and queries raised by the students over the years. This will explain why, in a subject as vast as Jewish Civil Law, a limited number of selected topics have been dealt with at length, while others of possibly equal interest and importance have been omitted entirely. Hence, in some instances, cases and examples quoted are not the most classical; they have been chosen not only to prove the point at issue, but also to give the student or reader a wider knowledge of the subject.

Apart from wanting to obey the Rabbinic exhortation, "Whoever reports a saying in the name of its originator brings deliverance to the world" (*Megillah* 15a), I felt it right to quote all my sources for two other reasons: first, to justify any particular statement made, and second, because of the Talmudic observation, "The Sages taught [were included] in the style [words] of the Mishnah; blessed be He who has approved of them and of their teaching" (*Baraita de R. Meir*, treated as the sixth chapter of the *Ethics of the Fathers*). This was interpreted by the Lubliner Rav as meaning that the greatness of the Mishnah lies not only in what was said, but also by whom it was said—hence the inclusion of their names (per R. Yaakov Broner of Bnei Brak).

It is not my intention, nor indeed within my competence, to quote final rulings on any subject, and therefore, normally, matters of disputation have been left open. The views of the Authorities quoted are not necessarily in accordance with the final ruling; they have been quoted merely to illustrate the point being discussed and, even where the Codes are quoted, the intention is merely to illustrate the point. (Only afterwards did I realize how much I had been influenced by the style adopted by Rabbi S. J. Zevin in his classic *Hamo'adim B'halachah*.) In a number of instances I have quoted the *Aruch Hashulchan*, a later compilation than the Codes themselves, not because the ruling differs from that of the Codes, but because it is written in a more modern idiom and, therefore, easier to quote to the contemporary reader. Where the subject is one giving rise to considerable discussion, I have quoted differing Authorities in order to encourage the reader to research the matter further. Indeed, there are many subjects, each of which, in itself, could form the basis of a more significant work than this, and it is my hope that I have given sufficient references to stimulate further study of Torah—the objective of any person privileged to teach it. Instances in which a lesser-known source is quoted in preference to a more familiar one are probably due to my own lack of knowledge.

Following the style of the Talmud itself, detailed treatment is often given to subjects not within the definition of Civil Law. This is done not only to add to the reader's knowledge, but to show the unity, uniqueness and comprehensiveness of the Torah. An example is that of **Chazakah**, dealt with at length in Chapter IV. *Chazakahs* not only affect Jewish Civil Law, but are important judicial tools in every branch of the Torah, and often the guidelines as to how they are to be used in Civil Law are to be found in other sections of the Torah.

The book is entirely in the Latin script without resort to Hebrew lettering purely in order to keep printing costs low; therefore, English translations and transliterations of Hebrew phrases have been used; the translations are mostly taken from the Silverman *Chumash* or the Soncino Talmud. In order to accommodate the novice without offending the more experienced student, I have used the glossary to explain the more common Hebrew terms. When quoting a comparative non-Jewish ruling, I have deliberately referred to books easily obtainable by laymen.

In any work based on the Talmud, it is imperative that the student be aware of the relationship between the various Authorities quoted and their authority relative to each other. Therefore, I felt it necessary to add a short Historical Overview explaining the various periods in the history of the transmission of the Torah, followed by short biographical and bibliographical notes on the Authorities quoted. This Overview is not intended as a detailed history, and therefore, dates are given (whether in accordance with the Jewish or non-Jewish calendar) only to help identify the period concerned. Scholars are mentioned either by name, by acronym or by title of work as they are best known in the world of Talmud study. I found it extremely difficult to list them in clear alphabetical order as I could not bring myself to use a "telephone directory" type of entry when mentioning an illustrious and much respected name. (An example which springs to mind is that of Rabbi Akiva Eger.)

The Index lists subjects actually dealt with, as opposed to those which only receive a passing mention. Often phrases can be translated in different ways and therefore, a particular subject may be mentioned in the Index in a number of places under different headings.

Hopefully the reader will now have some idea as to why and how this book has been written, and it only remains for me to express my thanks to all who have helped in bringing it about. I have already mentioned Rabbis Roberg and Bondi. I must thank my partners in our professional accountancy firm who allowed me the time to give *shiurim* over a period of six or seven years. I would like also to express my gratitude to those who helped with useful suggestions or quotations; normally these are referenced in the footnotes as "per." In particular I would mention two longstanding study partners. First, Mr. Shimon Schapiro, *z"l*, with whom I learned daily for many years, whose love of learning helped me find comfort during difficult times. Unfortunately he died at a relatively early age before this work was completed. Second, Dr. Gordon Weingarten, *sheyibadel lechaim*, with whom I have had a regular *shiur* for nigh on twenty-five years and with whom I hope to be able to continue learning for many more, God willing. Thanks are also due to Mr. Michael Goldman for his many helpful suggestions and amendments to the original manuscript.

It was, of course, my parents—my late father, Mr. Samuel Cohen, *z"l*, together with, *shetibadel lechaim*, my mother, Mrs. Leah (Anne) Cohen—who guided my education to the *battei midrashim* of the yeshivahs and who brought me into contact with my great Rabbis and mentors, among whom I am lucky enough to number Rabbi Shmuel Yosef Rabinov, *z"l*, Rabbi Leb Lopian, *z"l*, and Rabbi Leb Gurwicz, *z"l*, both of Gateshead; and Rabbi Nachman Shlomo Greenspan, *z"l*.

Finally, my thanks to my dear wife Sara for her unfailing

support and encouragement; the enthusiasm she and the children have for Torah is a major stimulus for my learning and writing. (In fact, our son, Yossi, devoted an entire *bein hazemanim* to checking the sources quoted in the footnotes.)

To the readers I must apologize for any mistake which may be found in this volume; as King David pleaded, "Who can discern his errors? Clear me from hidden faults" (Psalm 19, as interpreted by Rabbi S. R. Hirsch).

In closing, I want to offer thanks to the Almighty for the past, and pray to Him for the future; in the words of Rabbi Nechunia ben Hakannah: "I give thanks to Thee, O Lord my God, that Thou has set my portion with those who sit in the *beit hamidrash....*" "May it be Thy will, O Lord, that no offense may occur through me...." (*Berachot* 28b).

Arnold Cohen
London

It took me more than a year after the original preface was written to bring the manuscript to a state that I, at least, considered ready for publication. Only after it was taken over by the publisher, Mr. Yaakov Feldheim, and his colleagues did I realize how much editing was required and how important that editing is. To my editors Rabbi Ben Zion Sobel and Charmaine Ruderman I should like to express my thanks for the many valuable amendments they suggested. These amendments contributed much to the continuity of the text and to the clarity of a number of the more difficult passages. For the benefit of my British friends, I would just add that it was the editors, not I, who introduced the American idioms and spelling where these differ from that of the British!

A.J.C.
Tishrei 5751
October 1990

Abbreviations used in footnotes

a. References to the *Shulchan Aruch* (Codes) are given only by the name of the subdivision (e.g., *Choshen Mishpat*).

b. Rambam, *Mishneh Torah, Yad Hachazakah* is referred to as *Yad*, followed by subdivision (e.g., *Yad, Lulav*).

ad fin: to the end, at the end
ad init: at the beginning
ad loc: on that place
cf: compare with
et seq: and following
ibid: same work mentioned immediately above
infra: below (in this text)
lit: literally
loc. cit: in the place cited
op. cit: in the work cited
supra: above (in this text)
s.v: see under the word
v: see
z"l: may his name be for a blessing

ONE

Jewish Civil Law—
Its Place in the Torah

THE PHRASE "JEWISH LAW" encompasses the laws of the entire Torah—the six hundred and thirteen precepts of the Torah itself, together with the many ordinances and decrees issued by the Halachic Authorities over the generations.

Moshe, the first conduit in the transmission of the Torah, divided it into three major categories: "Now these are the **Commandments**, the **Statutes** and the **Judgments** which the Eternal your God has commanded to teach you...."[1] Each of these headings, often mentioned in the Torah, represents a different type of precept:

Commandments are ordinances of a religious character but understandable within the framework of society. An example of this category would be the Shabbat. A stated reason for the Shabbat is testimony: "It is a sign between me and the Children of Israel forever; for in six days the Eternal made Heaven and Earth, and on the Seventh Day He rested and was refreshed."[2] The detailed laws of Shabbat, its rituals—

---

[1] *Devarim* 6:1
[2] *Shemot* 31:17

even the punishment meted out to the transgressor—all indicate a day of an essentially religious character. But the Law of Israel led the world in understanding that man cannot labor seven days; he must have a day of rest.

Similarly, the Festivals are of a religious nature, but easily understandable in the context of Jewish nationhood. They are: Pesach, recalling and celebrating ancient Israel's rise to national independence; Shavuot, recalling and celebrating Israel's receiving that Code of Law which structured its society and which has proved to be its cohesive element throughout the long centuries of exile and wandering; and Sukkot, recalling Israel's metamorphosis during the forty years in the wilderness—from slavery to Divinely inspired, independent statehood.[3]

Under the heading of **Statutes** come those precepts which to us remain mysteries; those for which we cannot claim to know the underlying reason. The classic example is the *parah adumah* (the red heifer), the medium by which one became purified of *tumah* (Levitical uncleanliness). Indeed, the very concept of *tumah*, especially that caused by death, is itself a mystery. Also in this category is *Sha'atnez*: the prohibition of wearing a garment in which wool and linen are stitched together. All the detailed rules of the *avodah* (the ritual service in the Temple) must by their very nature remain mysterious to us.

And finally there are the **Judgments**, which comprise the civil and criminal laws which every society must enact to protect its members as individuals, and itself as a whole. These involve rules to avoid anarchy, to avoid theft, bloodshed, and oppression of the weak; rules to promote the welfare of the members of that society so far as is mutually beneficial. In short, these are the rules governing the relationship between man and his fellow.

Of all three categories—Commandments, Statutes and Judgments—it would seem that Judgments are the least religious, the least Divinely inspired, the least spiritual.

---

[3] *Meshech Chochmah, Devarim* 5:15.

Our Sages indeed remark upon this.[4] The first verse in the Torah dealing with Judgments, "*And* these are the Judgments which you should put before them,"[5] immediately follows, and is joined by, the conjunctive *ve* (and) to the previous verse, "...you should not ascend stairs to My Altar...."[6] The laws dealing with the mysteries of the Altar and those dealing with civil law are joined; they are one and the same in the Torah—of equal status. Moreover, in the words of the Preacher, "to do Justice and Judgment is more acceptable to the Lord than sacrifice,"[7] and it is this our Sages had in mind in their statement "that every judge who judges truly becomes, so to speak, an associate of the Almighty in the creation of His world."[8]

> The Almighty created the world for the continuity of society, and those wicked ones who steal and rob destroy society by their wickedness. We find that the decree annihilating the Generation of the Flood was only sealed because of theft, "for the earth is full of violence through them; and behold I will destroy them with the earth."[9] From this we can conclude that the judge who breaks the "arrogant arms" of the evil-doers and takes back from them that which they have stolen, returning it to its rightful owner, thus maintains the world and helps realize the wishes of the Creator, who created it so that it should remain in existence; therefore he becomes an associate in the maintenance of Creation.[10]

Indeed our Rabbis taught that the word "judgments" covers those commandments which, had they not been written in Scripture, would by right have been honored as they include laws concerning bloodshed and robbery;[11] precepts which

---

4   Talmud Yerushalmi, *Makkot* 2:6.
5   *Shemot* 21:1.
6   *Shemot* 20:23 et seq.
7   *Mishlei* 21:3.
8   *Shabbat* 10a.
9   *Bereshit* 6:13.
10   *Tur, Choshen Mishpat* 1:2.
11   *Yoma* 67b.

are easily understood as necessary for the continuation and development of civilization and which became obligatory on Man and his descendants, from the beginning of time.

In fact, these civil laws were part of the Torah studied and kept by our Patriarchs well before the Sinaitic revelation,[12] laws transmitted to Noah and his descendants.[13]

In Jewish life, in the Torah, there is no room for "the obvious." Even the simplest commonsense rules are Divinely inspired (they have no need of external reform, having been laid down for posterity[14]), and the closeness of the two subjects Altar and Jurisprudence, indicates that although the rules of justice may seem obvious and matters of common sense, nevertheless, being part of the Torah they also carry the depths and hidden meanings of the Torah in the same measure as do those laws covering, for instance, the ritual of the Temple.[15]

In the first mishnah in the tractate *Avot* (commonly known as *Ethics of the Fathers*), the *Tanna* gives a brief resumé of the way the Torah was handed down.

> Moshe received the Torah at Sinai and handed it on to Yehoshua; Yehoshua to the Elders; the Elders to the Prophets and the Prophets passed on the tradition to the Men of the Great Assembly.

Such a brief history would be more appropriate as an introduction to the whole Mishnayot, and its logical place should be at the opening of the first tractate, yet R. Yehudah Hanasi, the ultimate editor of the Mishnayot, saw fit to place it instead in *Avot*, a tractate found in the middle of the Talmud. R. Ovadiah of Bertinoro explains why R. Yehudah Hanasi took this step.

---

[12] *Yoma* 28b.

[13] R. Nissim Gaon, Introduction to *Berachot*; cf. *Likkutei Sichot*, vol. III, p. 896-900.

[14] *Otzar Chaim, Devarim* 11:32 & 12:1.

[15] Ibid., *Shemot* 21:1, in the name of R. Chaim Sanz.

I say it is because this tractate *Avot* is not based on any of the mitzvot of the Torah, as are other tractates, but is based exclusively on ethics and moral subjects; on these, scholars of other faiths have also written books according to their understanding of the ethical manner in which man is to conduct himself towards his fellow. Therefore, the *Tanna* begins this tractate by stating that Moshe received the Torah at Sinai, to indicate that the morals and ethics contained therein were not thought up by our Sages themselves, but were among the laws given to us by He who revealed Himself at Sinai.[16]

Good examples of what the Bertinoro means are to be found later in the tractate. "R. Shimon b. Elazar said, 'Do not appease your colleague in the hour of his anger, nor comfort him while his dead lie before him. Question him not in the hour of his vow, and strive not to see him in the hour of his disgrace.' "[17]

All these are matters of common sense; part of normal conduct for the well-mannered, yet in fact Divinely inspired *mitzvot* from Sinai, as is the injunction that the Jew should "pray for the welfare of the government of the country in which he resides since, but for the fear of authority, men would swallow each other alive,"[18] which is in fact sound political advice.

At this stage, it is both opportune and prudent to observe that while it may be convenient to divide the Torah into sections, each dealing with a different aspect of the life and faith of the Jew, it is in fact one complete, comprehensive, and monadic entity in which all sections overlap. Any Talmudic scholar can attest that a decision in one section may often inevitably lead to a decision in another; a ratio decidendi in one section must be the ratio decidendi of another. One cannot accept and obey just one section of the Torah only, as in no way does any part stand alone. Attempts to revive

---

[16] *Pirkei Avot* 1:1

[17] Ibid. 4:18 (in the *Siddur* it is mishnah 23).

[18] Ibid. 3:2.

Jewish Civil Law in the twentieth century have failed because the proponents were not prepared also to accept the Commandments and Statutes.[19]

In addition to these categories, the three major divisions of the Torah—Commandments, Statutes, and Judgments—were divided by R. Yehudah Hanasi into six further subdivisions, the six orders of the Mishnah:

(1) **Zera'im** (lit., "Seeds")—the laws of agriculture; inter alia, the laws of tithes and first fruits, the laws of hybridism and of the Sabbatical year.

(2) **Mo'ed** (lit., "Appointed Season")—Shabbat and Jewish Festivals.

(3) **Nashim** (lit., "Women")—the laws of marriage, divorce, and family life.

(4) **Nezikin** (lit., "Damages")—the section with which this book is most concerned—tort, mercantile, and other monetary laws.

(5) **Kodashim** (lit., "Holy Items")—the Temple and sacrificial ritual and laws.

(6) **Taharot** (lit., "Purities"[20])—the laws of Levitical uncleanliness in human beings, buildings, and chattels.

The Talmud[21] compares this division to a verse in *Yeshayahu,*[22] "And there shall be faith in your times, strength, salvation, wisdom, and knowledge; the fear of the Lord is your treasure."

Faith refers to the order of *Zera'im;*[23]

---

[19] V. M. Elon, "*Mishpat Hashalom Ha'Ivri,*" *Israel Law Review* 3 (no. 3) pp. 421-24.

[20] A euphemistic title, as this order deals with unclean items.

[21] *Shabbat* 31a.

[22] 33:6.

[23] "Faith" is applied to this order because agriculture demands faith in the Almighty; a farmer sows and for many months does not see the result of his efforts. He must have faith that in due course there will be a satisfactory crop.

Your times, the order of *Mo'ed;*[24]
Strength, the order of *Nashim;*[25]
Salvation, the order of *Nezikin;*[26]
Wisdom, the order of *Kodashim;*[27]
Knowledge, the order of *Taharot.*[28]

Yet above all these, the Prophet continued, "the fear of the Lord is *your treasure.*"

In fact, in early writings, we find the fourth section referred to not as *Nezikin,* but as the order of *"Yeshuot"* ("Salvation"). This title is not hyperbole, for this order is designed to protect, to bring aid and salvation to the weak and helpless, while at the same time guiding the honest man by stopping him from inadvertently becoming a thief. Indeed the Talmud quotes,[29] "A man used to say, 'Let him who comes from a court that has taken from him his cloak sing his song and go his way' "—he should be happy that he was relieved of an ill-gotten gain. "Said Shmuel to R. Yehudah, 'This is alluded to in the verse [in which Yitro tells Moshe, his son-in-law, that if his advice is adopted and Israel sets up an organized system of jurisprudence] "...then all these people [including

---

[24] "Times" as meaning Shabbat and the Festivals is self-explanatory.

[25] "Strength" refers to the order of *Nashim* dealing with family life, because it is through family life that heirs are created and the strength and continuity of the nation ensured.

[26] "Salvation" is appropriate since, through the order of *Nezikin,* society is saved from anarchy, as individuals are stopped from encroaching on their neighbors' rights or conversely suffering their own to be filched away; cf. Netziv, *Ha'emek Davar,* introduction to *Bereshit.*

[27] The order of *Kodashim* is extremely intricate and has clear but unfamiliar ground rules. The word "wisdom" is therefore applicable. One of the great scholars of the previous generation, Rabbi Yitzchak Ze'ev Soloveitchik, developed a yeshivah in which the emphasis is on the study of this particular section.

[28] Wide knowledge is a prerequisite to the understanding of the order of *Taharot.*

[29] *Sanhedrin* 7a.

the losers] shall come to their place in peace." ' "[30]

So important is this section of the Torah to both the nation's social and spiritual well-being that Rabbi Yehudah could declare,[31] "He who wishes to lead a saintly life, let him become involved in the teachings of [the order of] *Nezikin*." In order to live a saintly life, the Jew does not have to spend all his time in the Temple, nor to cut himself off from his fellowman. Our Sages advise him to study the teachings of the order of *Nezikin* so that he may know how to observe the difference between right and wrong, of **meum** and **teum** (what is mine and what is yours).

The close connection of religion and law is the essence of the Jewish legal system, and the Civil and Criminal Law is regarded by the Jew as an integral part of the Torah. Therefore, grounded in Scripture and centered on God, it is not like other legal systems, rooted in the creation of the State, nor did it ever draw its inspiration from political feeling. For the Jew, the Torah is an independent and positive source of inspiration, regulating individual and corporate action; and on the Torah is to be raised the whole structure of the Jewish legal system. Consequently, morality is a dominant factor in Jewish communal life and the underlying principle in all social and economic legislation. The object of the Jewish legal system is not to preserve a particular dynasty or certain form of government, but to establish social righteousness and to maintain thereby a close, constant, inseparable connection between ethics and law, both flowing from the same source.[32]

By appositioning laws of civil jurisprudence with details of

---

[30] *Shemot* 18:23.

[31] *Bava Kama* 30a.

[32] Soncino Talmud, introduction to *Seder Nezikin*. R. Samson Raphael Hirsch, *Tehillim* 147:20, on the verse, "He told His word to Jacob; His Statutes and Judgments to Israel."

how the Altar is to be built,[33] Scripture also indicates that the ultimate place of justice must be near the Altar; from this, the law is derived that the place of the senior Sanhedrin of the land was to be situated in the Temple Precinct,[34] a site which obviously served to enhance its status. The Talmud[35] quotes R. Yosei:

> Originally, there were not many disputes in Israel because the Beit Din of seventy-one [members] sat in the Hall of Hewed Stone.[36] There were two other Battei Din, each of twenty-three members, one which sat at the entrance to the Temple Mount, and one which sat at the entrance to the courtyard of the Temple. The remainder of the Battei Din of twenty-three members sat in all cities in Israel. If one had a query, he asked of the Beit Din of his town; if they had a tradition [the knowledge] and could answer, they did so, and if not they approached the Beit Din nearest their own town. If that Beit Din had a tradition, it answered; if not, they approached the Beit Din which sat at the gates of the Temple Mount. If they had a tradition, they gave the answer; if not, they approached the Beit Din which sat at the gates of the courtyard of the Temple. The scholar who differed from his colleagues declared, "This is how I have expounded the theme and this is how my colleagues have expounded it; this is how I have taught and this is how they have taught." If that Beit Din had a tradition thereon, they answered; if not, they all proceeded to the Hall of Hewed Stone, where the Great Sanhedrin sat from the early morning sacrifice until the evening sacrifice.[37] On Shabbat

---

[33] V. supra p. 9.

[34] *Sanhedrin* 86b.

[35] Ibid. 88b.

[36] Name given to a large room (one of six), opening off the courtyard of the Temple. V. *Mishnah Middot* 5:3.; *Yoma* 25a.

[37] *Korban Tamid*, morning and evening.

and Yom Tov this Sanhedrin sat in a different place.[38] The
question was put before them. If they had heard the problem and had a tradition, they answered. If not, they stood to
be counted. If the majority voted "unclean," they declared the
subject unclean. If "clean," they declared it clean.

Any member of any Beit Din, any Halachic Authority,
any scholar, however eminent he may have been, who dared
issue a ruling in defiance of the conclusion reached by the
majority of the Great Sanhedrin, was deemed a **zaken mamre**
(a rebellious elder). He became liable to the death penalty,
and it was beyond the powers of his colleagues to pardon
him, as the Talmud explains, "in order not to increase dissent
in Israel." Only dissent against the Great Sanhedrin, sitting in
its place in the Temple Precinct, could cause an elder to be
deemed "rebellious," for, **"the place is the cause"** [39] — the
source of the supreme authority of the Great Sanhedrin. The
fact that it was situated in the Temple, the religious hub of the
nation, imparted to its decisions and powers a weightiness
which they may otherwise have lacked.

The supremacy of the majority of the competent Halachic
Authority and the importance attached to its being obeyed is
clearly illustrated in the incident immortalized in the Talmud
as the dispute over the **oven of Achnai.**[40] R. Eliezer[41] held the

---

[38] For two reasons: Firstly, there was a larger crowd than on a working day: secondly, so as not to appear to be sitting in civil judgment
on the Sabbath (*Rashi*).

[39] *Sanhedrin* 87a.

[40] This refers to a particular type of large oven built up by placing
ceramic tiles one upon the other with a layer of sand between each
level. As no single unit on its own can be considered a utensil susceptible to Levitical uncleanliness, the dispute turns on whether it is looked
upon as a whole, unified by the outer coating of cement which holds
it together and therefore as a whole susceptible (the majority view), or
whether the sand between each layer, which itself is not susceptible,
acts as a divider (Rambam, Commentary on *Mishnah Kelim* 5:10).

[41] b. Hurkanos. Known as R. Eliezer the Great.

view that this oven could not become Levitically unclean, while the majority of his colleagues disagreed with him. The Talmud reports[42] that R. Eliezer put forward many arguments, all of which were rejected. When he realized that he was not being successful in persuading his colleagues to accept his view, R. Eliezer asked for Divine intervention, first by way of miracle and eventually by way of a Heavenly pronouncement which declared, "What have you against R. Eliezer, since the Law is always in accordance with his views?"

Even this was rejected. R. Yehoshua rose and quoted the Scriptural verse, "It is not in Heaven."[43] The Torah had already been given at Mount Sinai, and in that Torah was the injunction, "after many [the majority] to wrest judgment":[44] having received those instructions we have no authority to obey even a Heavenly decree if it is against the majority ruling. Because R. Eliezer was not prepared to submit, his colleagues challenged all his previous rulings and "on that day all objects which he had declared clean were brought [out] and burnt in fire as unclean." Seeing he would still not submit, a vote was taken to excommunicate him. Because of R. Eliezer's eminence, his opponents feared that unless they adopted these draconian measures there would be a schism among scholars which would damage the fragile unity of a nation suffering under the oppression of its Roman conquerors, a nation which had lost its political independence, lost its spiritual center with the destruction of the Temple, and which was left only with the Torah as a cohesive force.

Indeed, to appease any Divine wrath engendered on the day that R. Akiva delivered the decision of the excommunication, the President of the Court declared, "Sovereign of the Universe! You know full well that I have not acted for my own honor nor for that of my father's house, but for Your

---

[42] *Bava Metzia* 59b.

[43] *Devarim* 30:12.

[44] *Shemot* 23:2. V. *Chida, Shem Hagedolim*, s.v. *"Rabbenu Yaakov Hachassid."*

honor so that strife should not multiply in Israel!"[45]

It is because the Torah was given to human beings for their benefit that it depends on human understanding and human reasoning within the guidelines it sets out. Therefore all doubts are to be resolved by the understanding of the majority of competent authorities, albeit, because of the limits of the human intellect, this understanding may not be in accord with the ultimate and absolute truth.[46]

Thus can the Talmud declare:

> It is revealed and known before He who spoke and created the world, that in the generation of R. Meir there was none equal to him: then why was not the Halachah fixed in agreement with his views? Because his colleagues could not fathom the depth of his mind.[47]

This insistence on accepting the majority view has distinguished Jewish Law from other systems. Most systems of law function only where there is authority to enforce that law, normally by the Body Politic, whereas Jewish Law has functioned long after the destruction of the Second Temple, and long after Israel was exiled from its natural homeland, because, although the Torah could not be enforced, it received the recog-

---

[45] Bava Metzia 59b. Eventually R. Eliezer's hurt at being so treated caused the death of the President, who happened to be his brother-in-law. The Talmud reports this story in support of the Mishnaic comment that just as damage can be caused in buying and selling by overcharging or underpaying, so can damage be done by words. Indeed, in the case of monetary damage restoration is possible, but not in the case of verbal hurt (ibid. 58b). For sequel v. *Sanhedrin 68a,* where the death of R. Eliezer b. Hurkanos is reported.

[46] *Derashot HaRan, derashah 7,* s.v. *"veyesh"* in which he explains the Talmudic report *Bava Metzia 86a.* (V. *Malbim, Bemidbar 19:1 & 2* for different treatment of that report). V. *Yad, Tumat Tzora'at 2:9* and *Kesef Mishnah.* Cf. *Shabbat 88b-89a:* disputation between Moshe and the Heavenly Host.

[47] *Eruvin 13b.*

nition of its people. Its influence was so great that they submitted to it, and it was supported by the strong public opinion of those who studied it and were familiar with its message.

The Talmud reports[48] that forty years before the destruction of the Second Temple, the Sanhedrin voluntarily moved from its place in the Temple to meet in a room lower on the Temple Mount, in order to legally abolish capital punishment. At that time anarchy was rife throughout Judea, and the Sanhedrin realized that it would be impossible to punish all wrongdoers according to the letter of the law. Rather than allow the law of the Torah to be broken, it deliberately took a step to suspend that particular law. It was an acceptable step within the framework of the Torah itself, for in connection with capital punishment, the Torah rules, "and you should act according to that which is told to you from that place"[49]— clearly indicating that "the place" is the symbol of authority.[50] This is an example of how the Law can be made to meet changing circumstances using its own internal machinery; to remain relevant to each generation the Torah has no need of external reform—being Divine, it is itself eternal.

The Great Sanhedrin was responsible for the organization of justice throughout the Land. It was that Sanhedrin which appointed judges in each town; it was that Sanhedrin which promoted judges to the Beit Din of the Temple Mount and from there to the Beit Din in the courtyard of the Temple, and from there to membership of its own ranks.[51]

The standard of impartiality demanded of judges was rigorous, a standard set by Moshe himself, the first judge of the newly

---

[48] *Avodah Zarah* 8b.

[49] *Devarim* 17:10.

[50] V. *Zevachim* 54b, on how the requirement that the Sanhedrin be near the Altar determined the choice of the site of the Temple itself.

[51] *Sanhedrin* 88b.

independent nation,[52] for "the Judgment is God's"[53]; and rigorous was the standard of honesty required from him in his private life; any person who had to be sued in court and who lost his case was not considered fit to be a judge.[54]

As a means of achieving a more perfect standard of justice, attorneys were discouraged,[55] but to ease matters for the layman, the court would in some circumstances allow a litigant to alter his plea and in the pursuit of justice would, after a successful appeal, overturn its own ruling without regard to its reputation.[56]

As indicated by R. Yosei's statement,[57] the administration of justice was organized on a hierarchical system in that any problem or dispute had first to be put before the local Beit Din; only if that Beit Din could not solve the problem, or felt that the unsuccessful litigant had a valid point of appeal, was the case taken higher until ultimately it reached the Great Sanhedrin. No litigant could approach this Sanhedrin in the first instance. As it was responsible for the administration of the entire system of jurisprudence in the Land, it was essential that it not be bothered with trivia; only difficult points of law, meriting the attention of the eminent scholars who made up its membership, were put before the Great Sanhedrin.[58]

Apart from its function as the Supreme Court of the Land,

---

[52] V. *Devarim* 1:16 & 17.

[53] Ibid., v. *Sanhedrin* 8a.

[54] *Bava Batra* 58a & b.

[55] V. infra p. 158 et seq.

[56] *Bava Batra* 32a; cf. *Bava Metzia* 110a, dictum of R. Nachman: If the truth will out, the court is not to be troubled twice. For more detailed reading, v. R. Meyer Waxman, "Civil and Criminal Procedures of Jewish Courts," reprinted in *Studies in Jewish Jurisprudence*, vol. 1 (New York: Herman Press, 1971).

[57] V. supra p. 15.

[58] *Tiferet Yisrael, Mishnah Sanhedrin*, chap. 11, note 16.

the Sanhedrin had legislative powers to enact laws, both religious and civil, which it considered to be necessary.[59] It therefore operated in a dual capacity—as a judiciary and as a legislature, and as such was very much part of government in ancient Israel. For example, if it was necessary to increase the area of the Temple Precinct or to enlarge the Holy City of Jerusalem, it could only be done with the active participation of the King, Prophet, High Priest and Great Sanhedrin.[60] As an arm of government it was fitting that it should be sited at the center of Jewish life in Jerusalem, and as in the main it was responsible for the spiritual welfare of the people, that that site be at the spiritual hub of the nation—the Temple Precinct itself.[61] This arrangement also had a practical benefit, as it guaranteed the safety and therefore the independence of the judiciary.

The Torah encourages a single central authority and discourages collective leadership. When Moshe, the undisputed leader of his generation, prepared to hand over to his successor Yehoshua, he advised him to consult with the elders of his generation, to seek their opinions and follow their advice, but the Almighty countermanded this, insisting that Yehoshua alone should lead the people into the Land of Israel. "There can be but one leader for a generation and not two,"[62] and in the Jewish scheme, it was the King who was to be undisputed Head of State, entitled to ultimate honor and absolute obedience.[63] To distinguish between the King and his subjects, and to avoid the risk of any potential usurper

---

[59] V. infra chap. III.

[60] *Shevuot* 14a.

[61] V. supra p. 15.

[62] *Rashi, Devarim* 31:7, quoting *Sanhedrin* 8a. This may well be the reason that where collegiality is necessary, such as in the Sanhedrin, the minority are asked to capitulate to the majority so that the final decision is unanimous.

[63] V. infra p. 22.

setting up a competing power base, nothing which belonged to the King could be used by any other person in the Kingdom; even his widow or divorced wife was forbidden to remarry[64] so as not to elevate the social standing of her second husband. It was even beyond the King's own power to remit or forego any right, privilege or honor due to him.[65] Yet having given the King this exalted status, the Torah then proceeds to circumscribe it.

> And people appeared before him as he desired; they bowed to the ground and then stood before him, and even a prophet was obliged to bow and then to stand. But the High Priest was not obliged to come to the King unless he, the High Priest, so desired. He did not stand before the King, but the King stood before the High Priest. Nevertheless it would be meritorious of the High Priest to honor the King, to permit him to be seated, and to remain standing before the King when he appeared before him.[66]

Thus, so long as the King observed the Torah and ruled faithfully and fairly, he was to be, as a matter of policy, the undisputed ruler of the land, thereby avoiding the anarchy which often erupts where there is no strong central leadership.[67] But it was also part of this scheme that, should the King not be worthy of the trust placed upon him, the High Priest would be given the possibility of setting up a conflicting power base to limit the King's authority and if necessary to curb his excesses. Ensconced in the Temple, in a place of sanctuary, surrounded by loyal priests prepared to defend him, the High Priest was given a status by the Torah which enabled him, if circumstances required, to defy the King. The Sanhedrin situated in the same Temple could rely on the

---

[64] V. *Yad, Melachim* 2.

[65] Ibid. 2:3.

[66] Ibid. 2:5.

[67] *Sefer Hachinnuch*, mitzvot 71 & 497; v. Artscroll *Tanach* series, Overview to the Book of Ruth.

protection of the High Priest and could therefore retain its independence of the King and have no need to fear him.

The advantage of this arrangement has been shown by history. Only once did the Sanhedrin suffer at the hands of a King, the King referred to in the Talmud as Yannai Hamelech and by historians as Alexander Jannaeus.[68] A scion of the priestly Hasmonean family, he succeeded in having himself appointed both King and High Priest, and when he became a member of the Sadducee opposition he eventually ordered the massacre of virtually the whole membership of the then Sanhedrin.[69]

Apart from appreciating the ethos it creates in society and the conscience it imparts to the individual, our Sages also prized the order of *Nezikin* for its sagacity.

> Rabbi Yishmael further states: He who would be wise should engage in the study of civil laws, for there is no branch in the Torah more comprehensive, and they are like a welling fountain.[70]

The Talmud as a whole had always been considered a source of intellectual inspiration to the Jew:

> The importance in Jewish life of the Talmud (with which we may associate the contemporary Jerusalem compila-tion, the Midrash, containing homiletic and legendary em-bellishment of the Biblical story) is not by any means purely academic. It comprises the accumulated wisdom of the Jewish people over many generations. No aspect of Hebrew thought, and no subject of human interest, is unrepresented in it. The period of its redaction coincided with the growth of

---

[68] Circa 100 B.C.E.

[69] *Sanhedrin* 19a; Josephus, *Antiquities* 13:13; cf. *Pesachim* 57a. Presumably Issachar of Kefar Barkai was not protected by his fellow priests, as he did not conduct himself as he should have. V. 2 *Melachim* 11 and 2 *Divrei Hayamim* 22 & 23; cf. 2 *Divrei Hayamim* 24.

[70] *Bava Batra* 175b.

independent centres of life in far distant regions, cut off politically and linguistically from the former nuclei. The Jewish people were about to enter on an entirely different phase of [their] being, in countries of which their fathers had never heard, in callings with which they had previously been unfamiliar, in the face of difficulties hitherto unimaginable. But they possessed, to bring with them into a new existence, a code, not merely of religion or of law, but of civilization. The way of life which the Talmud so minutely illustrated and prescribed made the whole people of Israel one, wheresoever they might be found and into how many political factions they might be divided. It gave them the characteristic imprint which distinguished them from others, as well as their re- markable power of resistance and cohesion. Its dialectic sharpened their wits and conferred upon them a preternatu- ral mental acuteness.[71]

At a period when the vast majority of Europeans were illiterate, the Jews insisted, as a religious duty, upon a system of universal education of remarkable comprehensiveness. In every land to which they penetrated, schools of Rabbinic learning sprang up, in which the shrewd financiers became transmuted into acute scholars, while their clients sat toping in their castles....So generation after generation, the wits of the Jew were sharpened by continuous exercise, from earliest youth, upon the acute Talmudic dialectic. But the Talmud meant much more to him than this. It brought him another world, vivid, calm and peaceful, after the continuous humil- iation of ordinary existence. It provided him with a second life, so different from the sordid round of every day. After each successive outbreak was stilled and the shouting of the mob had died down, he crept back to the ruins of his home, put away his Jewish badge of shame and set himself to pore again over the yellowed pages. He was transported back into the Babylonian schools of a thousand years before, and there his anguished soul found rest.[72]

---

[71] Cecil Roth, *A Short History of the Jewish People* (London:Horovitz, 1943) XII:V.
[72] Ibid. XIX: VII ad fin.

It is this very Talmud itself, so essential to the existence of the Jewish people, that accords intellectual primacy to the order of *Nezikin*—that part of it which mainly deals with Jewish Civil Jurisprudence.

And what are the reasons for this?

Firstly, because of all sections of the Torah, this is the one least circumscribed by detailed laws; the section which, although affecting most people most of the time, receives little detailed mention in the Torah. The entire minutiae of the administration of civil law is based on just one verse: "in righteousness shall you judge your fellow."[73] In no other area of the Torah is the human intellect allowed so much freedom to investigate, to analyze and to decide according to the inclinations of the judge who, if he acts fairly, will receive Divine support. Yehoshafat, King of Judea, exhorted the judges he had appointed throughout the Land: "Take heed what you do; for you judge not for man but for the Lord, who is with you in the judgment,"[74] provided that what you do, "you do in the fear of the Lord faithfully and with a perfect heart."[75] The guiding principle as annunciated by our Rabbis is: "A judge has nothing to guide him but that which his eyes see."[76] It is true that today we have many definitions and guidelines, many rules which must be adhered to. But these were laid down by our early Authorities, the *Tannaim* of the Mishnah and later the *Amoraim* of the Gemara, followed by subsequent scholars and codifiers, the greatest among our nation. These leaders, afraid to allow complete intellectual freedom as the standard of scholarship deteriorated, felt compelled to set some guidelines, nevertheless leaving considerable room for subtlety, for comparison, for distinction, often by casuistry.[77]

---

[73] *Vayikra* 19:15.
[74] 2 *Divrei Hayamim* 19:6.
[75] Ibid., 7.
[76] *Sanhedrin* 6b.
[77] *Tiferet Yisrael, Mishnah Bava Batra* 10:8, note 84.

Secondly, civil problems are the only ones coming before a judge on which he must hear the arguments of both parties, who, if they themselves are not scholars whose knowledge of the law exercises him, are often advised by scholars.[78] Both sides may have valid arguments—either could be right. Unlike other branches of the Torah in which a problem is one-sided ("may this be done, or may this be eaten?"), where in the case of doubt a cautious negative or restrictive ruling can be issued, in a civil dispute a restrictive ruling against one disputant could give rise to unfair advantage and license to the other.[79] The judge must exercise his mind to arrive at a positive ruling, which at the very least should satisfy his own, hopefully, nagging conscience.

As shall be remarked at a later stage during a more detailed study of Case Law, the Torah only prohibits stealing from the rightful owner; that is, once ownership has been decided. The definition of and the decisions as to ownership are left to the human intellect—that of the honest judge.[80]

---

[78] Advisers, *not* attorneys (v. infra p. 158).

[79] *Tiferet Yisrael,* loc. cit.

[80] R. Shimon Shkop, *Sha'arei Yosher* 5:1.

* TWO *
Sources: Torah Shebichtav—
The Written Law

T HE ONLY ULTIMATE source of Jewish Law must be the Torah as a whole; and of all sections of the Torah, the prime source must be Scripture itself— **Torah Shebichtav** or the **Written Law**. The common expression used in the Talmud and subsequent Authorities in describing a law which emanates from Scripture is that it is a law **Mi-d'Oraita**. However, the written laws themselves, detailed as they may appear to be, are only a skeleton of the Law and cannot in any way be meaningfully understood without the traditions, Rabbinic interpretation and exegesis which form the **Torah Shebe'al Peh**—the **Oral Law** which surrounds it. Indeed, to be considered *Mi-d'Oraita*, a law does not necessarily have to be written in the Torah; in some cases, only the principles are mentioned clearly, while in others not even basic principles could have been understood without Rabbinic help.[1] For example, the prohibition of working on the Sabbath Day is quite clear: "on it you should not do any work."[2]

---

[1] For a detailed analysis v. Rabbi Z. H. Chajes, *Students' Guide Through the Talmud (Mevo HaTalmud)* (Translated by Rabbi Dr. J. Schachter), chap. I-IV.

[2] *Shemot* 20:10.

But what is called work? The Torah itself only mentions two specific prohibitions: that of kindling fire[3] and that of carrying.[4]

In fact, the Rabbis name thirty-nine types of action which are defined as work and therefore prohibited. These they deduced from the appositioning in the Torah of a repetition of the prohibition of working on Shabbat alongside the detailed description of how the Tabernacle was to be erected in the wilderness:[5]

> They [the builders of the Tabernacle] sowed, hence you must not sow; they reaped, hence you must not reap;[6] they lifted up boards from the ground[7] to the wagons,[8] hence you must not carry in from a public to a private domain.[9]

The prohibition of carrying clearly indicates that the definition of work is a legal one and not a practical one, for the restriction is only on carrying from one domain to another and not within the same private domain. Weight or effort plays no role in the definition; carrying a heavy load in a large private garden is not a punishable offense on Shabbat, whereas carrying a handkerchief in a pocket from a private residence into the public street is. It is because of this apparent anomaly that the Torah specifically singles out the act of carrying and mentions it as a prohibition.[10]

The fact that the Scriptural juxtapositioning of Shabbat and the erection of the Tabernacle is treated as significant is, of course, only a matter of tradition, and indeed there is

---

[3] V. *Shabbat* 70a.

[4] *Eruvin* 17b.

[5] *Shemot* 35.

[6] They required vegetables, which first had to be sown and subsequently reaped, to provide dyes for the hangings.

[7] Which is public domain.

[8] Which is private domain.

[9] *Shabbat* 49b. Conversely it is forbidden to carry out from private to public domain.

[10] *Tosafot, Shabbat* 2a, s.v. *"pashat"*; v. supra note 4.

virtually no law in Scripture which can stand on its own and which does not need some traditional interpretation or explanation.[11]

One of the basic requirements of the Jewish dietary laws is that only the meat of an animal correctly slaughtered may be eaten. What constitutes a correct Ritual Slaughter? The Torah itself is vague: "and you should sacrifice from your herd or flock which the Lord has given to you as I have commanded you; and you should eat in your gates to satisfy the longing of your soul."[12] From the words "as I have commanded you," R. Yehudah Hanasi infers that Moshe was shown how *shechitah* (Ritual Slaughter) was to be carried out; he passed this tradition on to the people, and so it was incorporated in Scriptural Law.[13]

A person who makes a vow which he subsequently regrets, can normally approach a Rabbi, tell him of the oath, explain the circumstances under which it was made, his original intentions in making it, and what causes him to regret that oath. On hearing him out, the Rabbi will be in a position to annul the oath entirely.[14] From where does he derive this authority? Indeed a *Tanna* declares, "The laws concerning the dissolution of vows hover in the air and have nought to rest upon,"[15] and although the Talmud does endeavor to find Scriptural sources for this authority, they are considered so weak that the right to annul an oath is accepted as being a law given orally at Sinai and handed down by tradition.[16]

And this brings us to a group of laws which are treated as being *d'Oraita* but of which there is not even a hint in Scripture itself. Called **Halachah LeMoshe MiSinai**, they are laws

---

[11] Ramban, commentary on *Sefer Hamitzvot, shoresh* 2.
[12] *Devarim* 12:21.
[13] *Chullin* 28a.
[14] *Yoreh De'ah* 228.
[15] *Chagigah* 10a.
[16] *Rashi*, ad loc., s.v. "*heter*"; Ramban, *Bemidbar* 30:2.

which God taught orally to Moshe who in turn passed them on to his successors in the same way. An example of such a law is the prohibition against eating the first three years' crop of any fruit tree, even outside the Land of Israel, although Scripture itself[17] quite clearly ties the prohibition to "and when you shall come unto the Land."[18]

Another example is the requirement that on the Festival of Sukkot, in addition to the necessity of taking the four species mentioned in Scripture,[19] a third bundle of willow had to be taken and held independently in procession around the Altar in the Temple.[20]

The Laws concerning minima[21] and other standards are also said to be *Halachah LeMoshe MiSinai*.[22] Thus we know that in order to carry out the precept of eating *matzah* on Pesach, the minimum to be eaten must be the size of an olive; to transgress the prohibition of retaining *chametz* on Pesach, the minimum retained must be the size of an egg; to transgress the prohibition of eating on Yom Kippur, the minimum swallowed must be the size of a date.[23]

By definition it would appear that there could be no controversy surrounding a tradition handed down. If it was handed down, it was handed down to all; who can disagree?[24]

Yet we do find controversy; for example, "Beit Shammai says [the possession of] yeast the size of an olive [is prohibited on Pesach] and of ordinary leaven the size of a date,

---

[17] *Vayikra* 19:23.

[18] *Kiddushin* 38b.

[19] *Vayikra* 23:40. V. *Yad, Lulav* 7:1-3.

[20] *Yad*, loc. cit., 20.

[21] The minimum required to comply with a precept in the case of a mandatory item, or to qualify for punishment in the case of a forbidden item.

[22] *Sukkah* 6a.

[23] V. *Rosh Hashanah* 13a on the exactness of these standards.

[24] *Tosafot Yevamot* 77b, s.v. "*halachah*"; *Yad, Mamrim* 1:3.

while Beit Hillel says [the minima] of both is the size of an olive."[25]

One explanation put forward is that the standards themselves are indeed traditional from Sinai, as are the subjects of those standards, e.g. *chametz*, food on Yom Kippur, or *matzah*. However, the matching of standard to subject was not decreed at Sinai; it was left to later Authorities to relate the standard they felt to be relevant to each particular prohibition or subject.[26]

An interesting example of *Halachah LeMoshe MiSinai* is to be found in the Talmud Yerushalmi:[27] "This book [Esther] was recounted to Moshe at Sinai." This statement resolved the controversy over the inclusion of the *Megillat Esther* (which commemorates Purim, an event that took place during the Babylonian exile) in Scripture as part of the Written Law. Indeed, by including it the Rabbis gave Scriptural authority to the laws of Purim. The Yerushalmi quoted maintains that these laws did not originate at the time of Purim—they were given to Moshe at Sinai, and he passed them on secretly to the leaders of the next generation, who in turn handed them down to their own successors, a process which continued until the generation during which the events of Purim occurred. This well explains the verse:[28] "And God said to Moshe, 'Write this for a memorial in the Book and rehearse it in the ears of Yehoshua: for I will utterly block out the remembrance of Amalek from under heaven,'" a pronouncement made after Amalek had set upon the Israelites, tired and weary after the exodus and tasting freedom for the first time in two centuries. If it was written "for a memorial in the

---

[25] *Beitzah* 2a.

[26] *Chavat Ya'ir, Responsa* 192. For more detailed discussion of this subject v. Rabbi S. B. Sofer, *Divrei Sofrim* (Jerusalem, 1957), vol. 1, s.v. "*Halachah LeMoshe MiSinai.*" (This point is made on p. 93b). Cf. Rabbi Y. Z. Soloveitchik, *Novellae, Yoma,* p. 49 (1979 ed.). (Brought to my notice by my son Yossi).

[27] *Megillah* 1:5; cf. Talmud Bavli, *Megillah* 7a.

[28] *Shemot* 17:14.

Book," why was it necessary "to rehearse it in the ears of Yehoshua"? The interpretation given is: This incident, the first battle with Amalek which occurred in *your time*, write in the Book; the incident which will take place six hundred years later can only be told to Yehoshua and should only be passed on by him *orally*, for if it were to be made public, the impact of the salvation which occurred on Purim would be lost—all participants would know in advance how the incident would end. Hence the need for the oral tradition of *Halachah LeMoshe MiSinai*—but only to selected individuals, one of whom was the hero of Purim, Mordechai. "And Mordechai knew all that was done,[29] [but nevertheless] Mordechai rent his clothes and put on sackcloth and ashes and went out in the midst of the city and cried aloud a bitter cry."[30]

There is yet one further group of laws, which can in no way claim either Scriptural or traditional sources, yet carries the same authority as those expressly mentioned in the Torah and are probably the most significant in Jewish Civil Jurisprudence—laws based on logic or, in Talmudic language, **Sevarah**, which can also be translated as "common sense." The legal authority given to this source is clearly indicated in the following ruling:

> R. Yochanan said in the name of R. Shimon b. Yehotzadak: By a majority vote it was resolved in the study of the house of Nitza in Lydda[31] that in every Law of the Torah if a man is commanded: "Transgress and suffer not death" he must transgress rather than suffer death—except when asked to commit idolatry, incest (which includes adultery), and murder.[32]

---

[29] I.e., the end of the story.

[30] *Esther* 4:1; a charade on his part to encourage his people to repent their misdeeds. V. Rabbi Yehudah Potock, *Otzar Likkutei Purim*, (London, 1944).

[31] A town known today as Lod, which the Romans called Diospolis.

[32] *Sanhedrin* 74a.

The general rule that human life is paramount comes from the verse: "You shall therefore keep my Ordinances and my Judgments; which if a man do he shall live with them"[33]—and not die by them. The three exceptions are deduced in the Talmud:[34] idolatry, from the verse "and you shall love the Lord your God with all your heart, and with all your soul, and with all your might"[35]—even though He take your soul; and incest and adultery, from their comparison to murder in a verse which equates the two.[36] The Talmudic discussion continues:

> And how do we know this? [that one must suffer death rather than commit the crime of murder itself]—it is common sense. Even as one who came before Rabbah and said to him, "The Governor of my town has ordered me to kill so and so; if not he will slay me." He [Rabbah] answered him, "Let him [the Governor] rather slay you than that you should commit murder. Who knows that your blood is redder? Perhaps his [your intended victim's] blood is redder."[37]

It is by sheer logic that we know that the Torah commands that one should suffer death rather than commit murder. Consequently as incest is compared to murder, two out of the three exceptions are arrived at because of common sense, yet are treated as having Scriptural authority.

In most systems of civil jurisprudence, and in particular the Jewish system, being in possession of what is claimed, gives the defendant considerable advantages at law.

> It is a fundamental principle in Law that the Onus Probandi falls on the claimant.

The Talmud tries to find a Biblical source for this prin-

---

[33] *Vayikra* 18:5.

[34] *Sanhedrin*, loc. cit.

[35] *Devarim* 6:5.

[36] Ibid. 22:26.

[37] I.e., you have no right to murder another to save yourself; his life is no less valuable than your own—and in saving your own you will be committing an act of murder.

ciple: "But R. Ashi demurred, saying: Do we need Scripture
to tell us this? Is it not common sense that if a man has a pain
he visits the healer?" In the same way that a patient must
convince the doctor that he has a pain in a particular spot, in
order to obtain the proper treatment, so must the plaintiff
convince the Court that he has a claim on a particular item.[38]

From R. Ashi's comment it is apparent that this principle
based on logic has exactly the same authority as if it had been
written in the Torah itself, for he was able to dispense with
Scriptural sources, holding that none were needed.

In every transaction there must be an act and a moment of
consummation—the *Kinyan*. With the formal act of *Kinyan*,
ownership and title pass—as does the risk; from that moment
on the object being transferred is at the risk of the acquirer.

> R. Yochanan said: By Biblical Law, the passing of money
> effects ownership. Why then was it said that *Meshichah*[39]
> effects possession? Lest the vendor say to the purchaser,
> "Your wheat was burned in the barn."[40]

The reasoning behind this Rabbinical order is that should
the passing of money transfer ownership to the purchaser
although the goods remain in the vendor's possession, the
vendor may be remiss in attempting to save them should fire
break out on his premises. If the ownership is still vested in
the vendor he will wholeheartedly try to save the goods; if
not, he might not do so.[41]

Where is the Biblical Law referred to by R. Yochanan, that
the delivery of money creates the change in ownership? While

---

[38] *Bava Kama* 46b; v. *Shitah Mekubetzet*, ad loc.; v. infra p. 103.

[39] Literally, "pulling." This legal mode of acquisition is performed by
the acquirer's drawing the object concerned into his, though not
necessarily exclusive, possession.

[40] *Bava Metzia* 47b.

[41] Ibid.; if the rule were to be *Meshichah and* money, the vendor would
be at risk if the vendee took delivery prior to handing over the
money. V. infra p. 65.

there is an attempt by some commentators to find written Biblical sources,[42] many follow the view that "we do not learn this Biblical Law from Scripture, but from general logic. Obviously, money must effect a transaction because most of our transactions are executed that way."[43] Clearly logic coupled with custom has the effect of creating a *d'Oraita* Law.[44]

An important factor in civil litigation is the *Miggo*—literally, "from the content of"; from the content of the litigant's argument it is apparent that he is being truthful. A satisfactory *Miggo*[45] should persuade the Court that the statement under scrutiny is to be accepted as the truth, on the grounds that, had the suitor wished to be untruthful, he had available to him a stronger statement with the same effect, which he could have made without fear of contradiction.

An example of *Miggo* is the case[46] of some goats that wandered into a field and ate some barley which they found there. The owner of the barley seized the goats and made a heavy claim against their owner.[47] The father of Shmuel ruled: He [the owner of the field] can claim up to the value of the goats, because if he so wishes, he could claim that the goats themselves were his by purchase.[48]

---

[42] *Rif & Rach*, ad loc.; *Rashi* 46b.

[43] *Nimukei Yosef* on *Rif*, ad loc.; v. *Shitah Mekubetzet*, ad loc. in the name of Ramban. V. *S'ma, Choshen Mishpat* 198:1.

[44] *Sha'arei Yosher* 3:3.

[45] The ground rules of what constitutes a satisfactory *Miggo* are both complex and contentious. One attempted codification is to be found in *Shach, Choshen Mishpat* 82, under the heading of *Dinei Miggo*.

[46] *Bava Batra* 36a.

[47] I.e., he asserted that the goats had eaten barley to a much greater value than their own worth.

[48] V. infra p. 105. Possession is a cardinal factor in deciding ownership. The goats were in the claimant's field. In default of contradictory evidence, he would be successful in a claim that the goats were his. This alternative possible claim helps the Court to accept the actual claim—but only to the value of the goats; beyond that there is no *Miggo*.

Another example of *Miggo* is to be found in connection with an interesting piece of social legislation.

Normally, the rule is that the onus of proof is on the claimant. However, the case of the laborer claiming his wages requires special consideration. The laborer clearly needs his daily bread and cannot afford to forego his wages; the employer, who may have hired a number of employees that day, could easily become confused and mistakenly believe he had paid this particular worker. The Rabbis therefore gave the benefit of the doubt to the laborer who (within a specified time) claimed that he had not been paid; but, to protect the employer, they decreed that payment would not be made unless the employee took a *Shevua* (an oath—the oath of the Mishnah, which according to most Authorities is a relatively severe form of oath).[49]

However, there is an exception to this rule "that the laborer takes the oath and receives payment," and that is in the event of his having been hired with no witnesses present. He is now in a position where the employer could deny ever having employed him. Therefore, the employer would be believed if he claims that he had paid his wages for that day, on the principle of *Miggo*; had he, the employer, been in doubt and wanted to tell a lie to free himself from the obligation of paying his employee, he could have claimed that he had in fact never hired him. The guiding ruling is that of:

> R. Nachman in the name of Shmuel: We rule that the employee "swears and takes" only when he is hired in the presence of witnesses, but if he is hired without the benefit of witnesses, then because the employer could say to him, "I never hired you," the employer is believed to say, "Indeed I did hire you, and indeed I did pay your wages."[50]

Another basic rule is that a defendant who makes a total

---

[49] *Shevuot* 45a, v. *Ran*, ad loc.

[50] *Shevuot* 45b.

denial of a claim is, *Mi-d'Oraita*, in the absence of satisfactory proof against him, absolved from all liability without even the necessity of taking an oath to support his statements.[51] Should, however, the defendant make a partial admission he is liable to take the oath of the Torah.[52]

The Talmud,[53] according to many Commentators,[54] questions the logic of this. Why does the Torah say a partial admission entails the taking of an oath? The defendant should indeed be believed that he is only liable to the amount he admits to, on the grounds that he could have denied the entire claim; or does this negate the principle of *Miggo*? To this the Talmud replies that normally a man does not have the impertinence to make a completely false denial in the presence of his plaintiff, which is in fact part of the reasoning as to why an absolute denial avoids an oath.[55] The defendant who makes a partial admission does not have the nerve to make a complete denial; in fact he would really wish to admit the entire debt, but finding this difficult he wants to delay until he is once again in funds. In these circumstances, the Torah insists on an oath in order to make him admit the truth.[56]

This powerful judicial implement of *Miggo* is considered to be *Mi-d'Oraita*—yet is not written anywhere in the Torah, not by way of hint nor even handed down orally to Moshe. It derives its authority solely from *Sevarah*—logic.[57]

Much of Jewish Law, both principle and detail, is derived from Rabbinical exegesis or exposition of Scripture. There

---

[51] V. infra p. 176; the Rabbis later instituted a Rabbinical Oath to test his truthfulness.

[52] Of the most severe type.

[53] *Bava Metzia* 3a.

[54] *Tosafot*, ad loc.; v. *Shitah Mekubetzet*.

[55] *Shevuot* 40b.

[56] And we do not consider him too untrustworthy to be allowed to take the oath; *Tosafot* and other *Rishonim*.

[57] *Kesef Nivchar*, rule 94; cf. supra p. 10, the statement of R. Nissim Gaon.

are a number of hermeneutical principles which the **Rabbis** adopted—the most famous group being the thirteen of R. Yishmael,[58] quoted as a prologue to *Torat Kohanim*, similar to the more expansive thirty-two hermeneutical principles of R. Eliezer and R. Yosei Hagelili. Earlier than either of these collocations, Hillel the Elder collocated seven principles.[59]

Hermeneutical principles can best be explained by way of example; the first principle quoted by R. Yishmael is that of **A Minori A Fortiori**. Scripture demands that if one finds a lost animal belonging to an opponent one must return it to him; a fortiori if it is the animal of a friend. Similarly, if one sees the ass of an adversary overburdened, and the owner himself is trying to ease its plight, one must help; a fortiori if it is the ass of a friend.[60] The Torah, while not wishing to write anything more than is absolutely necessary, wishes to make it clear that we have a social obligation even to our 'enemies,' leaving it to us to conclude that a fortiori we have the same obligations to our friends.[61]

Another of the principles often cited is that of **Gezerah Shavah**, the literal translation of which would be "equal cut." It is the application of a rule already known in connection with one subject, to another subject, on the strength of a common expression used in Scripture in connection with both of these subjects. This is strictly controlled in that no scholar may originate his own *Gezerah Shavah*; it is not a license for original punning. A *Gezerah Shavah* had to be a known coupling of phrases which was handed down from

---

[58] To be found in the *Siddur* before the *Pesukei d'Zimra*.

[59] *Avot de R. Natan* 37:10.

[60] *Shemot* 23:4 & 5. R. Sa'adia Gaon in his commentary on *Baraita de R. Yishmael*. The Hebrew term is *Kal* (lenient or lighter) *vachomer* (and more severe or heavier). As there appears to be no satisfactory equivalent English phrase, most translators resort to the Latin quoted in the text. Cf. translation in the Singer *Siddur*.

[61] *Rashi* on *Baraita de R. Yishmael*.

teacher to pupil.[62] Once this coupling was received into tradition, it could not be disputed; the only argument could be as to whether indeed it had been so received.

A valid *Gezerah Shavah* can both articulate a previously unknown law and interpret an already existing law.

An example of a law which is derived in its entirety from a *Gezerah Shavah* is that relating to the heirs of a gratuitous bailee. There are four categories of **Shomer**: unpaid, paid, hirer and borrower.[63] In the event of damage occurring to the item in his charge, the liability of the guardian varies with his status. Broadly speaking, the gratuitous bailee, not receiving consideration for the obligation of guarding the item, faces less risk of having to compensate the owner than does the paid keeper who is receiving payment. Thus, specifically, the Torah exempts a gratuitous keeper should the item entrusted to his care be stolen,[64] while a paid keeper is only exempt if the object "die, be hurt, or be captured."[65] Quite clearly a paid guardian is liable if the item is stolen from his home in the course of an ordinary burglary, but not if it is "captured" by armed marauders. In the event of the guardian's putting in a plea which would exempt him from the obligation of compensation—for example, if the gratuitous bailee claims the item was stolen or if the paid bailee claims it was captured, both have to take an oath "that he has not put his hand unto his fellowman's goods"[66]—that the bailee himself has not stolen the item.

What of the heirs of the guardian? In the event that he has died and there is a claim by the owner of the object against his Estate, do the heirs have to take an oath that to the best of their knowledge the bailee had not appropriated

---

62 *Pesachim* 66a.

63 *Mishnah, Bava Metzia* 93a.

64 *Shemot* 22:6.

65 Ibid., 9.

66 Ibid., 7 & 10.

the item for himself, or that they had not found it among his property? In the case of the paid keeper, the Torah is virtually explicit:

> Then shall an oath of God be between them both, that he has not put his hand to his fellowman's goods; and the owner of it [the object] shall accept it [the oath] and he [the keeper] shall not pay.

"Between them both"—between the bailee and bailor, the keeper and the owner, but not between the bailor and the keeper's heirs.[67] What is explicit in the case of the paid keeper is omitted in the case of the gratuitous keeper. Is it then to be inferred that the heirs of a *Shomer Chinam*—a gratuitous bailee—are liable to an oath? The answer is no. The phrase "that he has not put his hand unto his fellowman's goods" occurs in both cases; by *Gezerah Shavah* we compare one to the other and derive the rule, that the heirs of an unpaid keeper are exempt from any oath the keeper himself may have had to take.[68]

An example of a *Gezerah Shava* which only elucidates detail is given at the beginning of the Babylonian Talmudic tractate of *Kiddushin*.[69]

One method of betrothing a wife is by giving her money or money's worth.[70] The source of this law is the verse: "If any man shall *take a wife* and come unto her...."[71] What is the legal definition of "taking a wife"? Says the Talmud: The word *yikach* [shall take] written here is compared to the word *kach* [take] which comes in the reported dialogue surround-

---

[67] *Shevuot* 47a. However, between the keeper and the owner's heirs there remains the oath the keeper would have made for the owner himself. The rule is: It is the obligation of making an oath which is not transmitted, not the right to receive one.

[68] *Baraita de R. Yishmael* 4.

[69] 2a.

[70] Ibid. The other two methods are by document or by coupling.

[71] *Devarim* 22:13.

ing the Patriarch Abraham's acquisition of the Cave of Machpelah as a burial site for his wife and descendants.[72] "I will give you money for the field; *take* it of me and I will bury my dead there."[73] The *Gezerah Shavah* of the word *kach* and its derivative *yikach* indicates to us that in the same way as the Patriarch made his acquisition by means of money, so can the betrothal or acquisition of a wife be made.[74]

To this day, most of the Western world uses this method of betrothal—not in the form of ordinary money but in the form of a wedding ring, often following an engagement ring—which itself has no legal consequence, if no other form of contract is entered into.

Another important principle of exegesis is that of **Binyan Av**—induction or inference of general law from particular instances. One example of this is to be found in connection with the Festivals. The Torah instructs:[75]

> Three times in a year shall all your males appear before the Eternal your God in a place which he shall choose; on the Festival of Pesach, on the Festival of Shavuot and on the Festival of Sukkot; they shall not appear before the Eternal empty-handed.

The Torah clearly places all three Festivals on the same level; thus when we find that in connection with the Festival of Pesach the Torah specifically allows cooking on the Festival day,

> and on the first day there shall be a convocation of holiness and on the seventh day there shall be a convocation of holiness to you; no work shall be done on them save that which may be eaten by man and that only may be done for you,[76]

---

[72] *Bereshit* 23.
[73] Ibid., 13.
[74] *Kiddushin*, loc. cit.
[75] *Devarim* 16:16.
[76] *Shemot* 12:16.

we are entitled to relate that license to the other Festivals.[77]

An apparent contradiction in Scripture in situ can also serve as a source of induction.

> All agree that leaven [on the eve of Pesach] is [Scripturally] forbidden from noon and onwards; whence do we know it? Says Abbaye, two verses are written: "Seven days shall there be no leaven found in your houses"[78]; and it is written, "even the first day you shall put away leaven found in your houses."[79] How is this to be understood? If the leaven is only put away on the first day as the latter verse implies, there are not seven full days without leaven as is demanded by the earlier verse. Scripture must therefore include the fourteenth [of Nissan] as the day for removal.

It is therefore inferred that in this instance, "first day" means the day immediately preceding the Festival—i.e., the eve of Pesach.[80]

The final example of a hermeneutical principle to be quoted in this study is that of *Klal uPrat uKlal*.[81] The rule is: Where two general propositions are separated from each other by an enumeration of particulars, the general propositions are to be limited to include only such items or facts as are similar to those specified in the particulars.

This principle is applied in the Law of Bailment referred to earlier in this chapter.[82] The verse mandating the oath on a keeper who wishes to avoid paying compensation, which at the same time is the one that penalizes the thief with the penalty of repaying double that which he stole, reads:

---

[77] *Rashi, Baraita de R. Yishmael* 5; cf. *Rosh Hashanah* 4b.

[78] *Shemot* 12:19.

[79] Ibid., 15.

[80] *Pesachim* 4b.

[81] *Klal*—generalization; *prat*—specification; "generalization followed by specification followed by [another] generalization."

[82] Supra p. 39.

for all manner of trespass, whether it be for one of the
herd, for an ass, for one of the flock, for an outer garment,
or for any lost item...[83]

The opening phrase, "for all manner of trespass," is a
general proposition, as is the closing phrase, "for any lost
item"; between the two general propositions the Torah enumerates particulars. The generalities must therefore be limited to
such things as are similar to the specified particulars. Thus
we have the rule that there can in the first instance be no
oath in connection with land and documents. These items
are excluded because they are dissimilar to the specifications.
The specifications are clearly things which are moveable and
intrinsically worth money—land is not moveable, and bonds
and documents, although moveable, have themselves no intrinsic worth.[84] Similarly a thief who steals (trespasses on)
land, bills or other documents avoids the penalty of paying
double when apprehended.[85]

Does the source of a law alter its status? There is of course
the well-known opinion of Rambam who maintains that any
Scriptural law derived through the application of a hermeneutical principle is **MiDivrei Sofrim**—the words of the
Scribes or Scholars.[86] According to Rambam, therefore, a considerable number of laws which his opponents consider to
be entirely *Mi-d'Oraita* are, in fact, not so.

One major point of conflict between Rambam and those
who differ from him is the question of betrothal by means of
money.[87] In his *Yad*,[88] he rules that betrothal with money is

---

[83] *Shemot* 22:8.

[84] *Shevuot* 42b.

[85] *Bava Kama* 62b. Slaves, regarded for many legal purposes as land,
are therefore included among these exceptions.

[86] *Rambam, Sefer Hamitzvot, shoresh* 2; *Ramban*, ad loc. and others.

[87] V. supra p. 40.

[88] *Hilchot Ishut* 1:2.

only effective *MiDivrei Sofrim*. His meaning is itself a matter of controversy, and many maintain that Rambam only makes a semantic distinction—using money, as we do, being as effective and as binding *Mi-d'Oraita* as are the other two forms of betrothal.[89] Rambam's meaning does become somewhat clearer when read in conjunction with his responsum[90] stating explicitly that only a law expressly written in the Torah can be considered as of the Torah; even laws which we know through *Halachah LeMoshe MiSinai*[91] are considered *MiDivrei Sofrim* and not *Min HaTorah*. It follows therefore that a betrothed maiden who commits adultery does not face the death penalty if her betrothal was by means of money only; not being betrothed *Min HaTorah* she cannot face the ultimate penalty demanded by the Torah.[92]

Leaving Rambam's unique opinion and concentrating on the view prevailing among the majority of Halachic Authorities—that all laws derived by exegetical interpretation or received by the tradition of *Halachah LeMoshe MiSinai* are *Min HaTorah*—is there any difference in the status of any law, dependent upon its source?

On the one hand we do find limitations, for example: "No penalty is inflicted on the strength of a logical inference." Indeed, not only is no penalty inflicted but even "an admonition inferred by [such] argument [as a fortiori a minori] is not warranted."[93]

Similarly some Authorities hold the view that no punishment is meted out for infringements of laws received through *Halachah LeMoshe MiSinai*.[94]

---

[89] V. commentaries ad loc.; cf. *Rashi, Gittin 33a, s.v. "be'ilut"*; v. supra note 70.

[90] No. 144, Amsterdam Publication; no. 166, Fryman Publication.

[91] V. supra p. 30.

[92] *Devarim* 22:23 et seq.

[93] *Makkot* 5b.

[94] *Rashi, Sanhedrin 84a, s.v. "lo yavo."*

On the other hand, we have statements by several *Amoraim*[95] which begin "Never treat a *Gezerah Shavah*[96] lightly"; each *Amora* in that passage quotes a different example of serious punishment which is derived from *Gezerah Shavah*. There would therefore appear to be no general limitations, each source having its own rules.

We do, however, find an overriding, somewhat subtle distinction between a law expressly written in the Torah and one derived by exegesis.

There is a rule that a second oath cannot be made to add to an earlier one: once a person has taken an oath on a subject, he cannot at a later date make a valid duplicate. Therefore, it is questionable as to whether an oath to perform a mitzvah is valid, as all Jews are under a perpetual oath taken at Mount Sinai to observe God's precepts.

> R. Gidal also said in Rav's name: He who says, "I will rise early to study this chapter or this tractate," has vowed a great vow to the God of Israel. But is he not under a "perpetual" oath from Mount Sinai and one oath cannot fall upon another...? The second oath is binding, since one can acquit oneself of the Sinaiatic oath by the reading of the *Shema* morning and evening.[97]

The rationale is that the new oath is valid for those times of the day during which the *Shema* would not be recited and during which there is no other Scriptural obligation to learn Torah.

The Ran in his commentary[98] makes the point:

> It seems to me that a man does not really acquit himself of the obligation to learn Torah with the recitation of *Shema*, for each man is obliged to learn Torah regularly, day and night, so far as it is within his capacity to do so. This we

---

[95] *Kritot* 5a.
[96] V. supra p. 38.
[97] *Nedarim* 8a.
[98] Ad loc.

learn[99] from the verse "and you shall teach them diligently"[100] which means [playing on the word "teach," in this instance the Hebrew "*shinnantam,*" equating it with "*shannen*"—to be sharp] that the words of the Torah shall be clear-cut in your mouth, so that if anyone asks you something, you should not show doubt and have to delay answering, but you should be able to answer him immediately, and one would not be able to do this by merely reciting *Shema* morning and evening. Therefore, from this *gemara,* I have proof for that which I wrote in chapter 3 of *Shevuot,* that all laws derived from exegesis, although they are deemed to be from the Torah itself, because they are not expressly written therein can have a valid oath fall on them.

Thus an oath to recite the *Shema* morning and evening is caught by the "perpetual" oath taken at Sinai and would not have the full consequences of a valid oath, whereas an oath to learn Torah the remainder of the day is valid as a full-fledged oath with all consequences flowing therefrom.[101]

Of all the *d'Oraita* sources the strongest is tradition—those laws handed down "from trusted witness to trusted witness, teacher to pupil."[102] Thus we find that there can be no argument on a *Halachah LeMoshe MiSinai* or *Gezerah Shavah.*[103] Once a law has been decided by virtue of this type of tradition, it cannot be overruled, whereas a law arrived at through the application of any other method of exegesis could in theory be overruled at a later date.

This characteristic of tradition is used to explain a well-known Talmudic passage.[104] Although King David was the

---

[99] *Kiddushin* 30a.

[100] *Devarim* 6:7.

[101] V. Rabbi Elchonon Wasserman, *Kovetz Shiurim,* vol. II. *Kuntres Divrei Sofrim* 1:19.

[102] *Ravad, Sefer Hakabbalah.*

[103] V. supra pp. 30 & 38.

[104] *Yevamot* 77a.

anointed of God, the founder of the Royal House of Israel, and according to tradition the ancestor of the ultimate Redeemer, his acceptability was in doubt because one ancestress was Ruth the Moabitess. The Torah rules: "An Ammonite or Moabite shall not come into the assembly of God; even to their tenth generation shall they not enter into the assembly of God forever."[105] Thus no Ammonite or Moabite could be accepted as a Jew by proselytization, although members of most other nations could be so accepted. The question arises as to whether the prohibition relates only to male Ammonites and Moabites, since the Torah uses the masculine form, or whether it also covers the females of those races. This apparently was an argument which had exercised scholars for several generations after the time that Boaz, the ancestor of David, married Ruth the Moabitess. At that time the Court ruled that the prohibition affected males only;[106] Ruth, a female, could be accepted as a full-fledged Jewess. But the argument was only stilled when one of the leading scholars in the time of King Saul—after David had slain the giant Goliath—forcefully announced that he had it from the authority of the Beit Din of the Prophet Shmuel that it was *Halachah LeMoshe MiSinai*[107] that the prohibition related to the males only. Once it was accepted that it was *Halachah LeMoshe MiSinai*, there could be no further argument, and nothing could stand in

---

[105] *Devarim* 23:4.

[106] The original ruling was based on logic (supra p. 32). The complaint against the Ammonites and Moabites was based on the fact that "they did not meet you with bread and water on the way when you came out of Egypt" (*Devarim* 23:5). As your "cousins," they should have taken pity on your wandering in the hot desert after so many years of grinding slavery. That lack of compassion made them unfit to join a compassionate nation, which the Jews have always been considered to be. But as women were not expected to leave the privacy of their homes to greet strangers, this complaint could not be leveled against them; hence they were not included in this Law (*Yevamot* 77a).

[107] V. supra p. 32.

the way of David's becoming King and founding father of
the Jewish Royal Family. However, until that time arguments could be put forward for either view.

This explains the attitude of the *yavam*, the closest relative, whose duty it was to redeem the property of his kins-
man Elimelech and to marry his widowed daughter-in-law.[108]
He refused the challenge of Boaz to marry Ruth and to redeem
the property, expressing his refusal with the words, "And I
cannot redeem it for myself lest I imperil my own inheritance."[109] For himself he was not concerned, for he accepted
the ruling of the then Sanhedrin that the prohibition related
only to male Moabites, but he could not be sure that later
generations would not overrule this decision; hence his reference to his "inheritance." However, once it became known
that this rule was *Halachah LeMoshe MiSinai* no later generation could overrule it.[110]

To be accepted as authoritative, tradition did not necessarily have to be as strong as *Halachah LeMoshe MiSinai*. Traditions handed down from earlier scholars which were not
known to be opposed were accepted by later generations as
law; indeed there is an entire tractate of the Mishnah known
as *Eduyot* (testimonies), in which scholars testify to laws which
they heard in the name of earlier scholars. In the Babylonian
Talmud this tractate is also known as *Bechirta*, the "chosen"
or "excellent" tractate, as all its decisions, being traditional,
are binding ones.[111]

In a Mishnaic debate between R. Shimon and his colleagues they retorted to his arguments:

> If you are telling us a tradition [a law you have received
> from your teacher] we shall accept it; if, however, you

---

[108] V. *Ruth* 4:1-6.

[109] Ibid., 6.

[110] Shimon Schapiro in name of Rabbi B. Blau, based on *Chatam Sofer*.
V. *Riz Halevi* (Soloveitchik), *Novellae, Ruth*, ad loc.

[111] V. Soncino Talmud, introduction to *Eduyot*.

yourself are putting forward an exegetical argument, we can counter it—your a fortiori[112] has a weakness and we do not accept it; a tradition from your teachers, however, does carry weight with us.[113]

Tradition can help to restore a law which had been forgotten. Once the eve of Pesach fell on a Shabbat, and the then Authorities had forgotten whether it was allowed to slaughter the Pesach lamb on that Shabbat in preparation for the Festival.[114] This law was restored to them by Hillel the Elder, who ruled that the *Shechitah* of the Paschal lamb indeed overrides the prohibition of Shabbat. He was then asked, what was the rule if the slaughtering knife had not been, but could have been, prepared before Shabbat; did that also override the Shabbat, and would it be permitted to carry the knife? To this Hillel replied, "Indeed I have heard this law but I have forgotten it. Leave matters to the Jewish people, for if they themselves are not Prophets, they are descended from Prophets."[115] On the morrow he whose Pesach sacrifice was a lamb had stuck the knife in its wool, and he whose sacrifice was a goat had stuck it between its horns. Hillel saw the incident, recollected the

---

[112] V. supra p. 38.

[113] *Yevamot* 76b.

[114] Acts such as ritual slaughter or carrying are considered work and therefore prohibited on Shabbat. Where there is a contradictory ordinance the question arises of which prevails. For example: Making a wound is prohibited on Shabbat and therefore all surgical operations which can be delayed may not be carried out on Shabbat, but the Torah orders that the circumcision of a male baby must take place on the eighth day after birth—which may well be a Shabbat—and it is this rule which prevails over the prohibitions of working on Shabbat. A similar problem is that of the Pesach lamb which must be slaughtered on the eve of Pesach, which may occur on the Shabbat.

[115] A hyperbolic phrase signifying that the people themselves have Traditions.

halachah and said, "Thus have I received the tradition from Shemayah and Avtalyon."[116]

Because understanding of Scriptural Law is totally dependent on the accompanying traditions, interpretations and Rabbinic exegesis, the question must be asked: What exactly was Moshe taught when he ascended Mount Sinai, and in what form was the Torah given to him?

> R. Levi b. Chama says further in the name of R. Shimon b. Lakish: What is the meaning of the verse, "and I will give you the Tablets of Stone and the Law and the Commandment which I have written so you may teach them"?[117] "Tablets of Stone": these are the Ten Commandments; "the Law": this is the Written Law; "the Commandment": this is the Mishnah; "which I have written": these are the Prophets and the Hagiographa; "so you may teach them": this is the Gemara.[118] This teaches us that all these things were given to Moshe on Sinai.[119]

There is a similar statement based on the verse:

> And God gave to me the Two Tablets of Stone written with the finger of the Lord; and on them was written according to all the words which the Lord spoke with you from the Mountain."[120] This teaches us that the Holy One, Blessed be He, showed Moshe the minutiae of the Torah[121] and the minutiae of the Scribes[122] and the innovations which would be introduced by the Scribes;

---

[116] *Pesachim* 66a. Shemayah and Avtalyon were the two leading Talmudic Scholars of the previous generation. Hillel had specially left Babylonia for Israel to study under them.

[117] *Shemot* 24:12.

[118] Meaning Talmudic debate.

[119] *Berachot* 5a.

[120] *Devarim* 9:10.

[121] Minute indications upon which homiletical deductions are based.

[122] Inferences drawn from minute indications in earlier mishnahs.

and what are these? The reading of the *Megillah*.[123]

These two statements would, in the first instance, seem to cast doubts on the view of the Ran,[124] who maintains that there is no final ruling on any doubtful proposition until there has been a pronouncement by the majority of the competent Halachic Authority, for from these statements it would seem that the ultimate rulings were transmitted to Moshe. In fact there is no contradiction.

> And He gave unto Moshe when He finished speaking with him upon Mount Sinai, Two Tablets of Testimony, Tablets of Stone written with the finger of God.[125]

On this, the Rabbis say that He gave Moshe the entire Torah; a view consistent with the other two Talmudic statements. But the Midrash does ask:

> Is it possible that in forty days Moshe learned *all* the Torah— all the details? Is it not written:[126] "The measure thereof [the Torah] is longer than the earth and broader than the sea"? [Replies the Midrash] He taught Moshe the *principles* of the Torah.[127]

On the basis of this midrash, the meaning of the other two statements is not that Moshe was given all the conclusions and all the rulings and all the decisions which would be arrived at. Rather, he was given the hermeneutical and exegetical principles; the principles upon which Rabbinical decrees and ordinances are to be based; the rules of interpretation, of tradition;

---

[123] Book of Esther. *Megillah* 19b. There are numerous other examples but this particular Talmudic passage deals with *Megillat Esther*. This Amoraic view differs from that quoted by the Yerushalmi cited supra p. 31 note 27.

[124] *Drush* 7 cited supra p. 18; v. *Temurah* 16a. Many halachot were forgotten after Moshe's death.

[125] *Shemot* 31:18.

[126] *Iyyov* 11:9.

[127] *Midrash Rabbah, Shemot* 41:6.

the methods of arriving at the Halachah—metaphorically, the "tools of the Torah." It is from these rules and principles that the details would ultimately emerge. Once Moshe understood these principles, he understood the underlying reasons and causes of the minutiae of the entire Torah.[128]

This is born out by the report we have [129] that Moshe was permitted to see into the future and looked in on one of R. Akiva's lectures to his students. He was not able to follow the arguments and was therefore ill at ease, worried as to whether his own knowledge of Torah was complete in the light of what he was now hearing. However, during the subsequent discussion, when asked by a pupil for his source on a certain subject, R. Akiva replied, "It is derived from the laws given to Moshe at Sinai,"and on hearing that reply, Moshe felt comforted. Obviously, had the Torah been given to Moshe in the form of final rulings, he would have understood immediately what R. Akiva was expounding; it was because he only received the principles and had himself not pursued the subject of that particular lecture, that he was not familiar with the detailed argument and dialectic which would in the future be expounded by an illustrious successor in the eternal sequence of Torah.[130]

One point which must become obvious at this stage is that the role of the Talmudic Scholar cannot be over-emphasized.

---

[128] *Torah Temimah, Shemot* 24:12, note 28.

[129] *Menachot* 29b.

[130] Rashi, ad loc., avoids the problem by explaining that the laws he heard being debated were those he himself in his own time had not yet been taught. *Tosafot Yom Tov* in his Introduction observes that the Talmud in *Megillah* 19B (note 129 supra) is precise in its choice of words ".....He *showed* Moshe the minutiae..." Moshe was only *shown* all the later detail and innovations; he was not *given* it at that time for onward transmission as he was given the rest of the Torah. (V. also *Tosafot Yom Tov*, beginning of *Pirkei Avot*, per Rabbi Shloime Freshwater.) The disputation in *Zevachim* 115b is on a different point: were all the revelations made at Sinai or were some made then and others later?

Our Sages—**Chazal**—interpret and expand the written law by applying their tradition, dialectic, exegesis, and logic; so much so that they are also able to alter what is the apparent Scriptural meaning. The importance of the Torah Scholar was expressed by Rava when he observed:

> How dull-witted are those people [the less educated] who stand up in deference to the Sefer Torah but do not stand up [in deference] to a great scholar. In the Torah, forty lashes are prescribed for the transgressor, whereas the Rabbis by interpretation reduce the prescription by one, to thirty-nine lashes.[131]

This power of the Rabbis caused great contention between them and the Sadducees, or *Tzadokim* a group which took its name from one Tzadok who rebelled against Rabbinic teaching and claimed that the Oral Law had no place in the Torah. This group claimed that the Written Law was to be taken literally, and they allowed for no Rabbinic deviation from the written word. Towards the end of the era of the Second Temple, the *Tzadokim* grew more influential, and its members more prominent in the then political and economic arenas. Priests, aristocrats, and successful merchants, they belonged in the main to the wealthier elements of the population. Because of their position, they attempted to dominate the Temple worship and its Rites and in fact many of them infiltrated the Sanhedrin itself. One disputation, perhaps the most familiar, arose in connection with the counting of the *Omer*.

> And you shall count for yourselves from the morrow after the day of rest, from the day that you brought the *Omer* of the Wave Offering, seven weeks shall be complete.[132]

The words translated as "after the day of rest" read literally "on the morrow of the Sabbath." By Rabbinic interpretation the verse is understood to mean on the morrow of the

---

[131] *Makkot* 22b.
[132] *Vayikra* 23:15.

first day of Pesach; the *Tzadokim*, taking Scripture literally, would wait for the first Sabbath after the first day of Pesach and so begin their counting from the following Sunday, making Shavuot fall on Sunday each and every year.

This disputation is fully aired in the Talmud itself;[133] later scholars added their own proofs and deductions supporting Rabbinic tradition, when the problem resurfaced in the eleventh century with the advent and subsequent popularity of the Karaite Movement,[134] whose negative attitude towards the Oral Law reflected that of the *Tzadokim*.

Scripture itself is careful to distinguish between that which is written and the Oral Law which surrounds it—an important distinction in view of the Rabbinic power of legislation.[135]

> And God said unto Moshe, "Write you these words, for according to these words [literally, according to the mouth of these words] have I made a covenant with you and with Israel.[136]

The Talmud asks,[137] "What are we to make of this?" To which it answers, "The statement indicates that the words which are written, you are not at liberty to recite by heart; and the words which are transmitted orally, you are not at liberty to read from writing." What are the objections to quoting the Written Law orally and to writing down the

---

[133] *Menachot* 65b et seq.

[134] V. Rabbi S. Y. Zevin, *Hamo'adim B'halachah*, pp. 291, 293, 305 et seq. for further references. V. *Tosefta, Parah* 3:5 for report of an incident arising out of the dispute as to the state of levitical cleanliness required of the priest who sacrifices the *parah adumah* (the red heifer). V. *Yoma* 19b for report of the activities of a *Tzadoki Kohen Gadol* on Yom Kippur.

[135] V. infra Chap. III.

[136] *Shemot* 34:27.

[137] *Gittin* 60b; if the Torah is written, the phrase "according to the mouth" is inappropriate. Cf. *Torat Kohanim, Vayikra* 26:46; v. *Bava Kama* 58a; *Tosafot, Bava Batra* 113a, s.v. "*tarveihu*." The Written Law was not learned by heart.

Oral Law? It is obvious from examples of exegesis which have been quoted that much can turn on a single letter and certainly on a particular word in Scripture. Therefore quotations from Scripture have to be precise and no deviation can be allowed; statements transmitted orally could become distorted, so reference to the written text is imperative. As to the insistence on the oral transmission of the Oral Law,

> this rule was very opportune; for while it remained in force it averted the evils which happened subsequently, viz., great diversity of opinion, doubts as to the meaning of written words, slips of the pen, dissensions among the people, differences of usage and confused notions about practical subjects. The traditional teaching was in fact according to the words of the law entrusted to the great Sanhedrin.[138]

Having the Law transmitted orally without written rulings meant that as current practical problems arose, the Sanhedrin and others charged with finding solutions had to revert to original sources, a requirement which had the beneficial effect of keeping the theoretical studies of the Torah up-to-date with practical developments.[139]

It must be remarked that although the Talmud, based on Scripture, censures the committal of the Oral Law to writing, it is that very writing which has saved the Torah for the Jewish Nation. Questioning the propriety of scholars who used written books of Oral Law, the Talmud answers:[140] Since this cannot be dispensed with [otherwise it might be forgotten], now "is the time to work for the Lord, they [may] break your teaching."[141] By overriding the prohibition and committing the Oral Law to writing, our Sages created the Talmud

---

[138] *Rambam, Moreh Nevuchim*, part I, chap. 71.

[139] V. *Torah Temimah, Shemot* 34:27, note 40.

[140] *Gittin* 60a.

[141] *Tehillim* 119 & 126; cf. *Rashi, Berachot* 63a, s.v. *"misefer,"* quoting the example of Eliyahu on Mount Carmel.

as we have it even to this day: that Talmud which has, over the many centuries of bitter exile proved to be a pivotal point and a lifeline in the existence of an independent Jewish Nation.[142]

In no sphere of the Law is this more true than in the realm of Jewish Civil Jurisprudence. It has already been remarked[143] that of this, there is relatively little detailed Scriptural law; the only subjects dealt with at any length are those of tort and damages, bailor and bailee relationships, and inheritance. To make this section comprehensive and practical, we must therefore add the debates and Case Law reports contained in the two Talmudic compilations together with those contained in the rulings of the subsequent early Authorities, all of which form the basis of the rulings in the Codes. To contemporary jurists, the Codes themselves are an early compilation—to which must be added the mass of Case Law and Responsa handed down by the Halachic Authorities of succeeding generations up to and including our own, dealing with problems and situations as they arise.

Thanks to the foresight of our predecessors, we, today, have had handed on to us a mass of literature giving us a base upon which to pursue our studies of Jewish Civil Jurisprudence; without this literature we would have lost the possibility of applying Jewish Law to our everyday lives, a loss which would have impoverished our knowledge and understanding of the Torah as a whole.[144]

---

[142] V. supra p. 24; cf. comments of R. Yonatan Eibishitz in *Urim V'Tumim, Kitzur Tokfo Kohen*, regarding the Divine Inspiration granted even to later Authorities.

[143] Supra p. 24.

[144] Cf. Introduction, The Translator, Rambam's Commentary on the *Mishnah, Nashim*.

For further reading, covering this and the subsequent chapter, v. Rabbi Z. H. Chajes, *Students' Guide through the Talmud (Mevo HaTalmud)* translated by Rabbi Dr. J. Schachter; H. C. Schimmel, *The Oral Law*; Eliezer Levy, *Yesodot Hahalachah*.

THREE
Sources: Rabbinical

T HE IMPORTANCE OF THE Rabbis as interpreters of the Torah and as the conduit of Tradition
should, from examples quoted in the previous chapter, be abundantly clear. An equally important Rabbinic function was that of legislation; our Sages (especially in
Talmudic times) had a dual role—interpreters of Scriptural
Laws and legislators of Rabbinic Laws.[1]

The source of this Rabbinic power is questioned in the
Babylonian Talmud:[2]

> What benediction is uttered [when one kindles the Chanuk-
> kah lights]? This: Who sanctified us by His Command-
> ments and commanded us to kindle the light of Chanukkah.
> And where in fact did He command us?[3] R. Ivia said [it
> follows] from "You shall not depart [from the word which
> they shall tell you]."[4] R. Nechemiah quoted: "Ask your

---

[1] *Derashot HaRan* 7, s.v. *"v'yesh"*; H.C. Schimmel, *The Oral Law*, chap.
III.

[2] *Shabbat* 23a.

[3] The precept to kindle Chanukkah lights is of course not Biblical,
commemorating as it does the successful anti-Hellenist uprising of
the Hasmonean-led Jewish people circa 140 B.C.E. (v. infra p. 267).

[4] *Devarim* 17:11.

father and he will show you; your Elders and they will tell you."[5]

There would seem to be a fundamental disagreement as to the powers of Rabbinic legislation, for the source quoted by R. Ivia gives more authority than that quoted by R. Nechemiah, and generally it is the former which is the accepted one, supported as it is by the statement of R. Kahana:

> All the ordinances of the Rabbis were based by them on the prohibition of "you shall not depart."[6]

Nevertheless, there still remains doubt as to how far the Torah intended to include, within its own prohibitions and precepts, which are *d'Oraita*, those subsequent prohibitions and precepts ordained by later accepted Halachic Authorities. One view, that ascribed to Rambam, is that every transgression of a Rabbinic ordinance carries with it the transgression of the Torah ordinance of "you shall not depart."[7]

Those who differ consider that the prohibition of "You shall not depart" only embraces the transgression of a Rabbinic interpretation or conclusion in connection with a precept initiated by the Torah itself; it does not, however, raise Rabbinic ordinances to *d'Oraita* level or severity—although it is indeed the source of Rabbinic Authority to initiate legislation.[8]

The question is raised: As all Rabbinic ordinances are clothed with the Torah prohibition, why is it that we are permitted—for example in cases of doubt, or those involving personal humiliation—to adopt a lenient attitude and are not obliged to carry out the Rabbinic ordinance, whereas a much stricter attitude must be adopted in the case of a

---

5 Ibid. 32:7.
6 *Berachot* 19b.
7 *Sefer Hamitzvot, shoresh* 1, v. *Ramban,* ad loc.
8 *Sefer Hachinnuch,* mitzvah 496.

precept issued by the Torah itself?[9]

Firmly, the Ran explains:

> And included in this prohibition ["you shall not depart"] are two rules. Firstly, that we are commanded to follow their decisions as to the laws of the Torah itself, for example in relation to Levitical Cleanliness and Uncleanliness; and in connection with guilt or innocence. And secondly, that we should not turn our backs on the safeguards and regulations which they [the Rabbis] have ordained for us in order to safeguard the Torah. Therefore, anyone who transgresses a Rabbinic prohibition in connection with the Shabbat has transgressed the Torah prohibition of "You shall not depart"....And that which the Talmud says, that in the case of doubt regarding a Rabbinical law, we may be lenient; or in connection with Rabbinic law, a minor's evidence [for example] is accepted; or that their rules do not apply if [grave] loss of money or human shame are involved; or if the joy of the Festival is marred and other such matters; this is only because the Rabbis set this condition [ab initio when they legislated].[10]

Ran clearly sets out his views: firstly, of the dual role of the Rabbis in connection with Jewish Law and, secondly, that while the Torah does not in any way circumscribe their authority to legislate but, on the contrary, gives their legislation the same status as its own, nevertheless, they themselves were prepared to stipulate that in certain cases their laws need not be acted upon as strictly and severely as those of the Torah itself.

The Talmud, in connection with the blowing of the *shofar* on Rosh Hashanah, explains why our Sages deemed it neces-

---

[9] Ibid.

[10] *Ran*, ad loc.; cf. *Meshech Chochmah, Devarim* 17:11 for a synthesis; v. *Chatam Sofer, Responsa, Orach Chaim* 145; v. *Tiferet Yisrael, Pesachim* 4, explanation 13.

sary to blow two "orders": those known as "the blasts while sitting," and those known as "the blasts while standing."[11] The Torah itself only demands one order of *shofar*—the Rabbis added a second. *Tosafot*[12] immediately questions the propriety of this addition on the grounds that we are prohibited from adding to the Torah anything not already there, by virtue of the verse: "Whatever thing which I command you that you must observe and do, you should not **add thereto** nor may you diminish therefrom."[13] Prima facie we are adding to the precept of *shofar* by blowing twice when the Torah only demands of us to blow once.

Clearly there is support for Rashba's view that the prohibition of "not adding" is transgressed only when one adds to the instructions of the Torah without Rabbinic Authority—for example, a Priest who adds to the set three Priestly Blessings[14] a fourth verse....

> but in that which our Sages arose, and ordained for a purpose, there cannot be any prohibition of adding to the Torah, for the Torah has itself already instructed that we must observe "to do according to all that they shall teach you"....And the commandment "You shall not depart" makes it incumbent upon us to heed the words of our Sages.[15]

Not only is there authority for Rabbinic legislation; the Torah positively encourages it: "therefore shall you guard My charges"—make safeguards around My charges.[16] While

---

[11] Those blown during the *Amidah* of *Musaf* are the main blasts and are known as those "while standing"; those blown before are the additional blasts ordered by the Rabbis and are known as those "while sitting."

[12] *Rosh Hashanah* 16b, s.v. "*v'tok'im.*"

[13] *Devarim* 13:1; v. *Parables of Dubno Maggid*, ad loc.

[14] *Bemidbar* 6:22-27.

[15] *Novellae, Rosh Hashanah*, ad loc.; v. also *Tosafot*, ad loc., for its own answer.

[16] *Vayikra* 18:30; *Torah Temimah*, ad loc.; *Yevamot* 21a.

this is not of course the simple meaning of Scripture, nevertheless it is an **Asmachta,** backing and support for Rabbinical enactment. On the subject of *Asmachta* the Ritva has the following to say:

> On every point on which there is some sort of support [*Asmachta*] from Scripture, the Almighty indicates that it is right in the circumstances so to enact, but He did not make it mandatory. He left it in the hands of the Sages. This is the true interpretation [of an *Asmachta*] and differs from those who interpret *Asmachta* as merely a mnemonic chosen by the Sages [in order to memorize the law], holding that it was not the intention of the Torah so to legislate....The Torah indicates the requirement but leaves the mandating thereof to be fixed by the Sages if they think fit....Therefore you will find that when the Sages bring proof or hint of *Asmachta* from the Torah to support their words, they wish to show that they are not initiating an entirely new Law, but that all Oral Law (including their own legislation) is somewhere hinted at in Scripture, which itself is complete, lacking (God forbid) nothing whatsoever.[17]

The Rambam says:

> A Great Beit Din[18] which applies one of the hermeneutical principles and rules as it sees fit, and subsequently there arises a later Beit Din which sees fit to contradict that ruling, the latter may do so and can rule as it sees fit....Should, however, a Beit Din decree a prohibition, issue a regulation, or institute a custom, and the new rule is accepted by all Israel and after it there arises a later Beit Din which wishes to annul the words of its predecessor and to uproot that regulation, that prohibition or custom, it is not able to do so until [the later Beit

---

[17] *Ritva, Novellae, Rosh Hashanah* 16a.

[18] Meaning the *Sanhedrin HaGadol* (v. supra p. 16) in the Temple precinct, but taken by Rambam and others to mean any competent Halachic Authority.

Din] is greater than the earlier one both in wisdom and in
numbers.[19]

It may seem anomalous that when defining a Law of the
Torah, one Authority can be overruled by a later Authority,
although the latter is not as distinguished as its predecessor,
whereas to alter a Rabbinic decree or ordinance, the later Beit
Din must be more distinguished and drawn from a larger
circle of scholars than its predecessors. But that is the law; it
is easier to alter a ruling on a *d'Oraita* than on a *d'Rabbanan*.[20]

Rambam in the passage quoted enumerates three types
of Rabbinic ordinances: **prohibitions, regulations and customs**, and it is appropriate at this point to explain the distinction.

Prohibitions (*Gezerot*) were decreed to protect the laws of
the Torah and to improve the standard of religious life, while
regulations (*Takkanot*) were enacted for the welfare of the people,
to improve the standard of social life. **Customs** (*Minhagim*) were
adopted, as a matter of pragmatism, for the convenience of the
people.

A classical example of Rabbinical prohibitions are those
designed to keep the Jewish Nation from becoming assimi-
lated and lost among its heathen conquerors.

They [the Rabbis] decreed against heathen bread and oil
on account of their wine; against their wine on account of
their daughters;[21] against their daughters on account of

---

[19] *Yad, Mamrim*, 2:1 & 2, v. explanations of *Ravad*. The phrase "greater in
number" signifies that there is a wider circle of distinguished scholars
from which to elevate to the Bench; it cannot mean a larger Beit
Din, as the size of the Beit Din is fixed.

[20] V. *Chatam Sofer, Novellae*, on *Beitzah* 5a (on the subject of Formal
Prohibitions), an interesting interpretation of *Mishnah Avodah Zarah*
2:5, based on *Shir HaShirim* 1:2; v. also R. Yona of Gerona, *Sha'arei
Teshuvah* 3:4.

[21] Drinking wine would arouse desire for women present.

another matter;[22] and against this other matter on account
of still another matter.[23]

At home on Shabbat, surrounded by the paraphernalia of
daily life, one could easily forget the sanctity of the day. To
help keep it in mind, to ensure that the Jew treats it with the
gravity it warrants, the Rabbis instituted numerous prohibitions; for example, the laws of *Muktzeh*—a series of injunc-
tions forbidding the moving—or in some cases, even the
touching—of numerous workaday objects.[24]

In the sphere of Civil Jurisprudence, we find the rule that
predated documents are disqualified while postdated documents are acceptable.[25] A document properly witnessed gives
the creditor in whose favor it is drawn a lien, charge or
mortgage on all the property in the possession of the debtor
at the time the debt arose. This charge remained valid in
respect of real property notwithstanding a subsequent genuine
sale by the debtor. Thus a purchaser who acquired real property from a debtor, and was therefore subject to the creditor's
mortgage, was at risk. In the event of the debtor's not having
other assets from which to repay the debt, the creditor could
attach this land,[26] leaving the purchaser with nothing more

---

[22] Idolatry.

[23] *Avodah Zarah* 36b. The ultimate fear was pederasty.

[24] The Rabbinic laws of Shabbat are given a specific name—*Shevut*—
lit., "Shabbat Rest." Whether this difference in title is merely a
matter of nomenclature, or one of substance, is debated by comparatively recent Authorities. V. *Aruch Hashulchan, Orach Chaim* 243:3 &
308:4; cf. *Sefat Emet, Shabbat* 93a, who quotes *Maharsha, Shabbat* 42a (per
Rabbi Y. Levenberg); v. *Chatam Sofer, Responsa, Even Ha'ezer* II 173.

[25] *Mishnah Shevi'it* 10:5

[26] The charge on property in the form we have it, is shaped entirely
by Rabbinic activity. According to one Talmudic view, the very
charge itself is one created by the Rabbis in order to encourage
people to lend to those less fortunate; the opposing view is that the

than a claim for compensation against his vendor (who is of course the debtor who cannot currently meet his obligations). The only safeguard the purchaser had was the fact that a debt evidenced by a properly written document was more or less public knowledge in the neighborhood because of the number of people involved.[27] Therefore, before purchasing any property, a purchaser could make local inquiries to ascertain whether the vendor had incurred any debts which mortgaged the property being negotiated.

A predated document totally upsets this calculation, as it may well have been written after the property concerned had changed hands. Let Bertinoro explain:[28]

> For example, we are now in Nissan, and the document is dated the previous Tishrei [six months earlier]; it is disqualified because it would allow an illegal seizure from purchasers who acquired between Tishrei and Nissan.

This is of course obvious; but what would the ruling be should unimpeachable witnesses come forward and give evidence that in fact the true date of the document is Nissan? Could the creditor use it to seize property disposed of by the debtor after that date?[29] Continues Bertinoro:

> And the Rabbis penalized [this creditor who tried to take unfair advantage] by not allowing him to use this docu-

---

charge is created by the Torah in respect of every debt, but is limited by the Rabbis to debts evidenced by a written document, in order to make possible sale of real estate. For a more detailed discussion v. infra p. 146 et seq.

[27] The creditor, the scribe (v. infra p. 147) and the two witnesses.

[28] *Shevi'it*, loc. cit.

[29] Another problem does arise. The witnesses who sign a falsely dated document are legally committing perjury; they are therefore disqualified from acting as witnesses and automatically the document itself becomes a nullity and cannot be acted upon. V. *Bertinoro, Tiferet Yisrael* and *Tosafot Yom Tov*, ad loc.; *Aruch Hashulchan, Choshen Mishpat* 43:4 and others.

ment to seize any sold property, even that which had been sold subsequent to Nissan. We fear that [if validated to seize any property] it will be used [wrongly] to seize property which had been sold between Tishrei [the purported date of the debt] and Nissan [the true date of the debt].

Postdated documents are, however, valid (again Bertinoro), "because they limit the rights of the creditor, who can now only seize property sold after the date stated in the document" (and not that sold after the true date of the debt but before the date stated).

Reference has already been made[30] to the Talmudic law which decrees that the passing of money is not considered to be a *Kinyan*—the act of consummation of a transaction.[31] Ownership brings with it not only the advantages of owning the asset, but also the disadvantage of being "at risk." An asset which is destroyed is (subject to insurance)[32] the owner's loss. The Rabbis foresaw that in the event of a purchaser's paying the full purchase price and becoming the owner on the transfer of money without the transfer of goods, he would be at risk if there were, say, a fire in the vendor's barn or warehouse; the vendor would not deem it necessary to exert himself to save another's goods. Therefore the Rabbis decreed that the transaction was not completed until the buyer made *Meshichah*, a symbolic act, taking the goods into his possession.

This Rabbinic legislation would appear to be a typical *Gezerah*—a prohibition against completing a transaction with the passing of money because of possible ill consequence. However, it is often found to be quoted by Authorities as a *Takkanah*—a regulation considered socially beneficial. In fact, it is a hybrid; it is a *Gezerah* insofar as money does not complete

---

[30] Supra p. 34.

[31] *Bava Metzia* 47b.

[32] For more detailed reading, v. Rabbi M. Slae, *HaBituach BaHalachah* (Tel Aviv, 1980).

a transaction; it is, however, a *Takkanah* in that *Meshichah* does.[33]

As a result of this law, either party could legally withdraw from the transaction, after the money had passed, but before the *Meshichah* had been made. In a volatile market this would create uncertainty; it would also encourage something less than honorable behavior. In framing the law, therefore, the Rabbis also ruled that any person retracting from what the other party had considered a binding transaction was to be cursed by the Beit Din to which the complaint was made:[34]

> He who exacted vengeance from the generation of the Flood,[35] from the generation of the Dispersion,[36] from the men of Sodom and Gomorrah[37] and from the Egyptians who were drowned in the sea[38]—He shall exact redress from one who does not stand by his word.[39]

Some Authorities rephrase the curse from third to second person: "He shall exact redress from you if you do not stand by your word."[40] Other Authorities rule that the minister of the congregation will publicly and specifically announce the curse on the deviant in the synagogue.[41] These particular examples of God's vengeance were chosen because they concern sinners who had acted dishonorably and unfairly and whose punishment evidences Divine intervention.[42]

---

[33] R. Benzion Blau, London.

[34] *Bava Metzia* 44a.

[35] *Bereshit* 6 & 7.

[36] Ibid. 10:25 & 11:1-9.

[37] Ibid., 18 & 19.

[38] *Shemot* 14 & 15.

[39] *Choshen Mishpat* 204:4.

[40] *Remah*, commentary ad loc.

[41] *Aruch HaShulchan* 204:2.

[42] Ibid.; this clearly indicates the relationships between civil and canon law; v. supra p. 9.

The second type of Rabbinic legislation quoted by Rambam[43] is that of **Takkanah**—regulation for general public good. An example is the regulation that, although it is meritorious to ransom Jews in captivity, we are not allowed to pay excessive amounts of ransom; this was enacted so as not to leave the population open to blackmail by bandits and pirates who would realize that kidnapping Jewish victims could be very profitable. Similarly, we are not allowed to pay excessively for Jewish books or holy objects in heathen hands.[44]

Another example, one which crosses Family and Civil Law, is the marriage of a minor girl arranged by her mother or brothers. Under Torah Law, a father may arrange the marriage of his infant daughter. The Rabbis extended this, and in the case of an orphan allowed her brothers and her mother (or even the girl herself) to arrange her marriage, although none have the legal capacity to do so. The motive behind this license was to ensure that the young daughters of Israel should not be left unprotected. Naturally she was not considered a married woman according to Torah Law, and in fact did not, in the event of the marriage breaking up, require a formal *Get*—Bill of Divorce. Her refusal to live with her husband was, under Family Law, sufficient to dissolve the marriage.[45] This license however also affected Civil Law, for as she was not legally married to her husband according to the Torah, he was not her heir; her property in the event of her death should, according to Torah Law, be inherited by her brothers or paternal uncles. Nevertheless, the Rabbis transferred the right of inheritance to the man to whom she was married, under their edict, at the time of her death.[46] In fact, this may well be a double Rabbinic enact-

---

[43] Supra p. 62.

[44] *Gittin* 45a; v. *Unpaid Ransom* (Merkaz Le'inyanei Chinnuch), biography of Rabbi Meir (b. Baruch) of Rothenburg, for a historical instance.

[45] *Yevamot* 107a; v. *Yad, Ishut* 4:7 & 8 and *Gerushin* 11.

[46] *Even Ha'ezer* 90:3; v. infra p. 79.

ment, for there are many Authorities who consider that the law by which a husband normally inherits from his wife is of Rabbinic origin. Thus in the case of an infant bride, the marriage itself is Rabbinic, followed by a Law of succession which in principle is also only Rabbinic.

According to those who hold that the husband's right of inheritance is given him by Rabbinic order, there arises an interesting anomaly. While normally individuals may make stipulations to their pecuniary advantage, or disadvantage, notwithstanding the Torah Law,[47] the Rabbis, according to some Authorities, precluded a married couple from making any stipulation regarding the inheritance of the wife's estate, on the grounds that, while in monetary matters one may stipulate against a rule of the Torah itself, a rule propounded by the Sages must be strengthened and bolstered in order that it should not be held in contempt.[48]

In order to ease the last moments of a dying man, the Rabbis legislated that any dispositions made by him in anticipation of death must be acted upon and are to be enforced by the courts, although those dispositions may not accord with the order of precedence of heirs, as laid down in the Torah itself.[49] Without the backing of this legislation, the dying man's agitation would be increased by the fear that his legal heirs, as recognized by the Torah, would not carry out his last wishes.[50]

---

[47] *Davar Shebemamon*—on monetary matters, conditions made, although against Torah Law, are nevertheless valid. V. *Ketubot* 56a; v. infra p. 219.

[48] *Ittur* quoted by *Bach; Tur, Even Ha'ezer* 69:16; v. *Chelkat Mechokek, Even Ha'ezer* 69, explanation 6, who extends this ruling to the Statutory *Ketubah* according to those who consider the *Ketubah* itself of Rabbinic origin.

[49] *Bemidbar* 27:8-11.

[50] *Rashbam, Bava Batra* 147b; s.v. "*matnat*" ad fin.; v. infra p. 72 et seq. for the source of Rabbinical powers to overrule the Torah in monetary matters.

A problem arises in connection with the assignment of a debt; the debtor's obligation to repay is an intangible right of the creditor and, being intangible, is not easily transferrable in law.[51] However, in order to make commerce less complicated, the Rabbis ordained that if all three—the debtor, creditor and assignee—are together at the time of the assignment, it is valid and irrevocable in law. This legislation is to the advantage of merchants who are now able to transfer value to one another without any great formality.[52]

Again in order to facilitate trade, the Rabbis made a special rule for employees and contractors. Goods entrusted to an employee or a hauler, for example, to be transferred from one place to another, become his responsibility; he is a bailee, moreover a paid bailee, in which case he is responsible for any loss which is not entirely accidental and entirely beyond his control. He is responsible if the goods are lost or stolen in transit and would also be responsible if, for example, as the result of a sudden stop of his vehicle the goods were damaged. This would make life almost impossible for the hauler, and no one would be prepared to undertake this type of work. The Rabbis therefore instituted an oath which he is obliged to swear, to the effect that he was not negligent, and by taking this oath he frees himself of the obligation to pay:

> One who is paid to transport a barrel from place to place, and it breaks en route is, according to the strict law, obliged to pay, for this is not considered an absolute accident, as breakage is equivalent to having the items stolen or lost, which could have been avoided, and for which a paid bailee is obliged to pay;

---

[51] *Ritva, Novellae, Bava Batra* 147b, s.v. *"u'mechirat."* For this reason the sale of loan notes are considered a Rabbinical innovation by some Authorities, as, being merely evidence of the loan, a note itself has no intrinsic value and is therefore not assignable in strict law.

[52] *Rosh, Bava Metzia* 20a (para. 46). v. p. 239 infra note 44.

> nevertheless our Sages instituted the rule that he is obliged
> merely to swear that he was not negligent, for if we were to
> insist on strict law and oblige him to pay, there would never be
> any person willing to transport the goods of another.[53]

Another radical example of circumstances in which religious pragmatism clashes with civil jurisprudence is to be
found in the testimony of the *Tanna* R. Yochanan b. Gudgada
regarding

> a beam [of wood] which has been wrongfully appropriated
> and is built into a palace [or any other building]; restitu-
> tion shall be made in money[54] so as not to put obstacles in
> the way of penitents.[55]

The reason for this legislation in favor of penitents was so
as not to inhibit them from repenting; if called upon to destroy whatever they had built in order to return the beam
itself, as the original law demanded, more than likely they
would be dissuaded from any form of penitence, to their
own and the communal detriment.

The third example of Rabbinic legislation cited by Rambam[56] is that of *Minhag*—custom. An example of this is to be
found in a responsa of R. Sherira Gaon.[57]

Title to stolen goods is acquired, according to all Authorities, at such time as the original owner is *"Meya'esh"*—re-
signed to his loss,[58] and the article itself has been transferred
to the possession of another. Thus a person who buys an
object from a thief, in good faith, after the owner has ex-

---

[53] *Yad, Sechirut* 3:2 based on *Bava Metzia* 83a; v. supra p. 39; cf. infra p.
181.

[54] Instead of the actual beam having to be restored.

[55] *Gittin* 55a.

[56] Supra p. 62.

[57] Quoted in *Tur, Choshen Mishpat* 368.

[58] The time a statement is made by him announcing his acceptance of
the loss.

pressed his resignation to the loss, acquires a perfectly good and valid title. In most instances of valuables taken by outlaws, the owner gives up hope of ever having them returned to him, and therefore if a fellow Jew subsequently buys these goods from the outlaws, he, the purchaser, acquires good title. However, if the purchaser wishes to do what is absolutely right[59] he will return the goods to the original owner if he is known to him. This, however, is not a legal requirement; it is a moral one.[60] Nevertheless, some communities legislated that the purchaser be *legally* obliged to return the items to their original owner, and the question was put to the Gaon as to whether this legislation could stand.

> That which you have written, that there is a custom in your place that he who acquires from outlaws and thieves must return the items to their owners and be recompensed for his expenses; if this is definitely the custom then every man is obliged to carry it out and may in no way behave differently to that which is customary. For we say, from where do we see in the Torah that custom is to be reckoned with? From the verse: "You shall not remove your fellowman's landmark which they of old time have set."[61] Even more so[it is right to follow the custom] in a matter which is of public advantage and which avoids argument; therefore continue as your custom is; do not deviate.

The primary purpose of the verse cited by the Gaon is to prohibit one person from encroaching on land or territory of another. Although encroachment is a form of stealing and covered by the general prohibition of stealing, it also carries with it the prohibition expressed in this verse, which is extended to include encroachment on another's business activity and competing with him.[62] In this context the Gaon uses

---

[59] Lit., "Satisfy Heaven."
[60] V. infra p. 179.
[61] *Devarim* 19:14.
[62] *Aruch Hashulchan, Choshen Mishpat* 376:1.

the verse in a metaphorical manner.[63] Indeed it is on this basis
that the Talmud rules that any method of transfer adopted by
businessmen becomes valid in law and, if executed, irrevocable. Thus in Talmudic times the placing of the purchaser's
mark on the goods, which was accepted by the merchants as the
completion of a transaction, was so accepted in law.[64] In modern
times it is the custom in some trades to clinch a deal with a
handshake; this would be binding in law.[65]

The source of the underlying power of the Rabbis to
legislate in the way they did, is discussed in a Talmudic
debate—the one surrounding the institution of the *Prozbol*.[66]
The Mishnah reports:[67] "Hillel [the Elder] instituted the
Prozbol to prevent abuses." Amplifying this statement the
Talmud[68] explains:

> We have learned— A *Prozbol* prevents the remission of
> debts [in the Sabbatical year]. This is one of the regulations
> made by Hillel the Elder. For he saw that people were
> unwilling to lend money to one another and disregarded
> the precept laid down in the Torah: "Beware that there be
> not a base thought in your heart, saying, The Seventh
> Year, the year of remission, approaches; and your eye be-
> comes evil against your needy brother and you lend him
> naught; and he shall cry unto the Lord against you; and it
> be a sin upon you."[69] Hillel therefore decided to institute

---

[63] *Torah Temimah, Devarim*, ad loc.

[64] *Bava Metzia* 74a.

[65] V. *Rosh, Novellae*, ad loc., para. 72, in name of R. Chananel.; cf.
Radvaz, Responsum 1:503; *Nimukei Yosef, Bava Batra* 144b, s.v. *"omar"*
(p. 134 ad fin.); cf. infra p. 83.

[66] The hybrid of two Greek words, *Proz* and *Bol* meaning, "order" for
"rich", v. *Gittin* 36b & 37a; v. *Mishnah Shevi'it* 10:3, and commentaries ad loc.

[67] *Gittin* 34b.

[68] Ibid. 36a.

[69] *Devarim* 15:9.

the *Prozbol*, the text of which reads thus: "I declare before you, so-and-so,[70] the Judges of that place,[71] that touching any debt that I may have outstanding, that I may be able to recover at any time I shall desire."[72] The *Prozbol* was to be signed at the bottom by the judges or by witnesses.

By decree of the Torah,[73] every seventh year—*Shemittah* year—there was a remission of debts; amounts payable at the end of the year had to be released,[74] the creditor remitting the debt to the debtor. Consequently, as the cycle drew to its close and the seventh year came closer, creditors were reluctant to lend,[75] and the needy therefore suffered more than usual. In order to improve their lot, Hillel the Elder devised a method whereby without disobeying the Torah, the release of *Shemittah* could be circumvented. The principle underlying the *Prozbol* is found in the verse: "*He* [the creditor] shall not exact it [the debt] of his fellow."[76] By passing the debts on to the Court, it was the Court which was now exacting payment, not the creditor himself, and the Court, being an institution, is not "a fellow" of the debtor.[77]

The Talmud,[78] however, is not happy to accept this piece of legislation at its face value.

---

[70] The exact names being given.

[71] The name of the place being given.

[72] Even after the Sabbatical year. *Mishnah Shevi'it* 10:4; v. *Bava Batra* 150a, that a *Prozbol* is only written if the debtor owns land. Today presumably we rely on the fact that every Jew has a share in the land of Israel; v. *Bava Batra* 149a, *Ritva, Novellae* and note, and *Tosafot, Bava Batra* 44b, s.v. "*d'lo.*"

[73] *Devarim* 15:1 & 2.

[74] *Makkot* 3b.

[75] Especially as interest between Jews is prohibited; v. infra Chap. IX .

[76] *Devarim*, loc. cit.

[77] *Rashi, Gittin* 36a, s.v. "*masruni*" and *Rashbam, Bava Batra* 65b, s.v. "*harei*"; v. commentaries on *Mishnah Shevi'it*, ad loc. Prima facie this circumvention is in accordance with rules of the Torah. V. dispute *Rashi* and *Tosafot, Makkot* 3b and *Ritva, Novellae*, s.v. "*u'vemassar.*"

[78] *Gittin* 36b.

But is it possible that according to the Torah the Seventh
Year releases [a debt] and Hillel should take it upon himself to ordain that the year should not operate as a release?

Abbaye maintains that Hillel was only legislating for his
[and later] times during which the Torah Law of *Shemittah*
had in any event been suspended;[79] it was only resurrected
by the Rabbis in order to keep the memory of it alive, and
what the Rabbis ordain, they can annul.

The Talmud was still not satisfied;

But [conversely] is it possible that where according to the
Torah the Seventh Year does not release, and therefore
debts are correctly payable, the Rabbis should ordain that
it does release?

This enactment robs creditors of their just due. Abbaye
does give an answer but more significant is the reply given
by his contemporary Rava:

The Rabbis have power to expropriate property should it
be for the general public good.[80]

Rashi in his commentary[81] explains that Rava's solution
answers two questions:

To the first, how could the Rabbis circumvent *Shemittah* of
the Torah, the answer is: *Hefker Beit Din*—the Rabbis have
the power to expropriate the property of the debtor. To the
second, if the *Shemittah* of the Torah has been suspended,
how could the Rabbis reintroduce it at the expense of the
creditor, the answer is again: *Hefker Beit Din.*

---

[79] Because *Shemittah* depends on the operation of the Jubilee Year,
which in turn depends on having most of World Jewry living in
Israel, under its own rule. *Tosafot, Gittin,* ad loc.; v. *Aruch Hashulchan, Choshen Mishpat* 67:10 regarding the present day.

[80] Lit., anything declared ownerless (*Hefker*) by the Beit Din is indeed
Hefker.

[81] *Gittin,* ad loc., s.v. "*Rava.*"

Once established, this principle does become a powerful legislative tool in Rabbinic, and, as shall be seen, in communal hands, and the Talmud therefore insists on finding a Scriptural source of this power, and continues:

> For R. Yitzchak has said, "How do we know that the Rabbis have power to expropriate?" Because Scripture states, "Whoever comes not within three days according to the counsel of the Princes and the Elders, all his property shall be forfeited and he himself banned from the Congregation of the Captivity."[82] R. Elazar says: We derive it from this quotation: "These are the inheritances, which Elazar the Priest and Yehoshua the son of Nun and the heads of the fathers of the tribes…"[83] Now why is the word "fathers" [here] put next to "heads"?[84] To show that just as fathers transmit to their children whatever property they wish, so leaders transmit to the nation whatever they wish.[85]

The difference between the two sources may not be merely one of semantics; it may presage different legal conceptions. The decree of Ezra seems to be punitive; an ad hoc law to cover a specific occurrence (or non-occurrence). The powers taken by Yehoshua and his colleagues are more in line with the later usage of the power of *Hefker Beit Din*, in that they were used administratively, on a continuous basis.[86]

From the words of Ezra's decree, it would appear that he and his colleagues only exercised the power to confiscate property—literally, to make it *Hefker* (ownerless); for another person to acquire ownership he would have to make a formal *Kinyan* (act of acquisition). The source from the Book of

---

[82] *Ezra* 10:8.

[83] *Yehoshua* 19:51.

[84] It would have been sufficient to say "heads of the tribes."

[85] Leaders being compared to fathers.

[86] *Keren Orah, Yevamot* 90b. For punitive use see *Mishnah Shekalim* 1:1 & 2.

Yehoshua indicates that not only did the leaders have the power to transfer ownership by using the machinery of *Hefker Beit Din*, but they could remove the assets from the ownership of A to the ownership of B, without B's having to make any formal act.[87]

While there will be some practical differences resulting from the two approaches,[88] in most cases, the difference is purely academic, for as soon as a person acquires property, whether through the machinery of a direct transfer by the Authorities from the previous owner, or whether by his own acquisition of now ownerless property, it becomes recognized as his own for all purposes of the Torah.

This is clearly indicated in the one realm of the Torah in which civil, canon and personal law all meet—that of betrothal.

As a result of a valid betrothal[89] a woman becomes married in the eyes of the law; she is no longer to have a liaison with any man other than her betrothed; any indiscretion could result in her facing capital punishment (and any child born as a result of that indiscretion is illegitimate). At the same

---

[87] R. Akiva Eger, *Responsa*, 1:221 (a letter from his son R. Shlomo Eger), paras. 5 & 6; v. *Responsa* 222, para.21; v. *Rashba, Novellae, Gittin* 36b; v. *Chatam Sofer, Novellae, Gittin,* ad loc. & v. Rabbi Elchonon Wasserman, *Kovetz Shiurim, Bava Batra,* 512.

[88] Some are suggested in the responsum cited above.

[89] A Jewish wedding is divided into two parts: first the betrothal, by which the bride becomes prohibited to any other man, followed by the actual marriage, in which she is taken under the bridal canopy and becomes a full wife. Today both ceremonies are carried out together. The passing of the ring creates the betrothal; the subsequent seven benedictions under the canopy, followed by a session of privacy, brings the couple together fully as man and wife. In Talmudic times, up to a year could pass between the betrothal and the marriage, during which time the couple did not live together. The modern term "engagement" has no legal standing and no law flows from "being engaged," unless a valid contract is drawn up between the parties.

time, she is elevated to the status of her betrothed; if he is a priest, she may, according to the law, share in the tithes he receives. But this is, of course, only so if the betrothal is valid, and one of the essential conditions of a valid betrothal is that the value passed to her as consideration, for example the wedding ring, must be the bridegroom's absolutely before becoming hers as a result of the betrothal.[90] Any defect, under civil law, in his title annuls the betrothal, consequently affecting her personal status and that of any children of an extramarital liaison. Thus a Rabbinic civil enactment will affect the Torah law of personal status and the canon law of forbidden relationships.

For example, according to most Authorities, a thief himself cannot by rule of Torah acquire good title to a stolen article; title can only be acquired after the owner has expressed his resignation at its loss and (for example) it has been transferred to the ownership of a third person who then becomes the owner. Nevertheless, even among these Authorities, there is a school of thought that the Rabbis do give the thief a good title once the owner has expressed his resignation. Thus a thief who steals a ring may acquire title to it by Rabbinic edict only, not by Torah Law. Yet should he use this ring to betroth a woman, the betrothal will be a legally valid betrothal *Min HaTorah*, because an acquisition recognized by the Rabbis is indeed effective.[91]

The Rabbinical decree whereby the payment of money does not complete a transaction because a symbolic act of possession is required[92] also creates problems in the field of betrothal. What if the groom had paid the money and asks the vendor to give the bride the ring before he himself has

---

[90] V. *Rosh, Bava Batra* 8:46 concerning a borrowed ring; cf. *Even Ha'ezer* 28:19.

[91] *Yam shel Shlomo, Bava Kama* 7:7; v. infra note 93.

[92] V. supra p. 65.

taken possession? According to the Torah, it is his ring and she will be betrothed. According to the Rabbis, it is not yet his ring and he has therefore not carried out a valid act of betrothal, that of giving her a valuable item belonging to him. Conversely, if he had made the *Kinyan* but has not yet paid the money, according to the Rabbis the ring is his and he can now give it to his bride; according to the Torah it is not, and she would not be betrothed.[93]

On the Eve of Pesach [before the Festival itself], *Chametz* becomes entirely forbidden. The prohibition not only covers eating and drinking, it covers all forms of benefit. Thus, de jure, the leaven is no longer of any value, for of what use is it? This prohibition, from the sixth hour before the Festival, is a Rabbinical one;[94] nevertheless such leaven cannot be used for a betrothal as the Rabbis have effectively rendered it valueless.[95]

Reference has been made[96] to the Rabbinic enactment whereby a debt can be transferred by a creditor to a third party, provided both of them are together in the company of the debtor at the time of the assignment. This transfer is of course only Rabbinical, yet if a man were to betroth a woman by making this transfer while she, he and the debtor were together, she is considered to have received valuable consideration, and her betrothal is a valid one—recognized even

---

[93] V. *Rashi, Bava Metzia* 48a s.v. *"ka'ee."* Similar problems arise if the vendor uses the money for his own betrothal, before the buyer has "taken possession," or conversely if after receiving the money, the vendor himself uses the article for his own betrothal. These and related problems are debated by later Authorities. V. *Machanei Efraim, Mechirah: Kinyan Meshichah* 2 and *Kinyan Ma'ot* 11; cf. *R. Yosef of Slutzk, Responsa* 93; v. *Avnei Miluim* 28:33; *Ketzot Hachoshen* 235:4, s.v. *"omnam;" Aruch Hashulchan, Even Ha'ezer* 28:61-65.

[94] *Pesachim* 6b; for the Torah rule v. supra p. 42.

[95] Ibid. 7a; *Yad, Ishut* 5:1.

[96] Supra p. 69.

by the Torah, which itself does not recognize that particular mode of transfer.[97]

Similar is the Rabbinic institution whereby a minor daughter can be given in marriage by her mother or brothers: although the marriage is not recognized by the Torah, it overrides the normal laws of succession, and by Rabbinic edict this husband takes precedence over his "wife's" legitimate heirs; in the event of her death while still joined by this Rabbinical marriage, he would inherit her estate.[98]

A Rabbinical law can bring into play a *Shevuah*—an oath— by order of the Torah. A defendant admitting half a claim is, normally, ordered by the Torah to take an oath supporting his denial, this oath being of the utmost severity.[99] The Torah expressly excludes from an oath claims, denials and admission regarding documents.[100] In fact, according to many Authorities the destruction of a document does not give rise to a claim for damages; the document (the piece of paper itself) has no value. Other Authorities hold that one has to make good the damage caused, through the rule of *Dina d'Garmi*— liability for damage caused indirectly.[101] If for example a document witnessing a debt is deliberately destroyed, the damage to the document itself is valued at nil, but as this may enable the debtor to deny the debt, either the face value of the document or at least the discount sale value must be compensated for.[102]

Most scholars consider that payment under the doctrine of indirect responsibility is only *Mi-d'Rabbanan*—a Rabbinic

---

[97] *Even Ha'ezer* 28:13; v. *Tur,* loc. cit. at note 3, and *Beit Yosef,* s.v. *"hayah"* to middle of para. *"Vekatav"*; v. *Ketzot Hachoshen* 235:4.

[98] V. supra p. 67.

[99] V. supra p. 37.

[100] V. supra p. 42 – 43.

[101] *Bava Kama* 100a.

[102] V. *Rosh, Bava Metzia* 20a for discussion on this point.

requirement. What would the law be, should the plaintiff claim that the debt written into the damaged document was one of two hundred gold coins, while the defendant claimed it was a debt of only one hundred coins? According to the Torah the plaintiff has no claim; according to the Rabbis he does. Therefore, by their legislation, there is a partial admission, which in the case of a legitimate Torah claim would bring with it an oath of the Torah. The Rabbinical legislation is sufficiently strong, according to many jurists, to give rise to the Torah oath.[103]

Similarly, the Torah exempts from its oath any claim which affects real estate. Thus a claim for money secured by way of mortgage of real estate cannot require the defendant to take an oath of the Torah. What if the Rabbis legislate to abrogate the mortgage and remove the lien? *Tosafot*[104] rules that the Torah recognizes the removal of the lien; the dispute does not now involve land, and a full oath can be demanded of the defendant.

The powers given to the Rabbis to create legislation which transfers property from one to another were granted to them as representatives of the people. Thus any decree not accepted by the general public could not become law.[105] The more authoritative, the more representative the legislative body was, the more respected were the laws it enacted; so much so, that enactments of any great Sanhedrin could only be overruled with difficulty.[106]

Early examples of new legislation enacted by the leaders of the people were the ten stipulations made by Joshua[107]

---

[103] V. *Ketzot HaChoshen* 87:32.

[104] *Bava Metzia* 4b, s.v. *"ein."*

[105] *Avodah Zarah* 36a; v. *Ritva, Novellae,* ad loc. for Scriptural source; v. *Rashba, Responsa* 3:411.

[106] *Rashba,* loc. cit.; v. supra p. 61.

[107] *Bava Kama* 80b et seq.

when on leading his people, newly forged into a united nation, into the Promised Land he realized that he must make them aware of their duties one to the other, and that in an ideal society the guiding principle is not "each man for himself." Among his stipulations were: A spring of water emerging for the first time did not belong exclusively to the owner of the land upon which it appeared. It belonged to all the townsfolk equally, and they could use it free of charge. Similarly he stipulated that the public could walk through private fields until the main rain was expected, as before that time, although there may have been minor rainfalls, no harm was thus done to a field. On this the Talmud concludes that in Babylonia, even after the fall of mere dew, it is forbidden to walk on private fields as this would be harmful.[108]

This Talmudic observation does indicate quite clearly that Joshua's stipulations were not merely conditions of entry into Israel and valid only in that country—they are valid wherever a Jewish Community is to be found.

In addition to the ten stipulations originally quoted by the Talmud, several more are mentioned.[109] R. Yishmael the son of R. Yochanan b. Beroka reported:

> It is a stipulation of the Court of Law, that the owner of the bees [which settle upon a neighbor's tree] is entitled to go down into his neighbor's field and cut off the bough [on which his bees have settled] in order to salvage his swarm of bees; he only has to pay the value of the bough. It is [similarly] a stipulation of the Court of Law that the owner of wine should pour out his wine [from the flask] so as to use it to rescue the honey of his fellow;[110] he recovers the value of his wine out of the honey of his fellow. It is [again] a stipula-

---

[108] Ibid. 81b.

[109] Ibid.

[110] Carried by the other in a jug which suddenly breaks, leaving the contents, which are more valuable than the wine, in danger of being wasted if not salvaged in time.

tion of the Court of Law that [the owner of a bundle of wood] shall remove the wood [from his ass] and load [on his ass] the flax of his fellow [from the back of the ass which fell dead][111] and recover the value of his wood out of the flax of his fellow; for it was upon these stipulations that Joshua transferred the Land to Israel for an inheritance.

The last decrees form the basis of an interesting rule on a problem translated thus in contemporary terms: A is owed money by B. He sees B driving in the direction of the airport and is aware that if B succeeds in embarking and leaving the country, he, A, will not see his money again. It is imperative that he intercept B; he has no car of his own but notices C's car parked nearby with the driving keys in position. A inquires of C as to whether he needs his car for business and C replies that he does not. A thereupon seats himself in the car and drives off despite the protestations of C.

At first glance, A's legal position would appear to be that of a common thief, for someone who borrows without permission is just that.[112] However, this is not so; Joshua's legislation entitles a person to take an article belonging to his fellow to save his own money—he can cut off the bough, he can commandeer the jug, and he can lead away the ass. Therefore, why should he be prohibited (subject to the laws of the country he is in) from taking the car of his fellow? In the same way that he must pay for the bough, the wine and the wood, so of course must he pay for the petrol, the oil, and the wear and tear.

Terumat Hadeshen,[113] on whose responsum this example is based, goes further, ruling that even if C needed his car for business, if the profit involved was less than A was entitled to from B, A could still commandeer the car (horse, in the responsum) and out of the money he retrieves from B compensate C for his loss of business.

---

[111] And which flax is thus in danger of being wasted.
[112] *Bava Batra* 88a.
[113] *Responsum* 316.

The power of legislation vested in the nation as a whole, is also vested in individual smaller units such as self-contained communities, and in the Jewish scheme of law, each community as a whole has the power to bind its individual members. To make the process less cumbersome it may delegate its powers to its representatives so that not all members of the community must become involved in any particular piece of legislation. In a time when the writ of the Halachic Authority is accepted by the community, when problems are sent for resolution to the Talmudic Scholar, when rulings of the Beit Din are in force, the community has de facto delegated its powers to those authorities and it is on the basis of that delegation that the Court's powers of appropriation and redistribution are founded. It is also within the selfsame community's powers to delegate its authority to leading citizens; from this developed the practice of appointing representatives (normally seven) as the "Seven Distinguished Citizens of the Town" who, as they sit to discuss communal affairs, are taking the place of the Beit Din.[114]

So powerful is the community's right to legislate, that in Rashba's view their legislation can overrule *Din Torah*. In one question put to him in connection with a civic dispute, it was contended (inter alia) that "even if they [the witnesses] gave evidence, their evidence would have no value, since they are related to the members of the community. The respondent argues that it is customary among all communities to stipulate in their rules that members of the community may give evidence, and there is no need to bring outside witnesses to testify about their own rules." In a clear and unequivocal reply, Rashba wrote:[115]

He who contends that it is normal for local people to testify

---

[114] *Terumat Hadeshen* 2:214, dealing with a situation in which the townsfolk wished to appoint a person once caught lying, as one of the "Seven."

[115] *Responsum* 5:286.

on behalf of their own community regarding its rules is
right in his argument, since if it were otherwise, every
communal regulation would be ineffective. The custom of
the community is the Law. In all such matters, one may say
that Custom abrogates the Halachah.[116]

On another dispute, in which one party claimed that the
trial proceedings (in matters of taxation) were unfair in that the
parties, judges, and witnesses were all related, Rashba decided:

It is quite clear that after there is a decision by the community naught avails. And so it is the custom of all communities dealing in matters of taxation that disputes are decided
by the residents who adduce evidence from other residents, although these others may be related to the judges
and the disputants. Moreover [because of the nature of the
dispute] the Court itself and all witnesses are interested
parties[117] and they are [to an extent] judging and testifying
for themselves. [Nevertheless all this is perfectly permissible because of the power of Communal Legislation.][118]

The leaders of a community who were appointed with
powers to mete out both corporal and pecuniary punishment, and authorized by the terms of their appointment to
accept whatever testimony they saw fit, from relatives, from
women or even from children, inquired of Rashba[119] as to
whether they were entitled to act.

My reply: to me it is quite obvious that you are entitled to
do exactly as you see fit. For all the requirements and
qualifications are only necessary in a court of law which
judges according to the law of the Torah. An authority set
up under the State is not operating the law of the Torah,

---

[116] Ibid. 2:111 and *Responsa Hameyuchas LehaRamban* 65; v. *Bava Batra* 9a.

[117] Because for every person released from communal taxation others
must shoulder an increased burden, and vice versa.

[118] *Responsa Rashba* 6:7.

[119] Ibid. 4:311 and v. *Responsa Hameyuchas LehaRamban* 279.

otherwise it would not be able to punish... You have the
authority to act as you see fit in accordance with the statement of rules of your community; so is the custom in our
place and many other places, where they have a set of
rules and regulations between them.

However, not all Halachic Authorities agree with Rashba's radical approach, and Rivash, for one, tries to limit Rashba's ruling:

And also that which has been claimed that because the
community had accepted upon themselves: this we have
never heard, that a community should accept a judge who
is able to sit in judgment on his relatives... and that which
the Rashba allowed was only in a general case [one affecting a whole group of people of which the witnesses were
members but not where there is singular interest].[120]

Before either Rashba or Rivash we have a responsa from
a Gaon:

Shimon is quite correct in stating that he will not appear
before a Beit Din upon which sits a relative of his disputant. And even if your community has legislated to treat
relatives as strangers and accept testimony from them, Shimon cannot be forced to appear before them because of
your communal legislation.[121]

Let the final word on this subject be with the later codifiers:

We are now accustomed to receive witnesses from the community with regard to its laws, its charities, and all its other
affairs. And they are competent even if their relatives are
involved, because it [the community] had accepted them.[122]

So much for witnesses; on the question of the competence
of judges, the ruling is:

Judges may not hear any matter in which they have some

---

[120] *Responsum* 311.
[121] *Otzar Hageonim, Sanhedrin,* 171.
[122] *Choshen Mishpat* 37:22 and commentaries.

> beneficial interest... Accordingly, questions of taxation are
> not heard by judges of that city, since they or their rela-
> tives are concerned therein; but if a rule has been made or
> there is a custom in that city that its judges should also
> deal with tax matters, their decision is good in law.[123]

This ruling has been followed virtually up to the present
day. Rabbi Yechiel Michel Halevi Epstein, writing at the end
of the nineteenth century, confirms this:

> If a rule has been made or there is a custom in the city that
> the city's judges should deal with all matters affecting
> their own city, their decisions are good in law; this is com-
> mon usage. I have never seen or heard that in a question
> affecting a city, the judges of that city should not sit in
> judgment. Since this is the custom, it is as if it [the city] has
> accepted their jurisdiction, and the city's judges may deal
> with all the affairs of the city.[124]

Some communities felt the necessity to legislate in order
to avoid irresponsibility and licentiousness. According to law, it
is sufficient for a man to betroth a woman before two competent witnesses. She is then a married woman and requires
a proper Bill of Divorce to regain her freedom. Because this
gave couples an easy opportunity to flout parental and family
objections and to enter into unsuitable marriages, the community therefore legislated that any betrothal which was not in the
presence of ten people was not a valid betrothal; this legislation was supported by Rashba.[125]

> The strict law, it appears to me, is quite clear. The citizens
> are entitled so to legislate provided their Talmudic scholar
> does not disagree with them. The reason is because the
> community is able to confiscate all monies with the con-
> sequence that the betrothal money does not belong to him

---

123 Ibid. 7:12.
124 *Aruch Hashulchan, Choshen Mishpat* 7:22; cf. *Bava Batra* 43a.
125 *Responsa* 1:1206.

[the purported bridegroom]....and the community through the town court are able to confiscate money if they see in this an advantage for their citizens, and the Beit Din's confiscation is valid in the Torah...for we have learned that...[126] "The townspeople are at liberty to fix weights and measures, prices and wages, and to inflict penalties for the infringement of their rules." Nevertheless, if there is a Talmudic scholar in their midst, his consent must be obtained, as we have learned:[127] "There were two butchers who made an agreement to slaughter on alternate days and that if either slaughtered on the other's day the skin of that beast should be torn up, rendering it valueless. One of them actually did kill on the other's day and the other [with friends] went and tore up the skin. Those who did so were summoned before Rava and he ordered them to make restitution. Rabbi Yemar b. Shelemiah thereupon called Rava's attention [to the rule which says] that the townspeople may inflict penalties for breach of their regulations. Rava did not deign to answer him. Said R. Pappa: Rava was quite right not to answer him; this regulation holds good only when there is no distinguished scholar in the town, but where there is such a scholar, individuals certainly do not have the power to make such stipulations [without his consent]."

Rivash,[128] dealing with a similar problem in his time, also gives the required authority to the citizens to legislate as they see fit, but without the necessity of consulting the Halachic Authority. Similarly, he rules that a Union of Workers or a Professional Association can also legislate bindingly on its members—witness the case of the two butchers cited by Rashba— but because their internal regulations may affect the well-

---

[126] *Bava Batra* 8b; Rashba clearly links the power of communal legislation to the Talmudic concept of *Hefker Beit Din*; cf. *Kiddushin* 12b. Rav chastised any man who betrothed without prior arrangement and negotiation.

[127] *Bava Batra* 9a.

[128] *Responsum* 399.

being of the whole town, they must have the consent of the
Halachic Authority. Thus clearly does Rivash distinguish between regulations made by the entire community which, in
his view, do not require the consent of the Talmudic Scholar,
and the regulations of a minority group, which do.[129]

Rivash[130] also considers communal legislation binding on
succeeding generations unless formally revoked, which is in
agreement with an earlier ruling of Rashba who adds that in the
event of there being differing views in a community, the minority is subject to the regulations stipulated by the majority.[131]

Rosh, in refusing the minority the right to contract out of
legislation enacted by the majority, states:

> You should know that on all public matters, the Torah says
> "you must follow the majority ruling,"[132] and on all matters
> in which the community agree we follow the majority; the
> minority must accept that which has been prescribed for
> them by the majority, for if you do not stipulate so you will
> never have agreement in a community on any matter, for
> you will never achieve unanimity. Therefore, says the Torah,
> on everything that needs public agreement, follow the
> majority.[133]

The fact that Rosh invokes a Scriptural requirement to
rule on a public enactment indicates the weight he attaches
to such an enactment.[134]

"Now these are the Judgments which you shall put before

---

[129] Cf. *Choshen Mishpat* 231:28.

[130] Ad loc.

[131] *Responsa* 3:411.

[132] *Shemot* 23:2.

[133] *Responsa* 6:5. V. *Rashba, Responsa* 5:126; *Kol Bo* 142.

[134] There was considerable communal legislation in connection with
the preparation of documents, which is discussed elsewhere in this
work (p.188). V. *Tosafot, Bava Batra* 39b, s. v. *"leit;" Rashba, Responsa*
1:729, 2:11; *Hameyuchas LehaRamban* 65; *Rosh, Responsum* 7:4.

them."[135] Rashi: "Before them—but not before non-Jews, even if you know that a particular matter of law will be decided in the same way as in Jewish law, do not bring it before non-Jewish Courts."[136]

Many and vocal have been the protests against the practice of Jews of ignoring their own Battei Din and of putting disputes before the State Courts—tantamount, according to Rashi himself, to saying that the State system of civil law is superior to the Jewish one.

But that is far from being the whole story.

In this chapter, we have seen the powers given to the community to legislate, to enact laws to meet changing habits, and to lay down regulations to fit the structure of contemporary society. By the demands made upon it by litigants and by the solutions devised by judges, the Law was kept animate and therefore applicable as each new set of circumstances was thrust upon it. As long as it was practiced it could not become irrelevant, but, by being allowed to lapse in practice, the powers of the community as a whole, its courts and Talmudic scholars, fell into desuetude, leaving a void in the Law which could not now keep pace with the development and increasing sophistication of international commerce. What should have been an important part of the practical code of the modern Jew, has regrettably, in the main, become merely a theoretical study by a minority. With its firm Talmudic basis and its numerous precedents, its venerable Rabbinic tradition and the legislative powers available, Jewish Civil jurisprudence could well be revived as a practical force in the everyday life of the Jew.[137]

While Jewish Law was the salient base of national life, it

---

[135] *Shemot* 21:1.

[136] Ad loc., s.v. *"lifneihem."*

[137] There have been several attempts to revive Jewish Civil Law, the most notable being that of a Moscow-based group soon after the First World War.

made the Jewish community, in whatever its place of exile, "a state within a state," which helped it retain its uniqueness and independence; helped it maintain a coherent identity; and encouraged the individual Jew to retain his religious culture, which stood as a bastion against secular and less moral influences, influences which unfortunately dominate considerable sectors of modern society.[138]

---

[138] V. Elon, *Israel Law Review* (vol. 3, no. 1), p. 121 et seq., quoting Rabbi Raphael Hakohen of Altona and essayist Yechezkel Kaufman.

FOUR
Ownership and Possession

HE TWO WORDS "Ownership" and "Possession" are in no way synonymous; indeed while possession may indicate ownership and ownership gives right to possession, each word indicates an entirely different relationship with the object concerned.

The essence of ownership is that it is, subject to general rules of law, a right or aggregate of rights of use, enjoyment, and disposition; while possession is primarily a matter of fact.[1]

The difference between the two terms is clearly indicated by the ruling of R. Yochanan[2] that should a thief misappropriate an article and the owner not yet abandon hope of recovering it,[3] neither of them is able to consecrate it;[4] the one [the robber] because it is not his, the other [the owner] because it is not in his possession. The donation of an article for Temple use is the prerogative of the owner, not of the possessor; nevertheless, the owner's capacity to do so is limited by his lack of possession.

While it is clear that possession in no way equates with

---

[1] Geldart, *Elements of English Law*, p. 91.
[2] *Bava Kama* 68b.
[3] Which means he still retains ownership.
[4] Donate it for Temple service or use.

ownership, nevertheless it is of significant legal consequence, as it does bestow some legal privilege.

In a dispute over a movable chattel, the benefit of any doubt will be given to the disputant in possession, whereas in a dispute over real estate the benefit of the doubt will be given to the undisputed previous owner.[5]

The Jewish legal term for possession is **Chezkat Mamon,** which can mean either the **status** of possession or the **presumption** of possession. The fact of possession places the onus probandi squarely on the shoulders of the claimant; indeed the requirement that a court should have adequate proof before dispossessing the defendant is considered to be of the Torah itself.[6] But whereas, in the event of a dispute, the fact of possession may operate as the ratio decidendi, it does not always do so in the same way. As the alternative translations of the Hebrew legal expression *Chezkat Mamon* indicate, it can operate in one of two ways—as a status quo or as a presumption which indicates the truth. The different legal concepts can clearly be indicated by two simple examples:

In the first, A claims repayment of a loan he alleges he made to B; B denies the claim. In the absence of satisfactory evidence, B will be given the benefit of the doubt and will be left in possession of the sum claimed. There is no evidence to support B's denial but, because the court is in doubt, it will not interfere with the status quo.

In the second case, A claims that a certain object, currently in B's possession, does in fact belong to him, A, which again B denies. The court will assume that B's possession is in fact evidence of ownership and again, the judgment will be in B's favor, in this instance not merely because the court is bound to maintain the status quo, but because the balance of probabilities favors B, as normally items in a person's

---

[5]   V. infra Chap. V for detailed treatment of this subject.
[6]   V. supra p. 33.

possession belong to him.[7]

Although in both cases the court will rule against A, telling him that he has not satisfied the onus of proof which is upon him as the claimant, and that without sufficient proof the court will not deprive B, the possessor—nevertheless, the legal reasoning is clearly different in both cases.

In the case of A's claiming repayment of a loan, the status quo proves nothing. The fact that B is in possession in no way proves that he had not borrowed from A. **Possession** in this case is a **static**—an actual position which cannot be altered without proof, whereas in the case of the disputed articles **possession** may well be a **dynamic** or **probative** factor.[8]

The difference between the two concepts is significant in Jewish Law, and to understand that difference it is appropriate to examine the basic sources of **status** and **presumption** both of which, in Talmudic terms, are expressed in the one word, **Chazakah.** These are to be found in connection with *Shechitah*—the ritual slaughter of permitted animals, which is required in order that they be permissible to be eaten (kosher) in accordance with Sinaitic Law.

R. Huna (rules):

> An animal while alive has a status (*Chazakah*) of being forbidden (and therefore remains forbidden when dead)[9]

---

7   V. *Shevuot* 46b; v. infra p. 105. Other circumstances are also persuasive. For example, if A claims B has stolen the article (which is known to be A's) he is in no way believed (we do not presume a man to be a thief). However, if A claims he loaned the article to B and it is of a type which is frequently loaned, he may well be believed and B's possession is considered that of a borrower, not of an owner.

8   Rabbi Dr. I. Herzog, *The Main Institutions of Jewish Law,* vol. 1, p. 263; v. *Terumat Hadeshen* 207, which uses similar descriptions.

9   Because of the original prohibition of eating part of a living animal—*Rashi*; because it has not been ritually slaughtered—*Tosafot Beitzah* 25a, s.v. "*b'chezkat*"; v. Rabbi N. S. Greenspan, *Melechet Machshevet,* p. 162; v. note 39 infra.

until it becomes known to you that is was ritually slaughtered;
once ritually slaughtered it is presumed (*B'chezkat*) permitted,
until it becomes known to you how it became prohibited.[10]

The first ruling of R. Huna, that the dead animal retains
the same prohibited status it had while alive, is obviously
based on not interfering with the status quo ante. The Talmud inquires as to the source from which we know the legal
significance of the status quo and finds it in connection with
a plague-infested house, where it is assumed that the leprous
signs did not abate until at least after the critical moment—
after the priest had locked the door.[11]

What is the significance of R. Huna's second ruling that
once the animal has been correctly slaughtered it is presumed to be permitted? After being slaughtered, the animal
must be examined in order to be certain that it was not
suffering a terminal disease, which would render it *terefah*
and prohibited. A typical defect would be a small hole in the
animal's lung, and therefore before an animal may be eaten
its lungs must be examined. What if the lungs have been lost
and are not available for examination? It is on this point that
R. Huna rules that having been correctly slaughtered it is
presumed that the animal is kosher, not having suffered any
significant defect. This presumption is in no way based on
previous status; no one ever ascertained that it was free of
disease. On what, therefore, is R. Huna's presumption based?
Answer: on the fact that most animals are normal and do not
have, say, holes in the lung. The ruling is based on the precedent of the majority of cases—in Talmudic idiom, **Rov**.[12]

Varied are the sources from which the Talmud derives

---

[10] *Chullin* 9a.

[11] Ibid.; v. *Tosefta, Gittin* 2:13, which finds the source in connection
with the Cities of Refuge and the presumed continuance of the life
of the High Priest.

[12] V. *Ran, Novellae, Chullin* 11a; cf. *Yad, Shechitah* 4:7 and *Hagahot
Maimoni*, ad loc.

the authority to solve a problem by applying this precedent of *Rov*. One quoted by R. Mori[13] is derived from the case of he "who smiteth his father or his mother,"[14] for which offense the Divine Law prescribes death.

Now why do we not fear that the person struck may not have been his true father? Is it not because we follow the majority of cases, which are that a woman cohabits with her husband more often [than with a stranger—and therefore her children are presumably from her husband]?[15]

The difference between a decision based on the status quo and one based on a "majority" of cases is well illustrated in circumstances in which they clash.

> If a child is found next to a lump of dough [of *Terumah*][16] and there is dough in his hand, the Sages declare it unclean because it is a child's nature to dabble among refuse and with insects.[17]

The child has certainly touched the dough and has "most likely touched" unclean items which defile the dough. The dough has hitherto had a status of Levitical Cleanliness and was permissible; now there is a presumption based on the majority of such cases which becomes the prevailing factor in the Sages' ruling that the dough is to be treated as unclean.

The reason that a presumption derived from a majority of cases prevails over the status quo of a *Chazakah* is because the latter is static; it represents the position as it *was previously* and, in case of doubt, that status is not tampered with, whereas the "majority"—the *Rov*— is a *current* persuasive indicator, allowing us to presume as to what the facts really are.[18] To

---

[13] *Chullin* 11a.

[14] *Shemot* 21:15.

[15] *Chullin* 11b.

[16] The Heave Offering given to the Priests, which may only be eaten by them in a state of Levitical Cleanliness (*Bemidbar* 18).

[17] *Kiddushin* 80a.

[18] *Shev Shemateta* 4:24; cf. *Sha'arei Yosher* 3:3.

use the earlier idiom, the *Rov* is dynamic or probative whereas the *Chazakah* is static.

It should, therefore, follow that if there is a clash between a *Rov* and the *Chazakah* of possession, the *Rov*, in keeping with the general rule, should prevail. However, this is not so; in a case in which a farmer bought a bull which he subsequently finds to be dangerous and liable to gore, there is a debate as to whether the transaction is voidable. Shmuel rules (and that is the Halachah) that the sale is a valid one, for although the purchaser could claim that the vendor must have presumed that in common with most farmers he had purchased the animal for farm work, the vendor can respond by claiming that he actually presumed that the animal was in fact purchased for its meat value only. As the vendor, having been paid, is in possession of the money, the onus probandi is on the purchaser, who would base his claim on the fact that the **majority** of such purchases are for field work—a claim which would not succeed.[19] The *Chazakah* of possession prevails against the evidence afforded by the "majority of cases"— the *Rov*—because this particular *Chazakah* is one of the *current* status quo—the vendor is currently holding the money, whereas the normal static *Chazakah* is based on the status quo ante.[20]

Notwithstanding the fundamental difference between a *Chazakah* and a *Rov* and the two distinct sources from which the Babylonian Talmud derives them, the Jerusalem Talmud[21] finds as its source for the legally persuasive powers of a *Chazakah*, the law relating to the smiting of one's father or mother; from the very source that the Babylonian Talmud derives *Rov*, the Jerusalem Talmud derives *Chazakah*![22]

In fact, the Jerusalem Talmud is referring not to the static

---

[19] *Bava Kama* 46a & b.

[20] *Shev Shemateta*, loc. cit.

[21] Talmud Yerushalmi, *Kiddushin* 4:10.

[22] The Yerushalmi is followed by Rambam in *Yad, Issurei Bi'ah* 1:20; v. *Chullin* 11b, note of R. Akiva Eger.

Chazakah of status quo, but to the dynamic *Chazakah* based on presumption. For example, if children were brought up together as brother and sister, they are so presumed to be, and would be guilty of incest were they to cohabit. The "majority" of the Babylonian Talmud, that a woman cohabits with her husband more often than with a stranger, becomes the "presumption" of the Jerusalem Talmud, that we presume a woman's child to be that of her husband—a presumption based on a majority of cases. This *Chazakah* is described as a presumption derived from a majority.[23]

There are significant legal differences dependent upon whether the ratio decidendi is based on a static or on a dynamic presumption. For example, if we have doubt as to whether an animal has been correctly slaughtered, it may not be eaten, as it retains its previous status of being prohibited; nevertheless, one may not make an oath that this animal is not kosher. It may well be kosher, but the rules of *Chazakah* demand that we treat it as non-kosher. Yet in a case where a man named Chasa was drowned in shark-infested waters, R. Nachman took an oath: "By God, the fish have eaten Chasa,"[24] for in the majority of cases, people falling into such waters are indeed eaten by the fish and this "majority" indicates what happened to Chasa.[25]

It is tempting to believe that a probative *Chazakah* is le-

---

[23] *Tashbatz* 3:217 ad fin.; v. Rabbi N. S. Greenspan; *Pilpulah shel Torah,* foreword, note 4; v. *Chatam Sofer, Responsa, Even Ha'ezer 76.*

[24] *Yevamot* 121b. V. *Kovetz He'arot* 67:4.

[25] A charming story is told of the Ruzhine Rebbe. A childless woman came before him and told him of her sorrow with great bitterness. Deeply moved by her plight, he took an oath saying, "By God, you will have a child." Disciples present questioned him as to the propriety of his oath; after all, it was not within his powers to make such a promise. To this he responded, "I was entitled to utter my oath, for the majority of women do bear children and on the basis of the 'presumption arising out of a majority,' R. Nachman in the Gemara did, indeed, utter an oath."

gally stronger than a static one, but this is not necessarily so. Certainly, the static *Chazakah* has limitations. It proves nothing; it is only a method of arriving at a decision, and as such it cannot be invoked unless a decision is sought on the status of its possessor.

For example: To become Levitically Clean one must immerse oneself in a *Mikveh*. One requirement is that the *Mikveh* must contain no less than forty *se'ah* (a measure) of water. Normally, *Mikvaot* are regularly measured to make sure that they conform to this requirement. The bath in question was measured in the normal way and found to have a satisfactory content. Subsequently someone immersed himself, and after he emerged the *Mikveh* was once again measured and this time found to be wanting. Can we rely on its previous status and declare the bather ritually clean, on the presumption that it only lost water after his immersion?

The answer is no; the static *Chazakah* of the *Mikveh* relates only to the *Mikveh* and as far as the *Mikveh* is concerned there are no further doubts—it must in any event be refilled. As we are not asked to rule upon the *Mikveh*, we cannot call its *Chazakah* into play to assist the bather. The *Mikveh's Chazakah* only guides us as to how to react towards the *Mikveh* itself, and that is no longer in question.

Similarly (according to Rashi), a problem arises in the case of a woman who, hitherto having had the status of being allowed to marry a Kohen,[26] has that status jeopardized by doubt. In theory, she herself could rely upon her previous status and marry a Kohen. The issue of that marriage would also benefit from her *Chazakah* and would be declared a fit Kohen. However, after her death, when her personal status is no longer relevant to her, it cannot de novo be called into play to declare that her children are fitting priests. This

---

[26] A Kohen (priest) is forbidden to marry, inter alia, divorcees, proselytes, and women who have cohabited with forbidden partners, whether willingly or under duress.

was the problem which Alexander Jannaeus[27] faced. As he was of the Hasmonean family and therefore of priestly descent, he wished to act as High Priest. This the Rabbis of the time would not permit, as it had been rumored that prior to marrying his father, his mother had been captured and presumably raped. Had she been alive and the question put to the Rabbis as to whether she may continue to cohabit with her husband, the ratio decidendi would indeed have been her previous status—that of a fitting wife for a Kohen; that ruling could have flowed through to her son who, in turn, would have been declared a fit priest. After her death, however, it was not possible to use her personal *Chazakah* merely for the purpose of resolving the King's dilemma.[28]

But while indeed the static *Chazakah* does have this limitation as, in effect it proves nothing, it does at times have more influence than the probative *Chazakah* in leading the court to a decision.

In Jewish jurisprudence, the ultimate proof which can be laid before a court is the testimony of two competent witnesses;[29] faced with unimpeachable evidence, the court must act upon it and may not take cognizance of any other contradictory factor. If there is contradictory evidence laid before it by another pair of competent witnesses, the court becomes powerless to act, provided perjury is not proved against either pair; not knowing which testimony to accept, the court must leave the case in doubt. It would make no difference whether one side produced three, four or even a hundred witnesses. The unit of evidence demanded by the Torah is one pair of

---

[27] King of Judea 104-78 B.C.E. (Yannai Hamelech in the Talmud); v. supra Chap. I.

[28] Both cases are quoted by R. Shimon Shkop, *Sha'arei Yosher* 2:2.; v. Rabbi C. D. Kaplin, *Keter David Tinyana* 10. The strength of the status quo ante of *Kashrut* and fitness is clearly shown in the *Noda B'Yehudah* I, *Even Ha'ezer* 69.

[29] *Devarim* 19:15.

witnesses, and two have the same effect as a hundred.[30] It follows, therefore, that if one side attempted to give added credence to his witnesses by invoking a *Chazakah*, a *Rov*, or a *Miggo*,[31] the court would remain unimpressed. None of these three indicators has the persuasive effect of witnesses and, in the same way as an additional witness on either side will not sway the argument, so can no other indicator or probative factor.

Yet in a case where two witnesses were to declare that a woman had been validly divorced, while two others denied it (the classic example being the case of the husband's throwing a Bill of Divorce to his wife in a public thoroughfare and the witnesses' disputing as to whether it was nearer him, in which case she is not divorced, or nearer her, in which case she *is* divorced), the rule is that she retains her previous status of being a married woman. Her previous *Chazakah* prevails against the two witnesses who declare that the Bill fell nearer her and that she is indeed divorced. Why is this so? Because her *Chazakah* in no way contradicts the evidence of the witnesses; it is in no way probative; it does not attempt to prove that the Bill was nearer to him; all it tells us is that in cases of doubt, such as this is, the Beit Din must base its ruling on the status quo ante.[32]

This would not be so in the case of a probative or dynamic *Chazakah* or *Rov*, where the indicator is indicating a fact, not mandating a mode of conduct. As there is no indication of fact which can validly contradict competent testimony, this type of *Chazakah* or *Rov* is ignored in these circumstances, having no legal value. This is simply shown in the following case: A claims he loaned money to B for four weeks. B admits this but claims that he repaid the loan during the third week. If

---

[30] *Makkot* 5b.
[31] Supra p. 35.
[32] *Or Same'ach, Responsa*, 2:27; on the question of "public thoroughfare v. *Aruch Hashulchan, Even Ha'ezer* 139:36 et seq.

the matter stopped there, the Court would rule in A's favor on the presumption that "borrowers do not repay debts before the due date."[33] Although the borrower has the advantage of the *Chazakah* of possession, it falls before the presumption of non-payment. This itself is interesting in that the presumption is based on a majority of cases, a *Rov*, and it has already been shown that in monetary disputes, a *Rov* or majority is not the ratio decidendi.[34] It does seem therefore that a *Rov* which is designated with the title of *Chazakah* has the characteristics of both; it retains its probative function indicating the facts, but in addition it provides the matter upon which it reflects with a status quo which is not easily upset.[35]

To revert to the case of A vs. B, B produces witnesses who testify that, for example, on the fourth day of the third week, he indeed repaid A. However, A is able to produce witnesses who testify that on that day, he, A, was not in town and therefore could not have received repayment. The case now becomes one of conflicting testimonies, posing two problems. Firstly, who succeeds, A or B? Secondly, are the witnesses to be discredited and disqualified from further testimony, as one or other of these pairs has certainly committed perjury?

The answer to the first question is that B succeeds. A has on his side two witnesses supported by a probative *Chazakah* that B would not have paid before the due date; B has two witnesses and a static *Chazakah*. B's witnesses wipe out not only A's witnesses but also A's probative *Chazakah*. A's witnesses wipe out B's witnesses but cannot damage his *Chazakah* of possession which, being static and not probative, is on a different "wavelength" from witnesses who are probative.[36]

---

[33] *Bava Batra* 5a et seq.

[34] V. supra, p. 94.

[35] *Terumat Hadeshen* 314; v. *Kesef Nivchar* 144:35 & 36; R. Shimon Shkop; *Sha'arei Yosher* 3:3; v. *Chatam Sofer, Responsa, Choshen Mishpat* 67.

[36] *Shev Shemateta* 6:22. However, this point is disputed by Rabbi C. S. Lopian in his commentary *Ravcha Shemateta*, ad loc.

Are the witnesses to be disqualified? This is a point of dispute in the Talmud.

> If two pairs of witnesses contradict one another [so that one pair must be giving false evidence], R. Huna says that each pair may give evidence as a whole [in another case]; R. Chisda, however, says: what have we to do with false witnesses?[37]

R. Huna, who does not disqualify the witnesses on the grounds that they are possible perjurers, in fact relies on their previous status of being honest, trustworthy citizens. The **Chazakah of Kashrut** which has been theirs until now cannot be upset without definite proof, and this we do not have; but it can only hold good against the opposing pair of witnesses' testimony that these are lying, if it is a **static status**. If, however, it were to be considered a **probative status**, it would clash directly with the testimony of the other witnesses, and, being an inferior form of proof to that of witnesses, it must fail, leaving them as disqualified.

In fact, the argument between R. Huna and R. Chisda may well turn on this point; is the **Status of Kashrut** static or dynamic?[38]

Once the difference between a static and a dynamic *Chazakah*[39]

---

[37] *Bava Batra* 31b; R. Huna does not disqualify them because of the suspicion of their having given false evidence in this case. But even he accepts that one witness from one side may not combine with one from the other in any other case because one of the two has certainly given false evidence in this case and, therefore, in the subsequent case, one of the pair is certainly a perjurer.

[38] V. *Oneg Yom Tov, Responsa* 70. (On his subsequent discussion as to whether the status continues under a different law—e.g., an animal with the status of being prohibited because it is alive may retain the same status after death, although the prohibition is now of *Nevelah* [non-slaughtered carcass]—v. Rabbi N. S. Greenspan, *Melechet Machshevet: Gidrei Heter Shechitah*, chap. 5, p. 162); v. R. Akiva Eger, Responsa, 1:136.

[39] Supra p. 93.

is understood, it becomes reasonably obvious why most Authorities[40] consider that in the case of A's claiming repayment of a loan which B denies, that B's *Chazakah* of possession is a static one. In no way can B's possession be considered an indication of whether or not he did borrow money from A.

It also becomes relatively simple to understand why many Authorities consider that in the case of A's claiming a specific article, B's possession gives him, B, a dynamic *Chazakah*—the fact that it is in his possession indicates that the article is his.[41] This could help to ease the plight of an *Agunah*.[42] If, for example, after the husband's disappearance, a body is found, which itself is not recognizable, but which is wearing clothes identifiable as those of her husband, it may well be presumed that, as the clothes are in the possession of the dead man they are indeed his, in which case he was her husband and she is now a widow free to remarry.[43] Possession in this case is not merely a static status; it may well prove the point in doubt.

It is normally assumed that the Talmudic statement, "It is a fundamental principle in Law that the onus probandi falls on the claimant,"[44] is a corollary of the advantage given by law to the defendant in possession. It would follow, therefore, that where the defendant's claim to possession is defective, the onus of proof would not fall so heavily on the plaintiff—but this is not so.

In a barter transaction, where for example one party trades his cow for the other's ass, the moment the owner of the cow

---

[40] *Maharik, Responsa*, 72; *Netivot Hamishpat* 34:15; *Chatam Sofer, Responsa, Choshen Mishpat 67*, et seq.

[41] *Or Same'ach, Malveh V'loveh* 2:6.

[42] Lit., a deserted woman: one whose husband has disappeared without giving her a divorce, thereby keeping her bound to him and not able to remarry.

[43] *Noda B'Yehudah* I, *Even Ha'ezer* 37.

[44] *Bava Kama* 46b; v. infra p. 128.

takes possession of the ass he is acquiring, the owner of the ass automatically becomes the owner of the cow, wherever it may be.[45] Thus, while the ass may be with the transacting parties and visible to them, the cow may be some way away and not visible. What happens if, on repairing to the cow's pasture, they find that in the meantime it has given birth to a calf? The vendor will obviously claim that the birth took place before the barter transaction, while the purchaser will claim that the birth took place after the transaction was completed, and, having acquired a pregnant cow, the calf is now his. The Mishnah[46] rules that in such circumstances the value of the calf is divided equally between both parties. The Talmud[47] questions this ruling. There is a general rule of law, "that which is in a person's possession is presumed to be his";[48] if so, the Court should ascertain in whose field the calf was found and declare him the owner, unless the other can satisfy the onus of proof which is thrown on the claimant, as after all the owner of the field can be said to be "in possession."[49]

Tosafot[50] challenges this proposition on the grounds that the presumption of ownership does not flow from the possession of creatures such as sheep and cattle which can roam from field to field;[51] the fact that the calf is found in a particular field does not mean that it belongs to the owner of that field; it may have wandered into the field of its own accord. Tosafot holds that indeed the owner of the field does not

---

[45] *Mishnah, Kiddushin* 28a.

[46] *Bava Metzia* 100a.

[47] Ibid.

[48] An oft-quoted "Talmudic" dictum, which in fact is nowhere expressed directly in the Talmud, but which is inferred from the Talmudic debate in *Shevuot* 46a & b (*Mishneh Lemelech: Malveh V'loveh* 1:4).

[49] At this stage the Talmud is constrained to limit the Mishnaic ruling to such a case where the calf was found in a meadow belonging to neither disputant.

[50] *Bava Metzia,* ad loc., s.v. *"v'lechazeh."*

[51] *Bava Batra* 36a.

have the "presumption of possession," but because the matter is one in which the doubt arose *spontaneously* and not merely because of the claims of the disputing parties,[52] neither of whom seems to have more right than the other, the court will not upset the current status quo while the matter remains in doubt. By leaving matters as they are, automatically the calf would belong to the party who owns the field in which it is found—unless the other can satisfy the onus of proof upon him.

This ruling clearly indicates that while one party does not have the advantage of legal possession, nor indeed, any more rights than the other, it is up to the other, if he wishes to change the status quo, to satisfy the burden of proof upon him—a clear illustration that the onus probandi is not a corollary of legal possession.[53]

In fact, as a result of the Talmudic discussion surrounding that particular mishnah, the ultimate ruling is that we do look to who has the stronger claim to possession. As current possession is no guide, the Court will look to see who had previous possession; this would of course be the vendor, who owned the cow and the calf in its embryo state. The vendor having been in possession until the doubt arose, the onus probandi is on the purchaser to prove that the birth had taken place later.[54]

The presumption that an article in a man's possession is his, is based on the fact that without evidence we do not presume a man to be a thief;[55] therefore that which he is holding, he is rightfully entitled to. This would of course preclude the *Chazakah* operating in the possessor's favor in respect to items which it is customary to loan or hire out; in

---

[52] Talmudic term "*Derrara D'Mamona*."

[53] An orally reported lecture of R. Chaim Shmulevitch of Mir.

[54] V. Bertinoro, *Bava Metzia* 8:4; v. *Shitah Mekubetzet, Bava Kama* 46b, s.v. "*v'harav Rav*"; v. *Torat Chaim*, ad loc.; v. *Tosafot, Bava Kama* 35b, s.v. "*zot omeret*."

[55] *Shevuot* 46b.

such cases the undisputed previous owner would be believed with the claim that he had loaned or hired that particular item to the one in possession, who indeed is entitled to be holding the article, but whose possession does not give him "presumption of ownership."[56]

The importance of possession, or lack of it, is indicated in the Talmud by the following ruling:

> All the authorities concerned agree that when two men each leave an animal in the charge of a shepherd and one [we know not whose] dies, that the shepherd should leave the living animal with the two owners and depart [leaving them to sort out their difference].

The shepherd himself is not responsible—the animal died accidentially; neither claimant can claim possession of the living animal; the Beit Din does not have to protect the interest of either, and therefore the two claimants are left to settle the matter between themselves.

> Also in the case where one gave an animal in the charge of an owner [of other animals, and one animal in the pen dies], that the claimant must produce evidence that it was not his which died.[57]

The owner of the pen will claim that it was the visiting animal which died and the onus probandi is on the claimant, for, in this particular case, the owner of the pen is in possession of all the living animals.

This ruling is used by the *Terumat Hadeshen*[58] in dealing with the following interesting problem:

A arranged to travel to a distant city carrying with him twenty gold coins of his own in his purse. B and C both asked A as a favor to take some gold coins for them to that city, B giving him ten and C six. A accepted the assignment

---

[56] Ibid., as understood by most commentators.
[57] *Bechorot* 18b.
[58] *Responsa* 314.

but made it perfectly clear that he did not accept any responsibility whatsoever for any loss, however incurred. En route a hole developed in A's purse and four coins fell out. It is not known whose coins they were, and the question now is: how is the loss to be divided?

Quoting the case of the animals, the author begins by suggesting that A does not have to bear any of the loss. He is in possession of the coins; he will take his twenty, and it is up to the other claimants to prove that it was A's coins which were lost if they wish to deprive him of his possession of any of those twenty coins. This precludes what would seem to be the obvious solution of dividing the loss pro rata to the number of coins owned by each of the three. Against A is, prima facie, the general rule that when in doubt as to where an object comes from, one looks to the majority of the possibilities—as in the classic case of ten butcher shops, nine selling kosher and one selling non-kosher meat, in which it is presumed that any meat found outside those shops has come from one of the nine.[59] On that basis it should be assumed that the four coins which fell out were from the majority—from the twenty belonging to A. However, this is not so, because of the principle that "majority" or *Rov* cannot prevail against possession.[60] Consequently the dispute is now between B and C; between them, the principle of following the majority can operate, for it only fails against possession, and neither is in possession of his ten or six coins respectively. This would mean that C can argue against B, that as A's twenty coins are eliminated, the majority of the sixteen remaining were B's, and those which fell, fell from that majority, with the result that B suffers the entire loss and both he and C each receive six coins from A.[61]

---

[59] *Ketubot* 15a.

[60] Supra p 96.

[61] The author does not remain with this view. He distinguishes this case and that of the dead animal in the pen, in that each animal is

Even where the doubt is not one of fact but one of law—for example, an unresolved legal dispute—the decision must favor the defendant in possession.[62]

In Jewish Law, all property not yet disposed of, which is owned by a man at his death is inherited by his sons (with a firstborn son taking a double share). If in anticipation of death a Testator declares that all his property should be transferred to his wife, the assumption is that he made that declaration only in order that his sons should honor his wife; the declaration of gift is treated as a declaration trust, making his wife the trustee of his property, which makes his children dependent upon her cooperation. This ruling is based on the assumption that no dying man would ignore Jewish Law and totally deprive his sons of their rightful inheritance. The consequence of this ruling is that the widow is not the beneficial owner of the estate; she is merely the trustee and therefore cannot dipose of it to the detriment of the rightful heirs, nor, were she to remarry, would her new husband have any interest in it.[63] What would be the law if, while in the prime of life, and with no contemplation of early death, a man executes a deed transferring all his property to his wife, retaining for himself the rights of income during his lifetime? In such a case it may well be that he does intend making her the reversionary owner of the property absolutely, and consequently when he dies, his children have no claim against the widow. This problem is unresolved in the Talmud, and therefore remains a matter of doubt in law.[64] What should a court rule in these circumstances if faced by the opposing claims of the widow that she is the absolute owner, and of the sons that she is

in fact a different unit, whereas all the identical coins together form one "purse" (similar to a barrel of wine in which several people have a share); as all 36 coins form one unit, the loss is indeed in the event divided pro rata.

[62] *Choshen Mishpat* 25:2. Commentary of Remah.; cf. infra p. 118.

[63] *Bava Batra* 131b and commentaries. V. infra p. 239 note 14.

[64] Ibid. 132a.

merely the trustee? As in any case of doubt, the disputed property should be left with the party in possession; but who can be said to be in possession? Some Authorities hold that as inheritance is automatic and sons take their father's place, the heirs are said to be in possession and the onus probandi is on the widow to prove that her late husband intended to make her an absolute gift. Others are of the view that as the widow holds a document which is prima facie a valid deed of a gift, she is automatically in possession of the property, and it is up to the sons to disprove her claim.[65]

So strong is the presumption that ownership is with the possessor, that indeed it can be used against him. For example, A gives a valuable article to B to sell for him. B in fact owes C money, who on hearing that B has a valuable article in his possession, claims it as B's creditor. The Rosh[66] rules that unless C knows for certain that B is only an agent for A, he may foreclose on the article on the presumption that B's possession indicates his ownership. A as a single witness cannot upset this presumption. B's admission that the article is indeed A's would not be accepted, as he may well be party to a conspiracy to deprive C of the opportunity to collect his debt. Similarly, a landlord can distrain (seize as security) for rent on chattels in rented property although another party claims ownership.[67]

---

[65] V. *Ritva*, ad loc. (v. edition by Rabbi M. Y. Blau , New York, 1956, vol. 2, note 558 for more detailed discussion). As to whether the holder of a loan document with hypothecary rights is considered to be "in possession," v. *Rashbam, Bava Batra* 125a, s.v. *"l'ta'meihu,"* based on *Pesachim* 30b et seq.

[66] *Responsa* 107:1.

[67] Ibid., 3: This is a problem which faced hire purchase, rental, and leasing companies under British Law. In order to succeed in upsetting the presumption of ownership, A or B would have to produce very strong evidence. *Chatam Sofer, Responsa, Even Ha'ezer* 76 shows how the presumption prevails against a number of strong indicators because they fall below the standard of necessary evidence.

Obviously, there are occasions when possession fails. For example, if it is known that the possessor came by the article unlawfully—for instance, he snatched it, as in the famous case known as "the Ingot of R. Abba,"[68] its possession is discounted in attempting to establish ownership. "Possession which may be taken after a dispute has arisen is not considered possession, for we know that it came into the possessor's hands by snatching [and not by legal means]."[69] Tradesmen who receive articles for cleaning or repair obviously cannot claim that possession gives them the right of ownership, although a problem does arise if, for example, a tailor who had taken in a garment for repair claims that he subsequently purchased it.[70] Similarly, partners cannot claim that possession of partnership assets gives them the right of exclusive ownership.[71]

There is a general overriding rule that in case of doubt of a d'Oraita, or Torah law, the stricter and more rigorous alternative must be followed—for example, doubtful meat may not be eaten; a woman who may or may not be a widow, may not remarry. Stealing is prohibited by the Torah;[72] why then in a case of doubt do we give the defendant in possession the benefit of the doubt and allow him to retain the disputed article? He may well be wrong, in which case he is in possession of stolen money. Why do we not follow the general rule and remove the article from him to avoid his

---

[68] *Bava Batra* 33b. In that case the ownership of the ingot was disputed and the plaintiff snatched it in the presence of a single witness. He admitted doing so, but claimed that he had only repossessed his own ingot.

[69] *Rashbam, Bava Batra* 34b, s.v. "tifsuha."

[70] *Mishnah, Bava Batra* 42a; v. discussion 45a et seq.

[71] *Mishnah*, loc. cit.; for other exceptions v. *Torah Temimah, Shemot* 24:14 note 32.

[72] *Vayikra* 19:11. The prohibition in the *Aseret Hadibrot, Shemot* 20:13, relates to kidnapping (body stealing).

becoming a thief? Obviously we cannot give it to the other party, who is in exactly the same position; therefore perhaps it ought to be retained by the Court pending a solution.

The answer is: a person is only a thief if he deprives the rightful owner of that which legally belongs to him. Therefore, before the Biblical injunction "Thou shalt not steal" comes into force, the court must decide who is indeed the rightful owner.

This decision is arrived at by applying all the relevant rules of Jewish Civil Jurisprudence; and if under those rules, possession, or any other factor gives one party the right of ownership, only then, when his ownership is established, does the law of "Thou shalt not steal" apply to his opponent. The processes by which a decision as to ownership is arrived at are left to the courts, normally with no Biblical guidance; only after that decision has been made, does the Biblical law of "Thou shalt not steal" come into force.[73]

---

[73] R. Shimon Shkop, *Sha'arei Yosher* 5:1, who quotes other authors. Another answer may well be that as there is insufficient evidence to upset the defendant's denial, and as he is sure he is not doing wrong, the court is not obliged to interfere, although this may not be valid where he cannot know the truth, e.g. in the case of the cow which gave birth around the time of the barter (supra p. 103). For the principles, v. *Pnei Yehoshua, Novellae, Ketubot* 22b, s.v. "*va'adayin tzarich.*"

FIVE
Real Property—Ownership and Occupation

U
NLIKE MOVABLE OBJECTS, which can be passed
from hand to hand or from place to place, land, or
property built on land, cannot be said to be "in
the possession of" a person. On the contrary, he
who would claim possession would himself be on the land or
in the buildings. Land, therefore, by its very nature, cannot
be stolen;[1] it cannot be moved from its place.[2] A person who
illegally occupies land is a trespasser but not a thief.

This is an important legal distinction. A thief becomes
entirely and absolutely responsible for any article he has
stolen; as long as it has not been returned to its rightful
owner, the thief is liable for any damage done to it, however
accidental and however unavoidable. A trespasser, however,
is not responsible for any accidental damage occurring to the
land he has wrongfully occupied, provided he has in no way
caused it or been negligent in allowing it. Thus, if a river
floods a misappropriated field, the trespasser is entitled to

---

[1] *Bava Kama* 117b.

[2] *Tosafot, Bava Metzia* 61a, s.v. *"ela"; v. Maharsha, Novellae* and *Pnei Yehoshua,* ad loc.

say to the owner, "Here is yours before you."[3] If however, due to the trespasser's negligence, the property had, say, been appropriated by others, he would be liable under the general rules of tort to compensate the owner in the same way as he would for any damage that he himself actually caused. The difference between real and personal property can be summed up by the phrase, "Land always remains in the possession of its true owner."[4]

This phrase is not to be taken to give license to trespass, as a statement that the trespasser has not breached the law. Indeed, he has fully transgressed the prohibition of "Thou shalt not steal,"[5] and possibly that of "Thou shalt not remove another man's landmark."[6] What the phrase does mean is that while there are religio-moral objections to his trespassing and taking possession of another man's property, no legal consequences flow from so doing, provided the owner has suffered no damage due to the trespasser's activities.

A stolen object can become the property of the thief who stole it, which means he will, in that event, not have to return the object itself but will merely have to pay compensation, if, as often happens, the owner expresses resignation to his loss[7] and the thief himself makes some change in the stolen object. For example, stolen wool, once knitted into a garment, is no longer the object that was stolen. Similarly, once the thief has passed the article on to another person after the owner's resignation, the obligation of returning it is lifted from him, leaving in its place the obligation of making full restitution by means of monetary compensation.[8] This, however, is not so for real estate; wrongfully possessed land can never become the property of the trespasser or of any-

---

3   "Take it as it is." *Mishnah, Bava Kama* 117b.
4   V. *Tiferet Yisrael, Mishnah Bava Kama* 10:5, explanation 28.
5   *Vayikra* 19:13.
6   *Devarim* 19:14. V. *Rashi*, ad loc.
7   Infra p. 179 (the Talmudic term *meya'esh*—"despairs").
8   *Bava Kama* 66b.

one who derives his title from the trespasser.[9]

It follows, therefore, that although the "owner in present occupation"[10] has some claim in law, it is not as strong as that of the undisputed "previous owner."

An interesting case subject, of a difference of opinion between two *Amoraim*, clearly indicates the relative status of the present occupant and the previous owner.

A, the current occupant, produced an unchallenged document that the property was his—the document evidencing his purchase from the previous owner, B, now claiming restoration of the property. On being challenged, A admitted that the document he produced was, in fact, for some reason invalid, but he claimed that he had had a properly valid document which he had lost; the document produced was in fact not the basis of his claim; it was merely produced to bolster it. Had A remained silent and not admitted that the document produced was invalid, he would have been successful in his claim, as the document itself was unimpeachable. It only became valueless to his case when he admitted its invalidity. Applying the rules of *Miggo*,[11] A should prima facie be believed in his claim that he had at one time had a proper document and be confirmed in possession of the property. But this is not so; as the previous owner, B, whose previous ownership is undisputed, is considered to be in possession, A in fact becomes the claimant, seeking to deprive B of his property. In such circumstances the *Miggo* is of no avail to him, as there is a general rule that *Miggo* can only be used to defend—to help the defendant retain property—not to attack and deprive the defendant of property.[12]

---

[9] *Bava Batra* 44a. *Rashbam*, s.v. *"uparkinon."*

[10] *Tosafot's* term, *Bava Batra* 32b, s.v. *"vehilcheta."*

[11] Supra p. 35. A's unnecessary admission that the document was invalid indicates that he is being honest and therefore his claim should be believed. Had he wanted to submit a false claim, he would not have admitted the document's invalidity.

[12] *Bava Batra* 32b. *Rosh*, para. 13, quoting *Rivam*.

The principle that the owner is always considered to be in possession is a major judicial tool in deciding landlord/tenant disputes, and will, in the main, work in favor of the landlord.

One classical cause of dispute is the Jewish leap year, which is used to adjust the Jewish calendar. This is necessary because the Jewish calendar is based on the lunar orbit, which is just under eleven days shorter each year than the solar cycle. If unadjusted for several years, the Pesach Festival, for example, could fall in midwinter, and would not fulfill the Biblical requirement that Pesach is to be in the spring,[13] the advent of which obviously depends on the sun's position relative to earth. Therefore, the Head of the Sanhedrin, who was authorized to declare each new month and so to fix the calendar, would periodically declare a leap year, adding an additional month of Adar to the calendar. If the only consideration were the mathematical one outlined, there would have been no problem, as the advent of a leap year could have been known in advance as it is today, for which the calendar was mathematically fixed by Hillel, the last President of the Sanhedrin, circa 400 C.E.[14] However, there were other considerations, as we learn from the letter dictated by Rabban Gamliel[15] to:

> Our brethren, the Exiles in Babylonia and those in Medea and to all the Exiles of Israel; may you have peace forever! We write to inform you that the doves are still tender, the lambs are too young and the crops are not yet ripe. It seems advisable to me and my colleagues to add thirty days[16] to this year.[17]

---

[13] *Devarim* 16:1. V. *Torah Temimah*. After 10 years of non-adjustment, the Jewish year would be 110 days behind the solar year.

[14] *Ritva, Novellae, Rosh Hashanah* 18a, explaining the Mishnah.

[15] The second, called Rabban Gamliel of Yavneh (the center of Jewish scholarship and legal authority after the destruction of the Second Temple).

[16] One month, i.e., Adar II.

[17] *Sanhedrin* 11b. A similar letter was written by his son on a later occasion.

These signs of the late arrival of spring could not have been known in advance, and it could happen that after a year's tenancy had been granted, that particular year was expanded from one of twelve months to one of thirteen months. If the tenancy agreement was for, say, **one year** at a rental of twelve *dinarri*, the tenant would have for his twelve coins the benefit of the extra month. If the agreement stated that the tenant would pay twelve *dinarri* for **twelve months** he would have to pay an extra coin if he wished to retain the tenancy for the leap month. What would the position be if the agreement was couched in terms of, say, "Twelve gold pieces for the year—one gold piece per month"? The agreement itself raises doubt, as there is no indication where the emphasis should be—on the "twelve gold pieces for the year" or on the "one gold piece per month."

As in all monetary matters, disputes must be resolved by reference to possession, and the Talmud suggests that if the dispute arises at the beginning of the additional month, the landlord can demand the additional coin, as it is now the tenant who wishes to remain in occupation—depriving the landlord of his property for the additional month. Conversely, if the dispute arises at the end of the month, by which time the tenant has already had the benefit of the month's occupation, and it is now the landlord trying to take away a gold piece, the decision would be in favor of the tenant. If the question arises in the middle of the month, the Talmud suggests that the amount in dispute is to be divided.

However, these are only suggestions, and the final ruling is that of R. Nachman, that as the landlord is always in possession, it makes no difference when the dispute arises; the tenant must pay the extra gold piece.[18] Thus while the tenant can be said to be in occupation, it is the landlord who is in possession.

---

[18] *Bava Metzia* 102b; v. *Bertinoro, Bava Metzia* 8:3; note of R. Akiva Eger, ad loc; *Rashbam, Bava Batra* 105b, s.v. *"d'Hatam"* ad fin.

The rule that real property is always in the possession of its owner is a *Chazakah*—a presumption of ownership, similar to that of possession of movable property. To revert to the idiom of the previous chapter, what type of *Chazakah* is it: static or dynamic?—a presumption merely to maintain the status quo or a presumption considered probative?

The Talmud[19] reports the case of one who suffered periods of madness between periods of lucidity, who sold property he had inherited. Two witnesses testified that at the time of the sale he was mad, which meant that the sale was invalid, as a madman has no legal capacity.[20] Two other witnesses contradicted that testimony, claiming that the land was sold while the vendor was enjoying a period of lucidity. R. Ashi ruled that, as the two pairs of witnesses were contradictory, they cancel each other out, and as the court is now in doubt, it leaves the property in the vendor's possession as he was the previous undisputed owner. The fact of his possession in no way reflects his state of mind; in no way does it indicate that he was mad at the time of sale and therefore entitled to rescind it. It is, therefore, fair to say that the presumption of ownership in this case is merely static; the status quo is not upset if there is doubt.[21]

If indeed it is so, that the presumption of ownership given to the previous owner is a static presumption, it can be the decisive factor in the event of an unresolved legal point. Thus if Authorities cannot agree on the law in a particular case, later and lesser judges would be bound to leave the property in the possession of the previous owner.[22]

---

[19] *Ketubot* 20a.

[20] V. infra p. 229.

[21] *Keren Orah, Yevamot* 31a (shown me by Rabbi A. Gurwicz of Gateshead). V. also *Rashbam, Bava Batra* 33b, s.v. *"vehadri Pa'eri."*

[22] There is some controversy on this point. V. *Tosafot, Bava Batra* 32b, s.v. *"v'hilcheta;" Rashbam* & *Rosh,* ibid; *Kovetz Ha'orot* 27; *Ketzot Hachoshen* 146:13; Rabbi Dr. I. Herzog, *The Main Institutions of Jewish Law,* vol. 1, p. 263.

It may well be that a doubt in law is to be distinguished from a doubt of fact. When the doubt is one of fact, the law can operate in its full majesty and decide on a course of action, such as retaining the previous status. When, however, the doubt is one of law—when the law itself is indecisive—it would be invidious of it to force a decision or course of action on one or other of the parties. In such circumstances, it may well be preferable to leave matters exactly as they stood at the commencement of the trial—in which case, presumably, the current occupant would be left in possession.[23]

If the scales of Jewish jurisprudence are tipped so heavily in favor of the previous owner of real estate coming into conflict with the present occupant, what is the latter to do, if indeed he has purchased the property, to protect himself and his heirs? Obviously, if the transaction is executed in the presence of competent witnesses, who can be produced when required, the purchaser has little to worry about. But witnesses can wander off or die and may not be readily available when needed. Therefore, a purchase witnessed by a valid document is to be preferred—indeed more publicity is given to such a transaction, as the local scribe will act as an informal land registry.[24] This, in fact, the Talmud[25] quotes as advice from the Prophet. "Men shall buy fields for money and subscribe [sign] documents and seal them and take witnesses in the land of Benjamin and in the places about Jerusalem...."[26] Once the documents were executed, the Prophet further advises, "Thus sayeth the Lord of Hosts, the God of Israel; take

---

[23] R. Elchonon Wasserman, *Kovetz Shiurim, Bava Batra* 136; cf. supra p.108.

[24] *Tosafot, Bava Batra,* 39b, s.v. *"leit"*; it was later legislated by some communities that the local scribe's records become the formal records of the area and be decisive proof in settling disputes. *Rashba, Responsa, Hameyuchas LehaRamban* 65 & 2:111; v. infra p.147 & p.188.

[25] *Bava Batra* 28b and 29a.

[26] *Yirmeyahu* 32:44.

these evidences, this evidence of the purchase, both that which is sealed, and that evidence which is open;[27] and put them in an earthenware vessel, that they may continue[28] many days."[29]

But even the best-kept documents can, through mischance, be lost or unwittingly destroyed. What then? The rule is laid down:

> The legal period for undisputed possession of houses, cisterns, ditches, and caves, dovecotes, bathhouses, olive presses, irrigated fields, slaves and whatsoever produces steady [regular] gain is [obtained by occupation for] three years from day to day.[30]

This is the leading mishnah which establishes the Law of Usucaption (*Chazakah*): that undisturbed, undisputed possession of realty for three successive years, entitles the possessor to retain it against the claims of the former owner.[31]

There is a difference of opinion as to the legal basis for this rule of three years. R. Yishmael and his colleagues, who served in the Sanhedrin when it was situated at Usha,[32] consider that the law has a Biblical source, creating what in modern legal idiom would be called "Squatters' Rights," meaning that if one can remain in occupation for three continuous years, however weak or even non-existent his legal claim to the property may be, the mere fact that he has been in occupation gives him the legal right of ownership.[33]

However, this view is not accepted by the Talmud, which comes to the conclusion that the three-year rule of usucap-

---

[27] The custom was to have two documents, one sealed and the other unsealed.
[28] Remain in good condition and available.
[29] Ibid., 14.
[30] *Mishnah, Bava Batra* 28a.
[31] Blackman's *Mishnayot*, vol. 4, p. 179.
[32] V. *Rosh Hashanah* 31a & b.
[33] R. Shlomo Ganzfried, *Pnei Shlomo, Bava Batra* 28b.

tion is de novo Rabbinic legislation. It would be unrealistic to expect the average buyer to be able to keep his documents of title for more than three years,[34] and the Sages, therefore, instituted the law that if the person in possession can bring evidence that he has occupied the disputed property beneficially for at least three years continuously, he no longer has to produce his documents to establish title.[35] Standing on its own, this new legislation would tip the scales of Jewish jurisprudence very much in favor of the current occupant and, in itself, would be too draconian a measure vis à vis the previous owner, who, although he may have a valid claim, would seem to be legally defenseless against a determined squatter. Therefore, to counter the right of usucaption given to the occupant, the Rabbis in their legislation gave "a right of protest" to the previous owner; he has the right during the first three years of the other's occupation to protest against that occupation, and having done so immediately deprives the occupant of his right of usucaption, with the result that in the absence of documents, ownership of the property would revert back to the previous owner—the author of the protest. To be successful, the protest must be made before two competent witnesses whose testimony would be accepted by a court of law, and must include the words "A, who is occupying my property, is a thief," to which some Authorities require the additional words, "And I shall, in due course, take him to court."[36]

In framing their legislation, the Rabbis relied on the fact that news travels. Therefore, in normal circumstances, it is fair to assume that even an absentee landlord would know if another was trespassing on his property. Indeed, it would be normal to expect him to inquire of travelers arriving from

---

[34] *Bava Batra* 29a, as explained by *Rosh*.

[35] *Ketzot Hachoshen* 140:2; Rabbi Y. Kaniewsky, *Kehillat Yaakov, Bava Batra* 10.

[36] *Choshen Mishpat* 146:4.

that place as to what was happening to his property.[37] On hearing of the other's trespass, which would presumably be within three years of commencement of that trespass, he would be expected to use the power of protest given him by the Rabbis and in due course to adduce evidence to the satisfaction of the court that he had indeed done so. Conversely, the news of the protest would, in the same way, reach the ears of the current occupant, who, if he did originally have documents of title, would still be expected to have retained them, as three years of his occupation had not yet elapsed; he would now be especially careful to preserve them, knowing that the previous owner could one day return and reclaim the property. The occupant does not have to take possession in the presence of the previous owner, nor does the previous owner have to lodge his protest in the presence of the occupant. Normally, pleas that the previous owner did not know of the alleged trespass, or that the current occupant did not know of the formal protest, would go unheeded by the courts in the certainty that such news travels. To such pleas the court would respond with the popular saying, "Your friend has a friend, and the friend of your friend has a friend"[38]— someone is bound to have told you.

These rules would not apply in exceptional circumstances: for instance, if there is war between the country in which the property is situated and the country in which the previous owner is currently to be found, as there are no good lines of communication through which the news can travel.

How the right of usucaption is tightly bound to the right of protest is indicated by Rashbam.[39]

> If there are no lines of communication [between the place where the original owner is and the place where the land and

---

[37] *Tosafot, Bava Batra* 38a, s.v. *"mecha'ah."*

[38] *Bava Batra* 28b.

[39] Ad loc. 38a, s.v. *"l'olam."*

its current occupant are], if the previous owner does protest, the trespasser will in any case not hear of it and therefore will not take special precautions with his documentation [after three years]. Therefore, the protest is in any case useless and, because it is useless, the occupant does not obtain the right of usucaption, for his right normally arises from the fact that he can tell the claimant, "you did not protest during the three years [and therefore I did not keep my documents];" whereas in these circumstances the absentee could not have effected a valid protest as it could not have reached the occupants' ears.

Similarly, an absentee "previous" owner who flees because he is wanted on a capital charge would be afraid to draw attention to himself and to his place of refuge and would, therefore, deem it prudent not to protest. Because of his peculiar circumstances he does not lose that right of protest, and therefore even after three years, he can reclaim the property if the current occupant cannot produce the required documents,[40] as the Rabbis deemed it equitable not to give the occupant the advantage of usucaption in such and similarly exceptional circumstances.

Even if the court is certain that the protest did not reach the ears of the occupant during the three years in which he was expected to retain his documents—for example, the witnesses admitted that, without instruction from the protestor, they remained silent about his protest—nevertheless, it would be a valid one; the rules and conditions of this novel Rabbinical institution having been carried out as legislated, the result desired is achieved.[41]

It follows, that as the right of usucaption legislated by the Rabbinic Sages replaces the necessity of producing valid documents of title, it can only operate if the claimant has a valid and tenable claim. Thus, if in answer to a challenge by the

---

[40] Ad loc. 38b; *Choshen Mishpat* 146:3.
[41] Rabbi Y. Kaniewsky, *Kehillat Yaakov, Bava Batra* 10.

previous owner, the current occupant can declare, "I purchased the property from you over three years ago," and can prove his continuous beneficial occupation for the mandatory three-year period, he will succeed. However, if the claim is, "I acquired the property from so-and-so, who told me that he had acquired it from you," it would fail if the protestor were to claim that the alleged vendor himself never had good title. Unless such title could be proved, the occupant's claim would fail in the face of the challenge, "You do admit that the property was originally mine and that you did not buy it from me; against me you have no claim."[42] It is interesting that a small variation in the occupant's claim could, even in such circumstances, secure the property for him. If he can claim that he had purchased from his vendor **whom he knew** to have purchased it from the protestor, he would be successful; he would indeed be believed on the crucial point that he knew that his vendor did have a good title. Why is this so? Surely in a matter so germane to his entire claim, he cannot be considered an impartial witness—an uninterested party. The answer lies in the fact that having been in undisputed occupation for three years, he would be believed with a claim that he himself had initially purchased the property. Thus he has a *Miggo*;[43] had he wished to gain the property by falsehood, rather than claim that he knew his vendor had a good title, he could just as easily have claimed that it was he himself who had purchased it from the protestor.[44]

This does produce a peculiar legal anomaly. It would be expected that as the right of usucaption replaces the necessity of submitting title deeds, it should not give the occupant greater security; in fact, it does. Should the occupant, on being challenged, produce his documents of title showing that he had purchased the property from a third party ven-

---

[42] *Bava Batra* 30a et seq.

[43] Supra p. 35.

[44] *Rashbam, Bava Batra* 30b, based on Talmud, *Bava Batra* 41b.

dor, and in the event that that vendor's title be upset, the occupant would lose his case, as his rights only emanate from that vendor. In such circumstances, the occupant has no *Miggo*; in the face of documents that he purchased from X he has no alternative claim that he purchased directly from the protestor. Thus he must seek to justify his vendor's title, whereas, if he relies on his three-year occupancy, his statement that he knew of his vendor's good title needs no further substantiation.[45]

Because the right of usucaption depends on the occupant's being beneficially in possession without protest for three years, enjoying the property as an owner would, it follows that one whose possession comes about other than by a claim to ownership does not gain this right. For example, a mortgagee who takes possession and is, therefore, known to occupy the property as a mortgagee, cannot claim after three or even six years, that he had purchased the property and is now the owner—the difference to him being that as a mortgagee he is susceptible to the debtor's right to redeem and repossess the property,[46] which rights would be extinguished if the debtor had actually sold it to him. Similarly, occupation and possession as a guardian of orphans, as a partner in jointly owned property, or as a tenant farmer do not give rise to the right of usucaption, however long such occupancy and possession endure. A son occupying his father's property, or a father occupying his son's property, cannot claim this right. In none of these cases does possession or occupation indicate beneficial ownership, as the occupant is well entitled to remain in the property in the original role in which he entered it.[47]

To protect a mortgagor who has had his property foreclosed, or a landlord who lets his property for more than

---

[45] Ibid.

[46] Infra p. 151.

[47] *Choshen Mishpat* 149.

three years, the Rabbis varied the form of protest. The protestor would state that he had mortgaged or rented the property to A, "and if he claims I sold it to him or gave it to him [it is untrue] and I shall sue him in court."[48]

If, say, an orchard is occupied during the first three years of its existence—while the prohibition of *Orlah*[49] prohibits the eating of the fruit produced, the occupant will not gain the right of usucaption, as he has not enjoyed the fruits legally as an owner would have done.[50]

As with other civil legislation, these rules are subject to acceptance by the community; for while they are Halachah, there is an overriding rule in Civil Jurisprudence that custom abrogates the Halachah.[51] Indeed, many communities specifically legislated abolishing this right and accepting as evidence of title only valid documents or central registration in a recognized register,[52] legislation which put early Jewish mercantile practice far in advance of that of many other countries which have only comparatively recently introduced institutions such as Land Registries.

---

[48] *Bava Batra* 35b.

[49] *Vayikra* 19:23.

[50] *Bava Batra* 36a (according to *Rashbam*; but others including *Rach* and *Rambam* differ. V. infra chap. VI). *Orlah* is one of several possible prohibitions mentioned.

[51] Supra p. 70.

[52] Supra note 24.

SIX
Decisions

I T IS A PRINCIPLE OF jurisprudence, and the fundamental duty of any court hearing a dispute, that relief be given to the party which justifies its claim in accordance with the particular law being administered. Thus in a case of undisputed possession by the defendant and a legally unsubstantiated claim by the plaintiff, a Jewish court has no alternative but to support the defendant and to ensure that the plaintiff does not interfere with the defendant's right of enjoyment of the property concerned. Conversely, if the plaintiff justifies his claim with legally adequate proof, it is the court's duty to ensure that the property is transferred from the possession of the defendant to that of the claimant, who must henceforth be allowed full enjoyment as its owner.[1]

Having established the legal position, it is the duty of the court to ensure that the defeated litigant acts in accordance with its decision and in no way transgresses the prohibition of "Thou shalt not steal."[2]

---

[1] V. supra Chaps. IV & V on the relative merits of possession, previous ownership and other competing claims.

[2] *Vayikra* 19:11.; v. *Rosh, Bava Metzia* 1:1.

However, few cases which come before a court are so "cut and dried." What, for example, is the decision to be if both parties are seen by the court to be in equal possession? The classical example is the very first mishnah in *Bava Metzia*.[3]

> Two persons appear before a court, holding a garment.[4] One of them says, "I found it," and the other says, "I found it"....Then the one shall swear that his share in it is not less than half, and the other shall swear that his share in it is not less than half and [the value of the garment] shall then be divided between them.

The rationale of this decision is the fact that both parties appear before the court to be in equal possession of the disputed garment; the court must respect that possession and may not without reason deprive either party of that which it holds. It is conceivably possible that both parties picked it up at exactly the same time, in which case their entitlement is indeed equal; therefore the equal division of value may not be unfair to either party.[5]

The oath which is required from both parties "is an institution of the Sages, intended to deter an unscrupulous party from seizing another's garment, declaring it to be his own."[6]

In the debate surrounding this mishnah, the Talmud compares this ruling to that of Sumchos in another mishnah:[7]

> If a man exchanged his cow for an ass, and it calved; and likewise if he sold his maidservant, and she bore a child:

---

[3] 2a.

[4] So that they are both in actual possession—otherwise the one in possession would have the stronger claim with the onus probandi on the other.

[5] Ibid. 2b; v. *Rosh*, ad loc.; cf. *Tosafot*, ad loc. 2a, s.v. "*v'yachloku.*"

[6] *Bava Metzia* 3a. Statement of R. Yochanan. The terms of the oath are such that neither party directly contradicts the other; while claiming the whole, each swears only to being entitled to "not less than half."

[7] *Bava Metzia* 100a; v. supra p. 104.

> [and if] the vendor maintains that the birth occurred
> "before I sold her," while the purchaser says, "it was after I
> bought her"—they must divide.

The first case, that of the cow, is a barter transaction, and a barter transaction is completed the moment one of the subjects of the barter changes hands (in this case the ass), although the other subject (in this case the cow) may be far away. The second transaction (that of the maidservant) is a cash transaction which is completed the moment the cash is handed over, although the subject acquired (in this case the maidservant) may also be in a remote place. Therefore in both cases, the subjects (the cow or the maidservant) are not within sight of either party at the time of the actual completion of the transaction, and therefore, when subsequently it is found that the cow has given birth to a calf or the maidservant to a child, there is a legitimate problem arising, irrespective of the claims of either party, of when was the moment of birth—before or after completion?

Sumchos upholds the general rule that when the ownership of property is in doubt, it is divided equally among the claimants without an oath. But his colleagues, who are in the majority and whose views therefore prevail, rule "that the onus of proof is on the claimant," with the effect that if the subject is not at the relevant time in the legal possession of either party, the claim of the previous owner will prevail. The law assumes that the status quo ante remains until the last possible moment, and therefore in the eyes of the law the cow or the maidservant did not change hands until after the birth.[8]

These cases differ from that of the two claimants holding the garment, where both parties are in possession and neither has any legal advantage; their possession must be respected

---

[8] Ad loc.; v. *Tosafot, Bava Batra* 35a, s.v. *"umai"*; v. supra Chap. IV generally on status quo ante.

and in order not to deprive either party entirely, the only appropriate ruling is indeed equal division.

Even Sumchos, who maintains that in the case of the disputed offspring the value must be divided, distinguishes between those cases and that of the disputed garment. In the former cases the doubt arises naturally, not through the claims and counterclaims of either party; even if both parties remain silent there would be doubt as to exactly when the calf or child was born, whereas in the case of the disputed garment doubt is caused by the differing claims of the parties; consequently, the oath which is relevant to the dispute surrounding the garment is not relevant to the dispute surrounding the calf or the child.[9]

Before issuing a decision that a disputed article or its value be divided equally, the court must be satisfied that theoretically at least its decision could be fair to both parties—that there is a possibility, as in the case of the garment, that both do indeed have equal rights to the subject of the dispute.

Where this possibility does not exist, the court is not empowered to order an equal division. If a dispute arises between two parties each of whom deposited a sum of money with a bailee, one depositing, say, two hundred coins and the other one hundred coins and subsequently each claims to be the owner of the larger deposit,[10] the court will order that one hundred coins be returned to each claimant while the disputed hundred coins be retained under the court's supervision until such time as the dispute is satisfactorily resolved.[11] To give each party his undisputed hundred coins,

---

[9] *Bava Metzia* 2b.

[10] The deposits having been made in such a way that the bailee cannot be blamed for not knowing who deposited which.

[11] *Mishnah, Bava Metzia* 37a, which also quotes the view of R. Yosei that all three hundred coins be retained in the court's control so as to discourage the false claimant; after all, if he receives his own deposit back he loses nothing by making a false claim, whereas if the entire amount is frozen by the court he loses his money.

and then to divide the disputed hundred equally, can in those circumstances never be fair to the rightful owner; it is better for the court to temporarily hold the entire amount than to be a party to a legally wrongful permanent deprivation.[12]

The possibility that both parties have an equal claim is just that—a possibility, no great degree of probability being required. If for example a debtor and a creditor appear before the court both holding a loan document, the debtor claiming he is entitled to it, having paid his debt in full, and the creditor claiming he is entitled to it, being still owed the full amount, the court will order payment of half the debt on the grounds that it is possible that the debtor who is "in possession of half the document" has paid half the amount he owed, although the parties' own claims do negate the probability of this being the case.[13] This principle will hold good if two claimants are holding a garment which both claim to have woven; it is possible that each indeed wove half, and had they both remained silent, the court could well have come to that conclusion, seeing they both stand before it in equal possession.[14] This case differs from that of the two depositors, where, although both parties may be considered to "be in possession" by virtue of the fact that the bailee holds on behalf of both of them, nevertheless because of the way the deposits were made, he knows that it is impossible that each party should have given him one hundred and fifty coins; in such circumstances, even if the disputants remained silent, the court could in no way arrive at the conclusion that it is feasible that the money was equally owned by both.[15]

What is the decision to be if neither of the parties has a claim of possession or a claim of prior ownership?

There was a riverboat which was the subject of a dispute

---

[12] *Bava Metzia* 3a. V. *Tosafot* 2a, s.v. *"v'yachloku"*; *Rosh, Bava Metzia* 1:1.
[13] *Tosafot* and *Rosh*, loc. cit.
[14] *Rosh*, ibid. V. *Tur, Choshen Mishpat* 138, who disputes this.
[15] *Tosafot* and *Rosh*, loc. cit.

between two claimants, each claiming, "It is mine" [but neither actually having possession or evidence of previous ownership]. One of the parties appealed to the court, "Take the boat into the court's custody [so that my opponent should not be able to sell it in the meantime] until I bring witnesses to prove that it belongs to me." In such a case should the court attach the boat and take it into custody or not? R. Huna rules that the court should attach it, while R. Yehudah rules that the court should not. The court attached the boat,[16] and the claimant went to look for his witnesses but did not find them, whereupon he requested the court to release the boat, leaving it to the "stronger" to obtain possession. In such a case should the court release it or not? R. Yehudah holds that it should not be released, while R. Pappa differs, ruling that it should be released. The accepted ruling is that the court should not have attached the boat in the first instance, but if it did so, it should not release it [without acceptable evidence of ownership].[17]

Neither of the claims to ownership has legal merit; there is no party in possession to be protected, and patently the boat does not belong to them equally and in such instances the court cannot issue any order or judgment. It must therefore leave the two parties to sort the matter out between themselves, with, presumably, the "stronger" party ultimately being successful. As soon as it hears the opening claims, the court will recognize that there is a distinct possibility that it will have to take that course; therefore, when asked to take the boat into custody it must consider whether such a step is in the furtherance of justice and whether it will help the rightful owner to obtain possession. This will indeed be so if it gives one of the claimants the time he requires to

---

[16] It is in fact not clear from the Talmudic text whether this is a real case in which the court attached the boat, perhaps at the request of both parties, or whether the case is merely hypothetical (V. *Rashbam*, s.v. "*amar lehu*").

[17] *Bava Batra* 34b.

produce his witnesses; but if not, to whom should the court restore the boat? On the one hand, it may be argued that by restoring the boat to its previous situation no damage has been done to either of the parties—they can continue the dispute as before; on the other hand, it may not be right that a court of law releases or abandons property except to re-store it to its rightful owner—in this case impossible to deter-mine. Because, in R. Yehudah's view, a court cannot release property unless to its rightful owner, he consequently rules that in the first instance, the court should not attach the boat. In any event, attachment may not further the course of jus-tice; on the contrary—it could defeat it, for it may deprive the true owner of the opportunity to obtain possession.[18]

What is the basis of the judicial pronouncement, "Let the stronger prevail and obtain possession," and in this context what does the word "stronger" mean—physically stronger, or armed with superior proof and argument?

Under Jewish Law, a litigant may in certain circum-stances be entitled to take the law into his own hands.

> There was a well belonging to two persons which was used by them on alternate days. One of the partners, however, came and used it on a day on which he was not entitled to. The other party complained, but the wrongdoer paid no heed. The complainant took the blade of a hoe and struck him with it.

R. Nachman ruled that the assailant need pay no penalty for assault, as he was entitled to hit his recalcitrant partner; even those Authorities who hold that a person may not take the law into his own hands and resort to violence to protect

---

[18] *Rashbam*, ad loc., s.v. *"tafsinan."* The court is in a similar position to the bailee of the three hundred coins. Unless he can return the money to the rightful owner, he must keep it safe on that unknown owner's behalf (v. *Tosafot*, ad loc., s.v. *"hahu"*). V. *Choshen Mishpat* 65:1 and 300:1; cf. ibid. 222:2; *Shach*, ad loc., commentary 4 (v. *Aruch Hashulchan*, ad loc. 6).

his interests agree that he may do so where an irreparable loss will be suffered, such as in this case, where the water in the well is limited.[19]

From that report it is quite obvious that force may be used, although this, of course, should be a last resort.[20] Not only is he permitted to use force, but he is permitted to use any other stratagem in order to win back or retain property which he can definitely prove to the court is his; so much so that despite the stringent prohibition of taking a dispute before a non-Jewish court,[21] if the debtor or thief is one who will not obey a Jewish court, or is so powerful that a Jewish court is afraid to move against him, his victim is permitted to bring the case before secular courts or rulers to enlist their aid in saving or retrieving what rightfully belongs to him.[22]

In the case of the disputed boat, neither party has sufficient proof to convince the court of the justification of his claim and therefore, initially, neither party is allowed to take the law into his own hands. But, as the court finds it impossible to arrive at any decision which could be fair and not liable to be overturned at a later date by the introduction of new evidence currently not available,[23] its only course is to allow them to do so, with the "stronger" party prevailing.

But can such an order lead to a just result? Yes, argues

---

[19] *Bava Kama* 27b. R. Nachman's view is the accepted Halachah. If one knows he is in the right (even though no irreparable loss is suffered) "he need not trouble to appeal to the court" (*Yad, Sanhedrin* 2:12); v. *Rosh, Bava Kama* 3:3.

[20] *Choshen Mishpat* 4:1, commentary.(V. ad loc. and *Tur, Choshen Mishpat* 4 for more detailed guidelines.) V. *Rashba, Responsa* 3:81, forbidding the telling of an untruth to gain a just result. V. infra p. 175 et seq.

[21] V. supra p. 89 et seq.

[22] *Ramban, Responsa* 63; v. *Rashba, Responsa* 5:171 which is virtually word for word the same responsum; cf. *Beit Yosef, Tur, Choshen Mishpat* 26:2.

[23] *Bava Batra* 35a.

Rosh.[24] The claimant who is right is more likely to have some persuasive (although not conclusive) proof in his favor; he will also be more inclined to exert himself and put greater effort into obtaining that which he knows is rightfully his; the party who knows his claim is not justified will not put in so much effort, fearing that in due course his opponent will adduce conclusive evidence and be awarded the property by the court, while he will have gained nothing by his efforts.

Does this mean that the result produced by the two litigants is treated as a decision of the court? If it is, the unsuccessful claimant has no further claim (unless conclusive evidence proves that the result was wrong); if it is not, he can at least demand an oath from his opponent that he, the opponent, is not holding money belonging to him, the defeated disputant.

> Our ruling that the stronger prevail is not a legal decision, in which the successful one can claim that "the court has awarded me the article and I therefore need take no oath, but because the court cannot reach any conclusion and neither party is in possession,[25] the Sages ruled that the stronger prevail, relying on the fact that the rightful owner will do everything in his power to see that he is not cheated, while the false claimant will not go to so great a length as the other, fearing that the rightful owner will in due course bring witnesses testifying to his ownership, and he, the false claimant, will have to return the property. Seeing that this

---

[24] *Novellae, Bava Metzia* 1:1. Once one of the litigants has obtained possession, it remains his until the other brings conclusive evidence against him. If the other does take possession without evidence, the court will return it to the first possessor, as we do not wish to encourage permanent disputes. (*Choshen Mishpat* 139:1. *S'ma*, commentary 4; v. *Shach*, commentary 2, which quotes dissenting opinions.)

[25] *Rivash, Responsa* 434, adds the point that neither party has any prior right, nor does the court know of either party's connection with the disputed property, apart from their stated claims.

is not a conclusive ruling, the unsuccessful disputant can demand an oath that "you who have taken possession have done so in accordance with the law."

In other words, because of the peculiarity of this type of case, the court withdraws from the obligation of making a formal decision, abandoning it to the litigants themselves.[26]

Similarly, a squatter on real property, who has been in possession for three years[27] with no claim other than the fact that he has been in possession, will not be removed by the court at the request of a claimant who himself has no proof of ownership. For although the court is aware that the squatter has no legal claim, it is also aware that the claimant can produce no evidence of his own legal right—therefore why should it interfere?[28]

The point has been made that in the dispute surrounding the boat there is indeed an owner, and there may come a time when he is able to produce conclusive evidence of his ownership. But what if the circumstances are such that it is impossible for any further evidence to be placed before the court?

The Talmud[29] reports such a case and the surrounding debate. The mother of Rami b. Chama wrote over her property to Rami in the morning, but in the evening she wrote a document transferring all her property to Rami's brother, Mar Ukva b. Chama. Both documents were deeds of gift inter vivos,[30] and it was not known which deed was handed

---

[26] *Rosh, Responsa* 76:1; v. *Aruch Hashulchan, Choshen Mishpat*, 139:2. V. ibid., 3: if a third party seizes the disputed property; cf. *Shevut Yaakov, Choshen Mishpat* 162; v. Dayan Dr. M. S. Lew, *The Humanity of Jewish Law*, p. 71.

[27] V. supra p. 119.

[28] *Yad, To'an V'nittan* 14:12; *Choshen Mishpat* 146:9; *Aruch Hashulchan, Choshen Mishpat* 146:10. (R. Yechezkel Silber of London explains this decision as a withdrawal by the court.) V. supra p. 135.

[29] *Ketubot* 94b.

[30] V. *Rashbam, Bava Batra* 151a. s.v. *"imei"* on another case involving the same dramatis personae.

over first although, obviously, Rami's was written first. Rami appeared before R. Sheshet who confirmed him in possession of his mother's property, while Mar Ukva produced his document to R. Nachman who similarly confirmed him in possession of the same property. R. Sheshet complained to R. Nachman, querying why he had ruled in the way that he did, to which R. Nachman responded with the same query as to how had R. Sheshet had arrived at his decision. In reply, R. Sheshet pointed out that Rami's deed was written first, having been written in the morning, while that of his brother had been written in the evening. This argument was rejected by R. Nachman: "Are we then living in Jerusalem where the hours are inserted in deeds?" Since in Babylonia no time was entered on deeds, it was the custom that when two deeds were written on the same day, no preference would be given to one because it was written a few hours earlier than the other. Therefore, Rami could not claim preference over his brother, and as it is not known, and can now never be known, which one was handed over first, both deeds are equally valid over the property. R. Sheshet thereupon asked R. Nachman why, if that is so, did he confirm the property in the hands of Mar Ukva. As both litigants had equally valid deeds, surely the property should have been divided? "I treated this as a case to be decided by judicial discretion," retorted R. Nachman. If so, why did he overrule his colleague's decision? That of R. Sheshet could also be treated as an exercise in judicial discretion, and having already been applied, should have been respected and not reversed by a fellow judge exercising his own discretion. To this challenge R. Nachman replied with a two-point justification. Firstly, he, R. Nachman, was the officially appointed judge of the town, having been appointed by the Exilarch and the Yeshivah, while R. Sheshet, although a distinguished scholar, did not hold any official post as a judge. Secondly, R. Sheshet's decision was not an exercise in judicial discretion, but was based on his belief that Rami was entitled to the property as his deed had been written first; this was wrong and therefore the decision based on it could well be reversed.

Neither of the brothers was in possession of the disputed property; neither could produce stronger proof of ownership than the other and, while there is strong argument that an equal division be preferred[31]—for in that way each claimant would at least receive something—nevertheless it cannot be a correct judgment as the property must belong to one of them only. Consequently the ultimate ruling is that judicial discretion is to be preferred, for there is a possibility that the judge's discretion will be exercised in favor of the rightful owner.

How should this discretion be exercised? Some Authorities hold that the court's discretion is limited. It must examine the background and try to understand the intention of the donor;[32] to ascertain which of the parties was closer to him; to determine for which he had more affection and more regard.[33] Others hold that the court's discretion is absolute; it may award the disputed property to the party which *it* considers the most deserving.[34]

Thus in the case of the two brothers, either R. Nachman held that the mother had greater affection for Mar Ukva and therefore intended him to have all her property, or, he believed that Mar Ukva was the more deserving of the two brothers.[35]

In all examples of decisions so far discussed, the ultimate decision is tantamount to the court's saying that ab initio the disputed property belonged to the successful claimant. In

---

[31] The view of *Rav, Ketubot* 94a.

[32] Or the vendor in a case where the court is being asked to adjudicate between two documents of sale.

[33] *Rashi, Ketubot* 85b, s.v. "*shuda.*"

[34] *Tosafot,* ad loc., s.v. "*shuda*"; v. *Ritva, Responsa* 18.

[35] V. supra p. 254, the case of a testator whose instructions were not clear. If there is no way of identifying which of the claimants he had in mind, the final decision lies with the judge, who exercises his discretion.

fact, the final decision of the court if, for example, it is in favor of the plaintiff, will be couched in terms such as: "We find against the defendant in favor of the plaintiff. You, the defendant, are obliged to pay him [or transfer the property, as the case may be]; go and do so."[36] The decision concerns ownership of property,[37] and it is important to understand the difference between a claim on property and a claim on an individual to carry out an obligation. While a claim against a debtor appears to be a demand that he carry out his obligation to repay the debt, it is in fact a claim by the creditor to have his money returned;[38] and while the debtor's property is charged to secure the loan, his person is most certainly not.[39] What at first glance seems to be a claim "in personam" is in fact a claim "in rem."

A claim to completion of a barter transaction is another which appears to be a claim in personam but is in reality a claim in rem. For example, one barters an ass for a cow, and although the cow is in another place and only the ass changes hands,[40] nevertheless the deal is consummated, and in due course the owner of the cow must deliver it to the previous owner of the ass; neither party can retract.[41] This is not in law a personal obligation on the owner of the cow to honor a contract and transfer it to the other party; the cow actually belongs to the other party, and the previous owner has the normal legal obligation to hand over another man's property to him.

Similarly, if one makes a deal with a butcher that on the eve of Rosh Hashanah one will buy a kilo of meat of an animal which will then be slaughtered, and the shopper

---

[36] *Bava Kama* 69a, v. *Tosafot*, s.v. "*chayav.*"
[37] Decisions and orders as to penalties or forfeitures or compensation for tort, are not within the scope of this limited work.
[38] Infra p. 146.
[39] Ibid.
[40] Supra p. 128.
[41] V. *Choshen Mishpat* 195:1.

pays for that meat, he can, when the due day arrives, oblige the butcher to slaughter an animal to deliver him the single kilo of meat although the remainder of the carcass has not been sold.[42] This is not because the butcher is under a personal obligation to deliver the meat—it is because the purchaser has a share in that animal, and the kilo of meat is actually his and must therefore be delivered to him.

The problem therefore arises: Does Jewish law recognize a personal obligation as legally enforceable[43] with the consequence that it is within the court's prerogative to make an order for specific performance?[44]

This problem is especially pertinent to the marriage ceremony. One of its essentials is that the husband give his wife a *Ketubah*, a document which inter alia guarantees her a payment from his estate in the event of her surviving him, or from him in the event of his divorcing her. There are statutory minima as to the extent of the obligation, depending on the previous status of the bride; a woman previously unmarried is entitled to more than a woman now marrying for a second or third time.

It is, however, the custom of the groom, in order to show his esteem for his bride, to write into the *Ketubah* amounts often substantially greater than the statutory minima.[45] The amount so written now becomes a contingent liability on the husband should he divorce her, or on his estate should he pre-decease her while they are still married. If Jewish Law

---

[42] *Chullin* 83a.

[43] For a definition of the difference between a "charge in rem" and a "charge in personam," v. *Netivot Hamishpat* 39:17. (The former is an actual transfer; the latter an *obligation* to transfer.)

[44] Under the British system, such an order can only be made in Equity (v. infra p. 145); by Common Law the victim could, only after the event, sue for damages (v. Geldart, *Elements of English Law*, pp. 39 & 40).

[45] Today in Ashkenazic communities only the minimum amount is written into a *Ketubah*.

only recognizes an obligation in rem, and the groom undertaking the obligation does not currently have property equal to the amount obligated, on what can the charge fall? What has been given to the bride? This point is taken by *Tosafot*, which quotes the reply given by R. Eliyahu to R. Yitzchak: "Although he does not transfer any tangible property whatsoever to the recipient, the personal obligation he undertakes is valid and will be translated to any property which he may subsequently acquire."[46]

The basis of R. Eliyahu's ruling is a Talmudic passage in *Bava Metzia*:[47]

> It has been taught: A paid bailee may stipulate to be liable [to make restoration] to the same degree as a borrower. How [does this commitment become binding]—with mere words? Said Shmuel: because he makes a *Kinyan*.[48] R. Yochanan said: even without making a *Kinyan*; in return for the benefit he receives in that he achieves thereby a reputation of being trustworthy, he renders himself fully responsible.

There are, in law, four categories of bailee: the unpaid bailee, the paid bailee, the hirer, and the borrower. The more benefit accruing to the bailee, the more onerous is his commitment to make good in the case of loss; for example, an unpaid bailee is exempt from payment if the article in his care is stolen from him by a burglar, an event which compete vigilance could have forestalled, whereas a paid bailee must make good such a loss; more vigilance is expected from one who is being paid than from one who is not. Similarly, a paid bailee is exempt if an unavoidable accident befalls the object in his care, whereas a borrower who has total benefit from the

---

[46] *Ketubot* 54b, s.v. "*af al pi*"; V. *Rabbi Akiva Eger, Novellae*, ad loc.

[47] 94a.

[48] A symbolic act of transfer such as the handing over of a kerchief (v. infra p. 235).

object is, in most circumstances, liable.[49] The passage quoted investigates what the law would be in the event that a paid bailee agrees to take upon himself the onerous commitment of a borrower—in other words, to be liable even if an unavoidable accident occurs. The Talmud accepts that mere words or promises cannot place any additional responsibility unless accompanied by some absolute evidence of intention,[50] and Shmuel agrees that a formal transfer is necessary. R. Yochanan holds that as he has taken possession of the article he is to look after, and has received adequate consideration,[51] no formal act is required.

Be that as it may, to what is the bailee committing himself? Is he actually making a transfer of a charge on his property so that in the event of a loss, the bailor will have a claim against his estate as from now? If not, what is the nature of the commitment?

> And if you ask, on what does this *Kinyan* crystallize (after all, what has been given by the bailee is only a promise), the answer is that the *Kinyan* crystallizes on the **person** of the bailee, for now he is obligated to assume the same degree of responsibility as a borrower.[52]

Thus if one sells produce to another, which the purchaser is entitled to assume the vendor has, but which in fact he does not, the vendor cannot void the contract.[53] The court will order the vendor to acquire that produce in order

---

[49] V. *Bava Metzia* 93a and *Shevuot* 49a.

[50] V. infra p. 233.

[51] V. *Shitah Mekubetzet, Bava Metzia* 94a, s.v. "*hikshah HaRavad*," in which Rashba lays down the Doctrine of Consideration; v. *Rashba Responsa* 3:22 & 5:166.; v. commentary attributed to *Rashi, Nedarim* 31a, s.v. "*Alma*"; *Ran, Avodah Zarah* (on *Rif* 4b), s.v. "*umaksheh*"; cf. Currie vs. Misa (1875) 10 Ex. 162 & Wilkinson vs. Coverdale (1793) 1 Esp. 75.

[52] *Shitah Mekubetzet*, loc. cit., s.v. "*amar*," quoting a disciple of Rabbenu Peretz.

[53] *Tosefta, Bava Metzia* 4:5.

to honor his agreement even though its cost may well have increased.[54]

So much for an order of specific performance to deliver property—but can an order be made demanding specific performance of a personal service? Since it is a principle of Jewish Law that a debtor's person, as such, bears no responsibility for his debts,[55] is it responsible for his personal obligations?

An employer who wishes to dishonor a contract of employment he has with an employee will only be obliged to satisfy any claim against him by payment of compensation; after all, he has only undertaken to pay money in the event of the employee's doing the work allotted to him, and if he wishes to stop the employee from working, all that employee can demand is the sum promised.[56] The employee's own personal situation is covered by the Biblical injunction, "for the children of Israel are my servants,"[57] implying therefore that they cannot be servants of each other.[58] This means that in general no employee can be forced to undertake any task he does not wish to do, even though initially he agreed to be employed for that purpose. The employer's remedy lies in hiring a replacement and demanding compensation for any loss suffered

---

[54] *Mordechai, Bava Batra* 560, quoting a responsum of R. Nissim Gaon; cf. *Shitah Mekubetzet, Bava Metzia* 47b, s.v. *"omnam"*; v. *Netivot Hamishpat* 203:7; cf. ibid. 39:17; v. *Machanei Efraim, Hilchot, Mocher Davar Shelo Ba L'olam* 3. "Although one cannot transfer something not yet in existence [or in his possession], he can obligate himself to do so" [and the court will enforce that obligation]; cf. *Ketzot Hachoshen* 112:1.

For other examples, v. *Tur, Choshen Mishpat* 206:1, as interpreted by Rabbi Aaron Sassoon (*Torat Emet* 133); cf. both *Ketzot Hachoshen* and *Netivot Hamishpat* 206:1; v. *Tur, Choshen Mishpat* 39:19; *Choshen Mishpat* 60:1 & *S'ma*, ad loc.

[55] Infra p. 151.

[56] *Ketzot Hachoshen* 333:3.

[57] *Vayikra* 25:55.

[58] *Bava Metzia* 10a, lit., "not servants of servants."

due to the employee's not honoring his contract. Even if it is known that the employee will in no way be able to fund the payment of compensation due to the employer, nevertheless generally he cannot be forced to work against his will.[59]

The caveat "generally" has to be made because there are exceptions—contracts of employment involving the community as a whole.

> He who is a public bathhouse attendant, a public barber or a public baker, and there is no one in the area to replace him, should he wish to return to his own home as the Festival is approaching [at which time he is most needed], can be stopped from so doing until a replacement is found.[60]

The requirements of the community are as binding as the requirements of the law; it is illegal not to carry out the service demanded by and agreed upon with the community.[61] Therefore, a schoolteacher who tries to rescind his contract before it is completed and cannot be satisfactorily replaced, is forced to continue and to complete his contract.[62] In these exceptional circumstances the employee's obligation is not based on normal rules of civil jurisprudence; his personal rights are weighed up against the damage which would be suffered by the community. This is stated in no uncertain terms in the ruling from Salonika:

> The teacher is obliged and forced to continue his contract; if he leaves, this could contribute to the deterioration of an entire community, and although it may not be strictly legal, he is to be forced, for the court may smite and punish him although not strictly in accordance with the law....[63]

---

[59] *Har HaCarmel, Responsa, Choshen Mishpat* 10; v. *Chazon Ish, Novellae, Bava Kama* 23, para. 6.

[60] *Tosefta, Bava Metzia* 11:13.

[61] *Rashbash Responsa* 112.

[62] Ibid.

[63] R. Rafael Yaakov Menashe, *Be'er Hamayim*. The author, however,

If the number of options open to a court issuing judgment on a dispute, be it in respect to property or be it in respect to a personal obligation, is limited under absolute law, there are no such limitations if the litigants can be persuaded to accept a compromise.[64] As long as the decision is fair to both parties and so in accord with the Biblical injunction of "Justice, Justice, shall you pursue,"[65] it becomes a judgment, often to be preferred to, and always recognized by, Jewish Law.[66]

---

goes on to express the view that in the particular case before him the employee could *legally* be forced to continue his work. V. supra Chap. III for the basis of the extralegal powers of the community.

[64] V. infra p. 178. In the first instance the court should attempt to achieve a compromise.

[65] *Devarim* 16:20.

[66] *Choshen Mishpat* 12:2; v. *Sanhedrin* 32b.

SEVEN
Of Law, Equity, and Morality

I N ANY SYSTEM OF LAW, particular circumstances
may arise rendering it onerous or unfair. Therefore the law must possess within itself sufficient
flexibility to be able to remove anomalies—to render it fair and non-damaging. Somewhere, there must exist a
power capable of modifying the general law in order to arrive at a result which is not only just, in accordance with the
law itself, but which also satisfies all ethical notions of fair
treatment; in other words, a result which is "equitable."[1]

In Jewish Jurisprudence, this power is embodied in the

---

[1] V. Silberg, *Talmudic Law and the Modern State*, p. 96; *Israel Law Review*, (vol. 13, no. 3), p. 390. In the English scheme of Law, Equity developed independently of Common Law and originally there were two distinct judiciaries—the Kings Courts, which applied Common Law, and the Chancery Courts (so called because they operated under the authority of the Lord Chancellor), which applied Equity. These two judiciaries were merged into one High Court by the Judicature Acts of 1875 (although the title Chancery Division is given to that section of the High Court which deals, in the main, with cases involving Equity). Any High Court Judge is empowered to apply both Common Law and Equity, and if there is in his mind any conflict between the two, the rules of Equity are to prevail. (For more detailed reading see Geldart, *Elements of English Law*, chap. II.)

law by the Biblical injunction, "And you should do that which is right and good...";[2] good—in the eyes of the Lord; right—proper in the eyes of men.[3]

Basing themselves on this verse, the Rabbis instituted two specific Laws of Equity: that of the right of a debtor to repay his debt and reacquire property originally seized in lieu of payment;[4] and the right of a neighbor to preempt any other potential buyer of adjoining property.[5]

Brief mention has already been made of the rules of lien, charge or mortgage.[6] This is an important and far-reaching subject, and in order to understand the background to the Rabbinic Legislation, it is appropriate at this juncture to deal with it at length.

All property, whether real or personal, in a debtor's possession at the due time of repayment, can be seized or attached by a creditor in lieu of payment.[7] In cases of debts originating in law, e.g. liability to maintain a wife and her children, to pay an ex-wife what is due under her *Ketubah* or the obligation to repay monies borrowed, the lien attaches itself to real estate sold by the debtor after the inception of the debt; that is, in the case of a debt under *Ketubah*, property sold since the date of marriage, and in the case of monies borrowed, property sold after the original loan was received. However, in the latter case, there is a limitation; only a creditor in possession of a valid document, evidencing the debt and executed at the time the loan was made, has the right to follow the property through to a purchaser in good faith and to seize it from him. A debt, however well-witnessed, if not committed to writing at the time, does not generally give the

---

2 *Devarim* 6:18. V. *Avodah Zarah* 25a. *Devarim* is called the *Sefer Ha-yashar* (Righteousness) because it contains this injunction.

3 *Rashi, Devarim* 12:28.

4 *Bava Metzia* 35a.

5 Ibid. 108a et seq.

6 Supra p. 63.

7 *Bava Kama* 11b: "Even from the cloak on his [the debtor's] shoulder."

creditor the right of foreclosure against a purchaser.

There are two approaches in the Talmud as to why there is this difference between a loan committed to writing and an oral loan—although it must be stressed that in fact ultimately little practical difference arises.

> Ulla said: According to the word of the Torah, both a loan secured by a document and a verbal loan may be recóvered from sold property.[8] What is the reason? The hypothecary obligation involved is Biblical.[9] Why then has it been said that a verbal loan may be collected from free[10] property only? On account of possible loss to the buyers [who might not be aware of the existence of the loan and would thus purchase property which might at any time be taken away from them]. If so [that the interest of the buyers is to be safeguarded], the same law should apply also to a loan that is secured by a document? In this case the buyers would have brought the loss upon themselves.

The rationale behind this distinction is that a loan, secured by bond made or acknowledged in the presence of witnesses, receives due publicity, and intending buyers can, on enquiry, become aware of its existence.[11] In the case of an oral loan, there is no certainty that buyers can ever become aware of its existence and are therefore always at risk through no fault of their own.[12] Thus, according to Ulla, all real property in the possession of the debtor at the time of inception of the loan is liable to the lien according to the Torah, but for practical purposes, in order that commerce should flourish and buyers not be afraid to purchase land, the Rabbis re-

---

8 Which was considered to have been sold "subject to mortgage."

9 *Devarim* 24:11. Every debt carries with it a pledge of the debtor's property in favor of the creditor.

10 I.e., unsold.

11 In practice the local Scribe acted as an unofficial Land Registry (v. supra p. 63 & infra p. 188).

12 *Bava Batra* 175b.

moved it from all sold properties unless the debt was one of which the buyer could easily have become aware—one evidenced by a bond.

By what legal doctrine does the Torah raise this hypothecary obligation on the debtor's property? "...a man's possessions are his surety."[13] As a surety or guarantor is called upon to pay in the event of the debtor's not paying, so repayment is exacted from property if not forthcoming directly from the debtor himself.

As the Ran expresses the point—there are two charges, one on the debtor personally to pay back the debt, and the other on his property as guarantor. The latter charge is subsidiary to the former and in the event of the former charge being abrogated, the latter must fall, notwithstanding that the document creating the charge has been sold on to a third party.[14]

It follows, therefore, that once the date of payment has arrived, in the absence of the payment from the debtor, the creditor can follow through property which was in the possession of the debtor at the time of the loan although subsequently sold. However, he cannot seize property which the debtor had purchased *after* the loan was made and sold *prior* to the due date of repayment unless the loan document has stipulated a charge on future acquisitions; not being in the possession of the debtor at the time of the loan, this recently acquired property cannot be said to have "guaranteed" it. However, the creditor can seize property currently in the debtor's possession even though it was acquired after the loan was made, as the charge on this property follows the debtor's current obligation which is, of course, still extant.[15]

Opposed to Ulla is Rabbah, who said:

---

[13] Ibid. 174b.

[14] *Ketubot* 85b; V. *Chiddushei Rabbenu Chaim Halevi, Hilchot Shevuot* 8:13. The sale of a loan document creates problems in law. V. *Bava Batra* 147b, which is dealt with at length by early commentators.

[15] *Choshen Mishpat* 112:1 and commentary of Remah; *Ketzot Hachoshen*, ad loc.

According to the words of the Torah, both a loan secured by document and a verbal loan may be recovered from free property only. What is the reason? The hypothecary obligation involved is not Biblical.[16] Why then has it been said that a loan secured by a bond may be recovered from sold property? In order that doors may not be slammed in the faces of borrowers.[17] If so, the same law should apply also to a verbal loan! But in that case the loan is not sufficiently known.[18]

If, as Rabbah seems to hold, the Torah places no charge either on the debtor or on his property, what sanctions can be employed, or by what legal machinery can the recalcitrant debtor be made to repay his debt? Says R. Pappa: "The repayment of a creditor is a religious obligation."[19]

And what if the debtor is not inclined to be religious? Said R. Kahana to R. Pappa:

According to your statement that the repayment of a debt is a religious obligation, what can be done where a debtor says, "I am not disposed to perform a religious act?" The other replied, "We have learned: this [that a flogging is administered and the sinner is thereby purged] applies only to negative precepts, but in the case of positive precepts, as for instance when a man is told make a *Sukkah* and he does not make it, or he is told to perform the Mitzvah of the *Lulav* and he does not perform it, he is flogged [in an endeavor to coerce him to perform the precept] until his soul departs.[20]

---

[16] V. *Rashbam, Bava Batra* 175b, s.v. "*lav d'Oraita*," quoting *Bava Metzia* 114b.

[17] No one would risk making a loan if the security of land was not available.

[18] *Bava Batra*, loc. cit. Ulla and Rabbah each uses a different phraseology to make what is essentially the same point.

[19] *Arachin* 22a; v. *Ketzot Hachoshen* 39:1, but cf. *Sha'arei Yosher* 5:2.

[20] *Ketubot* 86a and *Rashi*. The source of the power of coercion is given in *Bava Batra* 48a. Coercion is resorted to even when willingness is required, as for example to obtain a Bill of Divorce from an unsuitable husband. Although generally a Bill of Divorce forced from an

In other words, no one is at liberty to declare that he is not disposed to perform a religious act and so avoid, in this instance, paying his debt.

In fact, even according to Rabbah, we do not find any form of coercion other than seizure being employed. The attachment of property is itself a form of coercion.[21]

Certainly, according to Rabbah, the ends of justice are served by the means of religious morality—it is a religious duty to repay a debt; therefore, this duty becomes a civil law obligation.

Both *Amoraim* agree that in fact a lien attaches itself to all property in the debtor's possession at the due date of payment. They also agree that only in the case of debt evidenced in writing can the creditor follow through land owned by the debtor at the time of the debt and subsequently sold. Only land is subject to this right of follow-through, because

> Land offers security—that is to say, land offers security to each party, the borrower and the lender, because it is always available and they depend on it.[22]

---

unwilling husband is invalid, if forced by a Beit Din on religious grounds, it is valid, as Rambam rationalizes (*Yad, Gerushin* 2:20) that that which makes the husband unwilling to cooperate with the Beit Din is "his evil inclination," which really he would wish to be rid of, as in truth he wants to be a good and correct Jew; by applying sanctions we merely drive away the "evil inclination," leaving him to carry out willingly his own real inclination.

[21] *Ramban, Bava Batra* 175b; and v. *Ketzot Hachoshen* 39:2, s.v. "*omnam.*" If a debtor has no money, no coercion is applied (v. infra p. 153).

[22] *Rashi, Kiddushin* 26a, s.v. "*sheyesh lahem.*" In Mishnaic parlance, real estate is often referred to as property which "offers security," while movable chattels are referred to as "property which offers no security"; v. supra p. 148—the document giving rise to the charge is a negotiable instrument which can be dealt in, although whether it is recognized as such by the Torah or only by Rabbinical edict is a matter of debate surrounding the Talmudic statement in *Ketubot* 85b et seq. and *Bava Batra* 147b.

The major difference in practical law between these two widely opposing views would be in the case of infants who inherit real estate from their debtor father. According to Ulla, as they inherit the property subject to the charge, the creditor can obtain repayment immediately, whereas according to Rabbah, the orphans inherit free of any charge or lien imposed by the Torah, and not being adults, are not obliged to carry out any precepts; therefore the creditor will have to wait until they attain adulthood, at which time they can be coerced into carrying out the precept of repaying their father's creditor.

And what is the machinery by which a creditor forecloses on real estate in order to obtain repayment? Let Rashbam explain.[23]

The order is as follows:

> The creditor comes to court and asks redress from the debtor, to pay his debt. We call the debtor to court. If he does not appear we excommunicate him, and we issue a writ of seizure to the creditor[24] that he may go and undertake a search whether the debtor has any landed property,

---

For legal purposes the charge on the property also gives a limited degree of "possession" (*Pesachim* 30b et seq.). Abbaye is of the opinion that when a creditor forecloses, he does so retrospectively; i.e., it is now shown that the property was his when the debt was initiated. Thus, if in the interim the creditor consecrated the property for the benefit of the Sanctuary, the consecration is valid, as it now transpires that the property was indeed his to consecrate. Rava disputes this principle, which is extended by Beit Shammai to their ruling, "A bond which stands to be collected is considered as already collected" (*Sotah* 25a), giving, in cases of doubt, legal advantage to the bond holder.

Destruction of a loan document also destroys the charge and is considered an "indirect damage," which some Authorities consider actionable by the victim (v. supra p. 79).

[23] *Bava Batra* 169a, s.v. *"v'ha amar."*

[24] This will be issued even if the debtor appears, if he does not repay or offer to repay, and it is felt that he has assets.

and wherever he shall discover the debtor's property, even in the possession of one who had purchased it from the debtor after the loan was made, he is to show the writ to the Beit Din of that city [which has jurisdiction over that land] and they will transfer the property to the creditor, by writing him a writ of assignment. By this he may control and utilize the property of the debtor until his debt is satisfied out of it. The writ of seizure is then to be destroyed in case the creditor would attempt to submit it to another Beit Din and duplicate the seizure. The property assigned is to be assessed according to the normal methods of assessment used by the Beit Din, and it is on the basis of that valuation that he is to collect his debt. The Beit Din will issue him with writ of assessment to prove at what value he took the property over, because the seized property is always returnable to the debtor when he has the funds to repay his debt, and when the Court issues the writ of assessment they will destroy the writ of assignment to stop the creditor attempting to use it again in violation of the law.

According to accepted principles of law, property which has been appropriated by a creditor in satisfaction of a debt due to him becomes his absolutely, and the debtor loses all rights or interest therein. However, because of the Biblical injunction "you should do right and good," the Rabbis instituted an Equitable Law, that the debtor may redeem his own property however many years may have passed. The reasoning behind this ordinance is explained by an eminent contemporary jurist thus:

What is the reason that after Search, Seizure, and Assessment, the property is assigned to the creditor? Obviously it is to pay the debt due to him from the debtor! This is the only legitimate interest the creditor has in acquiring the property. This and nothing else! He has no right to enrich himself through the loan which he extended to the debtor, and such enrichment is forbidden him even if it does not take the form of interest. It is for this reason that the Sages ruled that the "upright and the good" demands that if the debtor from whom it was seized finds the means of repaying the creditor...the creditor must return the land to its owners against the repayment of the sum due to him.[25]

The personal obligation of the debtor to repay his loan is a legal right (and no more) to repayment arising to the creditor, which he, in turn, would have to pass on to his own creditor:

R. Natan said: How do we know that if A claims a sum from B, and C claims a like sum from A, that we collect from B and give it to C? From the verse "and he shall give it unto him to whom he is indebted."[26]

This right does not throw any hypothecary charge on the person of the debtor; it is no more than an obligation to pay.[27] Consequently the debtor's person is not at risk; the Torah will not countenance the barbarity of ancient Rome which permitted creditors to satisfy themselves out of the actual flesh of the debtor, nor will it countenance the comparatively modern practice of throwing a debtor into a debtor's prison.[28]

---

[25] Silberg, *Talmudic Law and the Modern State*, p. 99. The debtor only has an "equity of redemption" so long as the property is in the hands of his creditor; should the creditor sell the property, the debtor loses this right (*Choshen Mishpat* 103:10).

[26] *Bemidbar* 5:7, translating "and he [the third] shall give it to him [the first] to whom he [the second] is indebted." This ruling is the dictum of R. Natan (*Pesachim* 31a); v. *Torah Temimah, Bemidbar*, ad loc.

[27] The term "charge on the person" is almost devoid of legal effect (Rabbi Dr. I. Herzog, *The Main Institutions of Jewish Law*, vol. 2, p. 4). While a debtor may sell himself as a Jewish servant, he is in no way obliged to do so (*Yad, Avadim* 1:1, a group of laws—the rules of acquisition—which Rambam includes in his section on Civil Law).

[28] An underlying theme guiding the rulings of the Torah was articulated by Shlomo Hamelech. "Its ways are ways of pleasantness and all its paths are peace" (*Mishlei* 3:16).

Even R. Pappa[29] allows coercion only where the debtor has the means to repay his debt, but is dishonest in refusing to honor his obligations and to carry out the Torah's precept; but, if the debtor is not able to pay his debt, there is no point whatsoever in coercing him. Where a person can pay, he will be coerced not only into repaying monies borrowed, but into providing sustenance for his wife[30] and for children under six years of age[31] and often between that age and the age of puberty.[32] Some scholars hold that a man of means may be coerced into providing sustenance for his parents who are unable to provide for themselves.[33]

Most Authorities are of the opinion that a man cannot even be forced to work to pay off a debt. This follows the principle that a debtor's person, as such, bears no responsibility for his debts.[34] Against this view is the apparent lone voice of Maharam of Rothenburg[35] who considers that while it is prohibited to take away a debtor's freedom, it is most certainly permitted to take away "the produce of his hands." Providing the work he is being asked to do is not especially unpleasant or humiliating, there is no reason why he should not do it; is there not a proverb "the borrower is servant to the lender"?[36]

Between these two extreme views we find a compromise quoted in the Bach[37] that while a man cannot be forced to work to pay off an ordinary debt, he can be forced to work in order to maintain his wife and infant children.[38]

---

[29] V. supra p. 149 & p. 150, note 21.

[30] Ketubot 77a.

[31] Ibid. 65b.

[32] Ibid. 49b.

[33] V. Talmud Yerushalmi, Pe'ah 1:1.

[34] Rosh 78:2; Mordechai, Ketubot 7:205.

[35] Responsa 146.

[36] Mishlei 22:7.

[37] Tur, Even Ha'ezer 70.

[38] The definitive publication on this particular subject is Freedom of the Debtor's Person in Jewish Law by Menachem Elon; v. supra p. 139 as

The second equitable law which the Talmud pegs to the verse "And you should do that which is right and good"[39] is that of the abutter—a neighbor who has the right of preemption over any other potential purchaser when adjoining property comes up for sale. The Talmudic term is **Bar-Metzra**—based on the word *metzer*, meaning border.

> It is an ordinance of our Sages[40] that if one sells his field, his house or his shop, should his bordering neighbor wish to buy it, this neighbor has preemption over any other person so long as he is willing to pay the price that a third party would; and the Rabbis relied on the verse: "And you should do that which is right and good in the eyes of the Lord." For the Almighty wishes people to deal with one another uprightly and fairly, and there can be nothing more upright and fair than this, for as the vendor wishes to sell, it is no loss to him that his abutter has preemption over any other person [whereas the abutter has a great advantage in being able to join the property he already owns with that which he is now able to purchase]. The Sages strengthen this law, in that even should the vendor complete a sale to a third party, that sale becomes invalid and the purchaser has to hand back the property to the abutter. Even more say our Sages: This buyer is considered an agent of the abutter for all purposes, and therefore, even if the value of the property were to increase while it was temporarily in the hands of the third party, nevertheless, the abutter pays him only the original purchase price [any profit accruing to the abutter]. Conversely, if the value drops, the loss is incurred by the abutter [he must pay the original purchase price].[41]

The Rabbis emphasize that the onus of doing "what is

---

to whether a person can be forced to honor a contract and whether a Court will order specific performance.

[39] Supra p.146.
[40] *Bava Metzia* 108a et seq.
[41] *Aruch Hashulchan, Choshen Mishpat* 175:1.

right and good" is on the buyer—for it is he who could buy property in another place; it is his interference which damages the interests of the neighbor. The legal machinery used to undo a transaction entered into by the seller and a third party, is to treat that third party as an agent of the neighbor; so much so, that there is a discussion in the Talmud[42] as to what is the law if the buyer overpays. The normal rule of agency is that the principal can claim compensation for any damage done by his agent on the grounds, "I sent you for my benefit, not for my disadvantage."[43] Can the neighbor take the property from the third party at what is generally agreed to be its true value—leaving the buyer with the loss on the grounds that as the neighbor's agent he should have made a better deal on his behalf? In fact, as land has no fixed value,[44] there never can be an "overpayment" as such—hence the neighbor must pay the buyer the amount he, the buyer, paid. However, it is clear that if not for the special rule concerning the value of land, the normal law of agency would have applied. This legal agency, invented by the Rabbis and later developed further, was an innovative step in the field of Equity.[45] Because it is an equitable rule, the burden of which is placed upon the buyer, it would be impossible to enforce it against women or orphans who, through a guardian, have agreed to purchase property: it would not be "right and good" to make women or orphans face additional inconvenience.[46]

The vendor is not asked as to his preference—provided he obtains a fair price, it makes no difference to him who buys his field. But if he would suffer any loss or inconvenience, this law cannot be enforced, as it would not be

[42] *Bava Metzia*, loc. cit.
[43] The Talmudic idiomatic expression.
[44] V. infra p. 223.
[45] Infra p. 158.
[46] *Aruch Hashulchan*, op.cit. 175:29.

"right and good" to hurt him in any way. Therefore, if, for example, he has entered into an agreement with a purchaser, whereby he sells *all* his property, however widely scattered, to this one purchaser, an individual abutter cannot intervene, as this could jeopardize the vendor's entire sale covering all the properties negotiated.[47]

A creditor in possession as mortgagee[48] is considered an abutter, and in the event of the debtor's wishing to sell the property, he has first refusal. There are differences of opinion as to whether his temporary possession as a mortgagee gives him the right of an abutter against adjoining property.[49]

The Court must ensure that the law is being applied equitably; any suspicion that it is being used unfairly would result in its not being enforced. The use of an equitable law perversely is the very negation of equity.

For example: A landowner may sell a small area of land in the middle of his own holding. At that stage, he would be the only abutter to the land being sold, as his retained land fully surrounds it. If subsequently he decides to sell the rest of his holding, he would prima facie have abutters of equal right on both sides—that is, his original neighbors surrounding the property, plus the new purchaser who is in the middle of his property. If we have reason to suspect that the original sale of land in the center of the estate was done for the purpose of giving the buyer the right of an abutter against other neighbors, the court will remove that right.[50]

Similarly, if a loan is made to a property owner who gives land as security, and the Court suspects that the motive is to give the mortgagee a standing against the neighbors, and the loan and mortgage is merely a sham intended to camou-

---

[47] *Bava Metzia* 108b.
[48] V. supra p. 151.
[49] *Aruch Hashulchan*, op. cit. 175:36.
[50] *Bava Metzia* 108b.

flage the sale and purchase, the court will not countenance a claim to preemption by the suspect creditor.[51]

The Rabbinic innovation,[52] that an interloping purchaser is to be treated as an agent for the abutter entitled to purchase, is an equitable law based on a legal fiction (for, after all, the purchaser was purchasing for himself and not for the abutter) and is itself the forerunner of the equitable rules of **Power of Attorney**.

Jewish Law does not encourage pleas before the court by attorneys[53]—it is preferable that the litigants themselves place their claims, defenses and counterclaims before the court. The underlying reason for this is that a person will hesitate to tell a blatant untruth face to face with one who knows the truth. Therefore, a defendant may not plead through an attorney or through an interpreter,[54] for what he would not have the impertinence to deny personally he may well be able to deny through an agent.[55] This rule does not apply in the case of the plaintiff; after all, he initiates the action, and there is the presumption "That a man will not claim from another unless he has a genuine claim upon him."[56] Nevertheless, the law does not look kindly on one who lodges his claim through an attorney.

And any person who appears [before the Court] with a power of attorney is included in that which was said [by

---

[51] *Aruch Hashulchan,* op. cit. 175:35.

[52] V. supra p. 156.

[53] The word attorney is not used in the American sense of lawyer or counsel who is only an adviser and spokesman; in this context it denotes a personal representative, one who deputizes for his principal.

[54] For this reason, members of the Sanhedrin had to be proficient in languages other than their native one.

[55] *Ran, Shevuot* 30a, quoting *Alfasi, Responsa.* V. *Choshen Mishpat* 124. But v. *Aruch Hashulchan, Choshen Mishpat* 124:2 for current practice.

[56] *Shevuot* 40b.

the Prophet],[57] "And that which was not good, they did among their people."[58]

However, as the Jewish horizon broadened and the Diaspora spread, this restrictive attitude made commercial life difficult and therefore Ravad[59] adds the following explanation to Rambam's rule:

> This is only true if the plaintiff and his opponent are in the same town and he [the plaintiff] gives a power of attorney to another to claim the amount due to him, but if the defendant is in a different town [and the power of attorney is given to a resident of that town], he [the attorney] is rescuing money belonging to another.

There is in fact no difference in opinion between Rambam and Ravad;[60] it is permissible to appoint an attorney and for the attorney to accept the appointment, provided the plaintiff himself cannot appear in person. From the Talmudic source from which Rambam takes his rule,[61] it would appear that the Rabbinical wrath was directed at the attorney himself,

> for he joins into a quarrel which is not his; it is possible that the plaintiff himself could more easily agree to a compromise than his attorney, who does not have the authority to compromise with monies belonging to another.[62]

The phrase, "a quarrel which is not his," does not indicate merely a moral weakness in the attorney's standing, but also a legal one. If the plaintiff sends an ordinary representative to represent him, the defendant can say to the representative: "This matter is no business of yours, *you* have no claim against

---

57 Yechezkel 18:8.
58 *Yad, Shluchin V'shutfin* 3:5, based on *Shevuot* 31a.
59 *Ravad, Yad,* loc. cit.
60 *Kesef Mishneh,* ad loc.
61 V. supra note 58.
62 *Rashi, Shevuot* 31a, s.v. "*zeh.*"

me."[63] A formula had to be devised to give the representative a legal standing, and the method employed was to assign to him the debt, and this assignment became the basis of the power of attorney in Jewish Law:

> An assignment which does not contain the words, "go forth and take legal action so that you may be entitled to it and secure the claim for yourself," is of no validity.[64]

In the course of discussion, the Talmud modified this and is satisfied if the assignment states

> You will be entitled to a half, or a third or a quarter of the claim;

the rationale being that, since he is entitled to litigate regarding the half, or the third, or the quarter, he is also entitled to litigate regarding the whole.

This legal form makes the representative the assignee of the debt; so what would be the position if, on being successful in litigation, the assignee refuses to return the money to the original creditor who appointed him? The view of Amemar is that however morally reprehensible his attitude would be, the assignee would be entitled to retain the money, and would be successful in any action brought by the assignor.[65]

However, R. Ashi maintains that, because in the formal assignment the original creditor puts the words "Whatever will be imposed by the Court of Law, I accept upon myself," it is quite apparent that the assignee was appointed an agent only.[66] Indeed, that is the final ruling in the Talmud, according to many.[67]

---

[63] *Bava Kama* 70a. The normal rule that a person's agent is as himself only holds good when no third party is in any way injured; here the appointment of an agent is to the detriment of the defendant.

[64] Ibid. For a contemporary text of power of attorney, v. *Aruch Hashulchan, Choshen Mishpat* 122:14.

[65] *Bava Kama,* loc. cit.

[66] Ibid.

[67] But Rosh and Alfasi omit this ruling of the Talmud.

This is a classic example of equity overruling law. In order to give the representative a legal standing, he has to become a party to the action—which he does by becoming the owner of the debt by means of a legal transfer; whereas, vis à vis the real claimant, he is treated only as an agent, which in equity is all that he really is.

There remains this problem: Once it is decided that the equitable position is the dominant one, what is there to preclude the debtor from relying upon it and saying to the attorney, "You have no business with me, you are not the plaintiff"? The fact that he cannot do so may be taken as an illustration of the power of legal fiction, a most useful artifact in the growth of law;[68] or it may be that, in reality, the principal of agency came to reassert itself, and that the fiction only served the purpose of avoiding an open clash with the old established practice, probably issuing from purely ethical motives of allowing the defendant to deny the agent's right of action.[69] The relationship between the assignor and the assignee is a clear example of early Jewish equity; put into modern idiom, it can be said that if the assignee is successful and obtains possession of the money, he holds it, in **absolute trust** for the assignor.

These rules deny the proud claim of British legal historians that the interests of the person for whose benefit the property was conveyed became a form of "equitable ownership" of a sort

---

[68] V. *Tosafot, Bava Batra* 77b, s.v. *"R. Pappa"; Tosafot, Ketubot* 55b, s.v. *"she'im"*; cf. *Tosafot,* op. cit. 54b, s.v. *"af,"* that a bridegroom's statement is taken at face value if that makes the *Ketubah* binding; cf. *Tosafot, Bava Batra* 127a, s.v. *"mi-dedarash,"* that the stratagem of power of attorney can also be used if the subject is not yet in the entitlement of the claimant (v. infra p. 236).

[69] Rabbi Dr. I. Herzog, *The Main Institutions of Jewish Law*, vol. 1, p. 204. But v. *Ritva, Shevuot* 33b, who maintains that power of attorney is of Rabbinic origin, the Rabbis using their powers of *Hefker Beit Din* (supra p. 74.)

"which has no parallel in any other system of Law."[70] As in many aspects of Civil Jurisprudence, Jewish Law embodied that principle earlier than any other system of law.[71]

It has already been noted[72] that if an owner makes a sale or grants a mortgage to a third party with the sole motive of defeating his abutter, that sale or mortgage is disregarded, and the apparent right enjoyed by the recipient is ignored in favor of the legitimate right of the neighbor. The underlying doctrine supporting this position is that, as far as it possibly can, the law will not allow itself to be used perversely; however "legal" the result may be, it would be totally inequitable. The application of this doctrine is clearly shown in two leading cases reported in the Talmud.

The first case:

> A certain slave was owned by two men in partnership, and one of them emancipated his half. [The result of this is that the slave is now half Jew and half slave, making his personal status intolerable: he cannot marry a Jewish woman because half of him is a slave, and he cannot marry a

---

[70] V. Silberg, *Talmudic Law and the Modern State*, p. 127 et seq. and note 160.

[71] It is only by adopting this principle, that the Rabbis can rule that a husband who leaves his entire estate to his widow has only appointed her as guardian, but has not given her beneficial ownership, notwithstanding the documentation (*Bava Batra* 131b).

Under Jewish Law a husband has considerable interest in his wife's property. Thus a woman contemplating marriage may wish to remove property she owns beyond the reach of her new husband. This she can do by executing a deed of gift in favor of a third party, which, although holding good against the husband, fails against the wife should she want her property returned; thus the donee is a trustee for the wife, but by legal fiction he is treated as the owner vis à vis the husband. This deed, acceptable in such circumstances and known as a "Deed of Evasion," (v. infra p. 166) is dealt with in *Ketubot* 86b and *Even Ha'ezer* 90:7.

[72] V. supra p. 157.

slave-woman as half of him is Jewish. The Court normally
coerces the remaining owner to emancipate his half, making
the former slave a full Jew and thus permitted to marry a
Jewess.] The remaining partner thereupon thought to himself: If the Rabbis hear of this they will force me to give up
my half. He therefore transferred the slave to his infant son
[who was not of legal capacity to emancipate the slave].[73] R.
Josef the son of Rava submitted the case to R. Pappa. He
sent him back answer: "As he has done, so shall it be done
to him; his dealing shall return upon on his own head."[74]
We all know that a child is fond of money. We shall therefore appoint a guardian for him [the child]; the slave will
rattle some coins before the child and the guardian will
write out a deed of emancipation for the slave in his [the
guardian's] name.[75]

To avoid a legal consequence which would be unfair to
the slave, the Rabbis invoked the principle of *Hefker Beit Din*[76]
to deprive the child of his legal ownership, thereby enabling
the guardian to right the wrong.

The second case:

A man once bought a boat load of wine. He did not know
where to store it and asked a certain woman: "Have you a
place for renting?" She replied: "No." Then he proposed
marriage and betrothed her, whereupon she gave him a
place for storage. He then returned to his home, wrote a
Bill of Divorce and sent it to her. So she went, hired car-
riers against the wine[77] and had it put out in the road. Said
R. Huna son of R. Yehoshua: "As he has done, so shall it be
done to him; his dealing shall return upon his own head."[78]

---

[73] V. infra p. 229.

[74] Based on the verse in *Ovadiah* 1:15 (which is in the second person).

[75] *Gittin* 40a & b. V. *Tosafot*, ad loc. 40b, s.v. "*v'katav*." See a similar
approach in another context, *Yevamot* 110a.

[76] Supra p. 74.

[77] I.e., paying for them out of sale proceeds of that very wine.

[78] *Bava Metzia* 101b.

In fact, the woman concerned was breaking the law, for the landlord/tenant relationship is, under Jewish law, also controlled by the principles of equity.

In order that neither side can take advantage of the other, adequate notice must be given. The law is that if the tenancy agreement is for a fixed term, no notice need be given by either side—both know how long the tenancy has to run.

If, however, there has been no agreement as to the length of the tenancy, the minimum period is one year and the notice which must be given varies with the circumstances. For example, in the summer, when it is considered easier to find accommodation, thirty days notice is required. On the other hand, in the winter people do not move, and it would be difficult to find new accommodation, so thirty days notice must be given *before* the onset of winter. Similarly, because there is a shortage of accommodation in very large towns, a year's notice must be given, irrespective of the season in which it is given.

There are also rules governing the letting of business or shop properties. Because there is a problem of transferring goodwill, normally at least one year's notice is required. If the tenant is engaged in a business which has a longer credit cycle, he is allowed a longer period of notice; in other words, he is given time to collect all his debts and to advise his customers of his impending move.

Because tenants know of the difficulty of finding accommodation, they do not readily give up what they have. To some extent, this jeopardizes the landlord's position if he has a vacancy. Therefore, it is only fair that the same notice that he must give, he is entitled to receive, although a tenant may move out without giving notice, provided he can find a satisfactory replacement.

As the arrangements are to be fair and equitable to both parties, the rule is that should the landlord's house be destroyed, and he finds himself homeless, he can, after the initial period has expired, ask the tenant to quit without giving him notice, on the grounds that the tenant should be no better off than he. Similarly, if he requires the house for his son who is about to be married, the court will consider the matter; if it were possible for the landlord to have given notice, then the tenant is entitled to such notice; if not, the tenant must quit. Conversely, the sale or gift of the house to another landlord in no way invalidates the tenant's rights.[79]

To revert to the incident of the wine dealer who tricked the landlady by his false betrothal: In order that his cunning recoil upon his head, the Rabbis allowed her in the name of equity to evict him without giving any of the required notices.[80]

In arriving at a decision on any matter, a court is entitled to rely on a reasonable presumption, as did King Solomon in the case of the two women claiming the one live child.[81] On the presumption that it would be the mother who under no circumstances would want her child killed, he gave it to the one who pleaded for its life. On the same lines, there is this case reported:

> A man heard his wife say to her daughter, "Why do you not observe more secrecy in your amours? I have ten sons and only one is from your father." When that man was on his deathbed he said, "I leave all my property to my *one* son." They had no idea which of them he meant, so they consulted R. Bana'ah. He said to them: "Go and knock at the grave of your father until he gets up and tells you which one of you he has made his heir." So they all went to

---

[79] Ibid. and v. *Choshen Mishpat* 312 and *Aruch Hashulchan*, ad loc. Obviously, these rules, laid down in the Talmud, vary with custom and with prevailing socioeconomic conditions.

[80] *Ritva, Novellae, Bava Metzia*, loc. cit.

[81] 1 *Melachim* 3. V. *Malbim*, ad loc.

do so. The one who was really his son, however, did not
go. R. Bana'ah thereupon said: "All the estate belongs to
this one."

On the presumption that it would be the real son who
would have the feeling of filial love and respect for his dead
father, he awarded him the estate.[82]

Similarly, if a mortally sick man writes over all his property to another and then recovers, the court would undo the
gift; they would presume that, as he has written over *all* his
property, he did so only in anticipation of death, which fortunately did not occur,[83] and therefore the gift is invalidated.

The same presumption is followed in the event of a man,
who, on hearing of the death of his only son, writes over all
his property to another. Subsequently, when it is found that
the son is alive, the gift is invalid, on the presumption that
it was made only because the donor thought he had no
heir.[84]

Thus, in the circumstances that a man writes over all his
property to another and then continues dealing with it, we
are entitled to rely on the presumption that the deed of gift
is nothing more than a document prepared for evasion, to
keep the donor's property from his creditors, and accord-

---

[82] *Bava Batra* 58a; although all the putative heirs are legally "in possession" (v. supra p. 109), nevertheless this presumption is sufficient to remove property (*Rosh, Responsa* 78:3). The author has not
found a ruling as to whether the other sons were now to be considered illegitimate by virtue of the court's interpretation of the
father's statement; normally a father's declaration that a younger
son is his firstborn would illegitimize the older ones (*Bava Batra*
127b and *Tosafot*, ad loc., s.v. "*kach*"). In this case the father never
made the statement that this is his only son; the court has presumed it from the statement he did make. V. *Kovetz Shiurim, Bava
Batra* 260 that this was only an exercise in judicial discretion (v.
supra p. 136) with the judge finding comfort in the presumption.

[83] *Mishnah, Bava Batra* 146b.

[84] Ibid. (V. infra p. 251).

ingly it is voided.[85] If such a document comes before a Court of Law it is in fact destroyed.[86]

Rosh[87] justifies his attitude towards a document prepared for the purpose of evasion by the fact that, if we accept it, no creditor would ever feel safe and would therefore never extend credit to any needy person.

> A true Torah, virtuous Statutes and upright Laws were given by the Almighty to His people Israel through our teacher Moses. "Its ways are ways of pleasantness and all its paths are peace; the righteous walk with them." The Sages of Israel are obliged to confuse the plots and void the schemes of those who conspire to prevent righteousness, to weight down the scales of justice with falsehood.

Thus does Rosh open his responsa on the subject, and thus does he close:

> It is most certainly the law, and I have explained that it is right to void all documents of evasion and maneuver which have been prepared, and when they come to the hands of the court, they should be destroyed. And let the law be laid down in Toledo to all scribes and witnesses, that under no circumstances should they write or sign deeds of gifts of property which they fear may be prepared for the purposes of a maneuver or for cheating; but they should bring the matter before the Rabbis of the town and according to their judgment should they act. And if the scribes do not obey this rule, they should be removed from their profession.[88]

Similarly, it is not advisable to allow a creditor to claim a debt from a debtor's estate in the latter's absence, as the

---

[85] *Rosh, Responsa* 78:1 & 3.
[86] *Ketubot* 79a; cf. supra, note 71. In the case of a woman contemplating marriage, such a document is allowed, whereas if in order to avoid creditors, it is not; v. *Rosh,* loc. cit.
[87] Ibid., 3.
[88] Ibid.

debtor may in fact have a justifiable defense. Nevertheless, the ruling is that creditors may do so, "in order that people should not take others' money and abscond and settle in a country beyond the sea, and thus cause the lenders' doors to be shut in the faces of needy borrowers."[89]

In the same way as Jewish law requires an equitable balance between landlord and tenant,[90] so also must there be equity in taxation.[91] According to current political thinking, there are three major purposes for levying taxes: firstly, to raise funds to cover the expenditure of government and of national, civic, and parochial institutions; secondly, to promote social justice and equality; thirdly, to further general economic, fiscal, and monetary policies. Often, secondary, socially desirable objectives are given as reasons to support taxation on certain items, which explains, for example, the high rate of taxation on alcohol and tobacco.

Jewish Law regards only the first reason as valid for levying taxes. "The King is permitted to tax the people for his requirements or for the requirements of war."[92] And the authority to collect taxes lies either with the sovereign power, or with the community, under the rules of communal legislation.[93]

How is the burden to be apportioned? Per capita? According to ability to pay? (In which case, is it capital wealth, income, or consumption which provides the basis?) According to benefit derived from the utilization of the money? Or according to causation?

---

[89] *Ketubot* 88a.

[90] Supra p. 164.

[91] For more detailed treatment of this subject v. Dr. Aaron Levine in *Intercom* (vol. 16, no. 1), p. 7 et seq. A major part of this section (in both form and substance) is taken from his work.

[92] *Yad, Hilchot Melachim* 4:1.

[93] Supra Chap. III. The alleviation of poverty, and other socially desirable objectives, are looked upon as religious obligations and are covered by the laws of tithes and charity.

> R. Elazar enquired of R. Yochanan: "Is the impost [for the wall of the town] levied as a poll tax [per capita] or according to means?" He replied: "It is levied according to means."

According to another version, R. Elazar asked R. Yochanan whether the impost was levied in proportion to the proximity of the resident's house to the wall, or in proportion to his means. He replied:

In proportion to the proximity of his house to the wall.[94]

The conclusion drawn is that there are two levels of apportionment; firstly according to wealth and secondly according to proximity to the wall, so that

> the poor nearer the wall are charged more than the poor further away, and the rich nearer the wall are charged more than the rich further away, but the rich who live away have to pay more than the poor who live near, for taxes are collected according to wealth.[95]

Rashi explains why a heavier tax burden is imposed on households located closer to the wall—because they have the greatest benefit; in the absence of a wall, it is these households that suffer the greatest likelihood of being victimized by bandits based outside the town limits.

Wealth attracts thieves, and the benefit of protection against them is pro rata to the wealth and therefore to the risk involved. However, in the event of war, when an enemy wishes to wipe out an entire community, it is the existence of the people which attracts the enemy, and therefore, the benefit of protection is equal for all the townsfolk. Thus, says Rosh,

---

[94] *Bava Batra* 7b.

[95] *Tosafot,* ad loc., s.v. *"lefi"*; cf. *Rosh, Novellae.* Normal people would give all their wealth to save their lives; thus levying tax according to means achieves a result as if all the townspeople put in all their wealth and received back what was not needed on a pro rata basis.

in the event of war, half the cost of the wall must be charged equally to all citizens on a per capita basis, while the remaining half is apportioned in accordance with property ownership, as property is also at risk to a plundering victor.[96]

It follows, therefore, that if the wall is primarily to protect property against theft, only movable property which can be stolen is to be taken into account in calculating a tax based on wealth—it is only such property which attracts thieves and which can be said to be a "cause."[97]

R. Menachem of Merseburg, a fourteenth-century German Halachic Authority, calls for a heavier levy on those houses whose rooftops conspicuously tower above the average rooftop height of the town. The logic offered is that these houses cause the town to be visible from a greater distance than it would otherwise be, and this greater visibility generates greater risk to the community by attracting to it a larger number of potential predators.[98]

During the Middle Ages, the rulers of several lands in which Jews settled and established communities found it expedient to tax those communities. The tax was charged to the community in total, the amount varying with the government's estimate of the total wealth of each particular community. Was the government estimate based only on income, in which case only income-producing assets must be included in calculating the taxpayer's wealth, or did the government also include non-income-producing assets, in which case these too must be included in the individual taxpayer's statement of wealth?[99] Interestingly, by the fifteenth century it was a universal custom to include jewelry in the tax base. This was

---

[96] *Rosh*, ibid. V. *R. Reuven Grozovsky, Novellae, Bava Batra*, chap. 6, who develops the "causation" principle.

[97] *R. Reuven, Novellae*, loc. cit.

[98] Cf. *Mordechai, Bava Batra* 1:475.

[99] V. *Terumat Hadeshen* 342; *Rashba, Responsa Hameyuchas LehaRamban* 184; *Maharal, Responsa* 121, etc. V. *Aruch Hashulchan* 163:8.

to bring into charge those who invested earned money in precious stones in order to gain tax exemption on the grounds that these are not income-producing assets.[100]

Using these principles, how is a Jewish Community to apportion the costs of the services it renders its members? A practical example is the salary of the **Shochet**—the ritual slaughterer. Without his services, no kosher meat would be available.

One ruling we have is that his salary be charged to those who used his services most, and this is done in the form of a production charge on the meat. With the price of the meat reflecting the salary of the *Shochet*, an individual's share in the expense would be determined by his level of meat consumption—the benefit he has from the *Shochet*.[101] This, incidentally, would also to some extent be a tax on wealth, for presumably the level of meat consumption of the rich is higher than that of the poor.[102] It may well be, therefore, that scholars may claim some waiver of their proportion of the costs of communal teachers' salaries: being able to teach their children themselves, their benefit is not so great.[103]

In applying the "benefit" principle to members of a community, consideration is given not only to the benefits actually reaped from that expenditure, but also to the assumed demand for those services. An illustrative example is the responsum of R. Hai Gaon dealing with the question as to how the salary of the Communal Cantor (Reader) is to be charged.[104]

> Another exponent of the benefit principle as the appropriate equity rule to be used in connection with the financ-

---

[100] *Terumat Hadeshen,* loc. cit.

[101] R. Moshe Fresco of Salonika, *Yadav shel Moshe.*

[102] *Heishiv Moshe* 94.

[103] *Knesset Hagedolah, Choshen Mishpat* 163.

[104] Quoted in *Beit Yosef, Tur, Orach Chaim* 53 ad fin., as summarized by Dr. Levine, p. 19.

ing of communal projects of a religious character is R. Hai Gaon. His benefit principle advocacy is clearly evidenced by the tax formula he proposes to defray the expense of the Cantor's salary. Taking notice of the multi-faceted role the Cantor plays in Jewish communal affairs, his formula breaks down the Cantorial function into its religious, ceremonial, and entertainment elements. Communal demand patterns for these various functions are not uniform. At one end of the continuum stands the communal demand pattern for the distinctly religious function of the Cantor. The Cantor performs his distinctly religious duties when he officiates at public prayer sessions. Since participation in these events is obligatory on all male members of the community, the communal demand pattern for the services of the Cantor in this context can be described as income inelastic. With every male member of the community generating a demand for the distinctly religious functions of the Cantor, the minimum salary necessary to engage a Cantor to perform at distinctive religious functions alone is allocated among the townspeople on an equal per capita basis.

Rav Hai Gaon points out that the public prayer sessions correspond to the daily communal Burnt Offerings of the Temple. The equal per capita levy prescribed by the Torah for the financing of these communal sacrifices should therefore apply also for the financing of that component of the Cantor's salary that corresponds to his distinctive religious function.

Should the Cantor, by virtue of his vocal skills, command a higher than average remuneration for his role of leading the congregation in prayer, this salary differential is allocated among the townspeople on the basis of a proportional income tax. This follows from the assumption that the communal demand pattern for the aesthetic and artistic dimensions of the Cantorial function is highly income elastic. Similarly, the communal demand pattern for Cantorial renditions at festive and mournful occasions can also be regarded as income elastic. The differential in earnings that the Cantor demands for rendering these services is, likewise, to be raised on the basis of a proportional income tax.

The name Sodom has become a synonym for wickedness and perversity. In Jewish Civil Law, equity will not allow a man "to act in the manner of Sodom"[105]—meaning the law will not allow him to adopt a "dog in the manger" attitude, refusing to confer upon another a benefit which costs him nothing.[106] Provided he suffers no real or contingent harm, a man will be coerced to bestow the required privilege on his fellow.

This ruling is foreshadowed by Yehoshua's ten stipulations—a good example being the one which permits the public to walk through private fields until the main rain is expected. As before that time, fields will suffer no damage through pedestrians,[107] the owner loses nothing; the public gains a shortcut.

In fact, the Law of Trespass is limited, as indeed it is in English Law.

> Trespass where no willful damage is done is no crime, and the notice that "Trespassers will be prosecuted" has been well described as "a wooden falsehood."[108]

The following are among the applications of this principle: One Jew cannot stop another taking shelter under his balcony, provided the wayfarer does him no harm, either tangible or intangible, such as putting himself in a position from which he can see into the house, thereby invading the householder's privacy.

---

[105] *Eruvin* 49a, *Ketubot* 103a, *Bava Batra* 12b, 59a & 168a.

[106] For the wickedness of Sodom, v. *Sanhedrin* 109a; *Midrash Rabbah, Bereshit* 49. Rabbinic Literature emphasizes the cruelties and injustices perpetrated by the Sodomites, rather than the homosexual activities for which the town's name has been perpetuated in the English language.

[107] Supra p.81.

[108] Geldart, *Elements of English Law*, p. 190. (There are currently suggestions that the English law be amended.)

Should one wish to make a window in a wall which has hitherto been windowless, his neighbor can stop him, via a Beit Din, on the ground that, as the new window will overlook the neighbor's property, there will be an invasion of privacy. If, however, it can be proved that there is no risk of his being able to look into the neighbor's property, the neighbor cannot object, because he will be compelled not to act in the "manner of Sodom."[109]

If one has a holiday home which he does not let throughout the year, and during the non-holiday period someone moves in, while the owner can indeed have him removed, he cannot claim any rental for the period during which the squatter was in occupation. Provided no damage has been done, the owner has lost nothing, as in any case he would not have let the house, and meanwhile, the other has benefited.[110]

This rule can affect the process of inheritance. If two brothers inherit two fields, and one brother is already the abutter to one of those fields, he can ask to inherit that one, provided that there is no difference, either actual or contingent, between the two fields—that, for example, they are watered from the same source so that one does not have a greater risk of drought than the other, or that one is closer to a border and has a greater risk in time of war.[111]

The equitable principle of "Compelling a man not to act in the manner of Sodom" overrules the legal principle that a legally valid contract cannot be voided unilaterally:

A certain man once leased his mill to another in consideration of the latter's services in grinding the landlord's grain

---

[109] Bava Batra 59a and Ritva, Novellae, ad loc. The Torah values privacy. V. Rashi, Bemidbar 24:5, "How goodly are your tents, O Yaakov," because the entrances were not facing one another, and one neighbor therefore could not see into the home of the other. V. Bava Batra 60a which quotes Bemidbar 24:2; V. Rashbam, ad loc., s.v. "chalon."

[110] Aruch Hashulchan, Choshen Mishpat 363:15.

[111] Bava Batra 12b.

[without charge]. Eventually the landlord became rich and bought another mill and an ass. Thereupon he said to the miller, "Until now I have had my grinding done at your place, but now pay me rent."

The Talmud concludes:

> If the lessee has sufficient orders for grinding at his mill, he may in such circumstances be compelled not to act in the manner of Sodom [and must release the landlord from the original contract].[112]

Since the lessee has enough customers, he will incur no loss, for instead of grinding the lessor's grain, he grinds that of another, and with the payments he receives from this other customer he can pay the rent to the owner of the mill; meanwhile, the lessor benefits in that his own newly acquired mill does not stand idle.

Rashba[113] was faced with a dispute in which A required a statement from B, who contended that such a statement could jeopardize his own position. Rashba upheld B on the grounds that the principle of "Compelling not to act in the manner of Sodom" is invoked only when no harm or contingent harm can occur to the bestower of the privilege. The theory of **Compelling** is an equitable one and therefore must be just and fair to both sides.[114]

The difference between Equity and Morality has been defined as: "**Equity** guides the law, **Morality** the litigant." Thus, while equity becomes part of the law, morality does not. It may be the basis of some laws, such as usury and extortion;[115] it may be demanded by law; but normally it is not part of the law.

---

[112] *Ketubot* 103a.

[113] *Responsa* 3:91.

[114] V. *Ketzot Hachoshen* 154:1., *Even Ha'azel, Shechenim* 12:1 and more. For more detailed treatment of this particular subject, v. S. Shilo, "Jewish Law's Concept of Abuse of Rights," *Israel Law Review* 15, no. 1, p. 49.

[115] V. infra Chap. IX.

The Talmud quotes an example of a demand by the Torah:"Just balances, just weights, a just *efah* and a just *hin* shall ye have."[116] The word "*hin*" can be read as "*hen*," meaning yes.

> Why should the Torah add the word "*hin*"; after all, it is only a form of measurement and can be included with an *efah*? The reason is to teach you that your "Yes" shall be a just Yes, and your "No" shall be a just No.[117]

Because of the Torah's demand for a high moral and ethical standard, however certain a disputant is of his rights, he is nevertheless exhorted not to resort to any form of subterfuge or trickery to win his case.

For example: In Jewish Law, a defendant who makes a complete denial is exempt from taking an oath on the grounds that no man would have the impudence to deny a valid claim—therefore, his denial is to be believed; whereas one who makes a partial admission may well owe the amount claimed and may be merely stalling, in which case he would not take a false oath and under oath would indeed admit to the truth.[118] Once a litigant is compelled to take an oath on one claim, the oath can be extended to other claims, which in themselves do not carry the obligation to make an oath, such as claims on land.[119]

Suppose A has a claim against B for an ordinary monetary amount. He can at least hope for an oath, whereas in normal circumstances, B will not be obliged to swear in response to the claim to property.

> How do we know that he who has a claim of one hundred *zuzim* against his neighbor should not say: "I shall claim

---

[116] *Vayikra* 19:36. *Efah* is a dry measure; *hin* is a liquid measure. *Rashi*, ad loc., but v. *Rashi, Bava Metzia* 49a, s.v. "*hin*."

[117] *Bava Metzia* 49a, quoted in this context by *Rashi, Ketubot* 86a; s.v. "*Periat*" but v. *Ritva, Novellae*, ad loc.

[118] *Bava Metzia* 3a; v. supra p. 36–37.

[119] *Shevuot* 42b; v. supra p. 43.

two hundred so that he [being an honest man] will admit one hundred and be liable to an oath [because of the rule of partial admission], and then I will be able to impose an oath upon him from another place [i.e., in connection with my claim for land—because of the rule that an oath against a monetary claim can attach an oath against a property claim[120]]"? Because it is said, "Keep far from any falsehood."[121]

And how do we know [conversely] that if one has a claim of one hundred *zuzim* against his neighbor and sues falsely for two hundred, the debtor should not say, "I will deny it totally in court but admit it outside the court, so that I should not be liable for an oath, and he may not impose on me an oath from another place"? Because it is said, "Keep far from any falsehood."

And how do we know that if three persons [together] have a claim of one hundred *zuzim* against one person [and have no witnesses] one should not be the litigant, leaving the other two as the witnesses in order that they may extract the three hundred *zuzim* and divide them among themselves? Because it is said, "Keep far from any falsehood."[122]

But these of course are only examples of very basic morality; the Jewish concept of morality is stretched further, calling upon the Jew to give up legal rights and entitlements in order to maintain a high standard of moral and ethical behavior.

In a sweeping indictment, the Rabbis declare that Jerusalem was destroyed only because its inhabitants judged in accordance with Torah Law. The Talmud queries, and how should they have judged—in accordance with the laws of untrained arbitrators? No, replies the Talmud [what is meant is], because they based their judgments strictly upon Torah Law

---

[120] *Mishnah, Kiddushin* 26a.

[121] *Shemot* 23:7.

[122] *Shevuot* 31a; v. *Rashba, Responsa* 3:81, that while one may take the law into his own hands and even resort to force to save his property, nevertheless he is not allowed to resort to falsehoods, even though through them the Court will arrive at a just result.

and were not prepared to go beyond the strict requirements of the law.[123]

It follows, therefore, that before litigation begins, the litigants should be persuaded to accept a compromise, with neither insisting on the rigorous application of law.

> It is incumbent to say to the litigants at the beginning of the case, do you wish us to apply the strict law or will you be satisfied with a compromise?[124] If they desire compromise, a compromise is made between them. And any Beit Din which concentrates on compromise is praiseworthy; it has followed Scripture: "execute the Judgment of Truth and Peace in your gates."[125] And so, regarding King David, it is written: "And David executed Justice and Righteousness to all his people."[126] What is Justice which has *with* it Righteousness?—it is compromise.[127]

However, in asking a litigant to agree to a compromise, the court may not, in fact, be asking him to give up any right of which he is certain. In every case there are weaknesses; no litigant is absolutely certain of what the result

---

[123] *Bava Metzia* 30b. Lit., "beyond the line of justice." In several places, the Talmud indicates that God himself does not always insist on a strict application of Justice. Among His Attributes, are both the Attributes of Justice and of Mercy. It is His desire that the Attribute of Mercy should prevail. V. *Berachot* 7a.

The Maharal of Prague explains that had the Israelites been prepared to make concessions and not enforced their full rights under law, God would have been prepared to make concessions, been merciful, and not have inflicted the full penalty of the destruction of the Temple and the State. V. *Torah Temimah, Bemidbar* 14:17; cf. *Bava Metzia* 30b, which finds the source for this requirement in *Shemot* 18:20.

[124] V. *Tur, Choshen Mishpat* 12:2, which reverses the order, mentioning compromise before law.

[125] *Zechariah* 8:16.

[126] *Shmuel II* 8:15

[127] *Yad, Sanhedrin* 22; v. *Mechilta* on *Shemot* 18:16.

will be, and he may in fact fare better with a decision based on compromise than with a decision based merely on the law, and therefore, the element of self-sacrifice demanded of the litigants may be singularly limited, as would therefore be the demands of morality.

Jewish Morality, in fact, does not hesitate to demand more.

The Talmud[128] relates that R. Yehudah once followed [his teacher] Mar Shmuel into a market of wholemeal vendors, and asked him:

"What if one found an [identifiable] purse here?"

The question of law is as follows: If, in a place frequented mainly by fellow Jews, a Jew finds an article which has distinctive identifying characteristics, the finder is obliged to announce his find in the Synagogue in order that the owner can come to him, describe the identifying characteristics, and reclaim his property. If the same article was found in a place frequented in the main by non-Jews, the owner despairs of having it returned to him, as it was not the custom of non-Jews to announce finds in the Jewish Synagogue. In such circumstances, even if the owner were to come to the Jewish finder, cite the distinctive identification marks, and reclaim his property, the finder is not legally obliged to return it to him. He can claim that, as the owner had despaired of his property, he had renounced ownership, and by the time it came into the finder's possession, it had become ownerless property, and he, the finder, is entitled to keep it.

The question posed by R. Yehudah was in respect of a place where the general public is to be found—the majority being non-Jews. Does the Jewish finder have to announce his find in the Synagogue?

Mar Shmuel answered, "It would belong to the finder."
[He does not have to make an announcement.]

---

[128] *Bava Metzia* 24b.

The implication is that the law recognizes that the owner has given up hope, because the majority of the crowd is non-Jewish, and that therefore the purse comes into the finder's possession as ownerless property. R. Yehudah continued questioning his mentor:

> "What if an Israelite came and cited the identification mark?"
> Mar Shmuel answered: "The finder would have to return it."
> "Both?" [I.e., you are contradicting yourself.]
> Mar Shmuel answered: "He [the finder] is required to go beyond the strict line of justice."

It is not by law that he is obliged to return the article; it is morality which obliges him. As Rambam writes:

> He who wishes to act in a fair and virtuous manner and to act beyond the strict requirement of the law, will return the lost article to the owner who cites the identification marks.[129]

To make one return another's property may not be too exacting a standard of morality. After all, the find was a fortuitous and unexpected enrichment, and the return merely puts one in the same position as before the find, no better but certainly no worse off.

Can the demands of morality be more exacting, and may they require one to take a loss in meeting them? Based on the following Talmudic report, the answer must be yes!

Liability for error has always been a risk faced by professional advisers, but Jewish Law, while being severe on the negligent, does exempt a fully qualified professional from

---

[129] *Yad, Gezelah V'Avedah* 11:7, but v. *Remah, Choshen Mishpat* 259:5. From Rambam's phraseology it would seem that returning the article, while meritorious, is not compulsory. Others disagree. V. *Shach* on *Choshen Mishpat* 259:3; cf. Talmud Yerushalmi, *Bava Metzia* 2:5, which quotes instances of virtuous men returning lost property although legally not obliged to do so. In each case they were guided by the desire that through their behavior people would declare "Blessed be the God of the Jews"; cf. *Chullin* 44b.

reimbursing his client for loss suffered because of bad advice given in good faith. According to most Authorities, however, this exemption is limited to advice given free of charge and not to that for which a professional fee has been demanded.[130]

R. Chiyya was a qualified money changer and therefore a specialist in coinage. A woman showed him a denarius and [without charging a fee] he told her that it was a good one. Later she came back to him and reported that she had shown it to other experts, and they had advised her that it was a bad coin and in fact she could not pass it on. R. Chiyya then instructed a disciple to change the bad coin for a good coin and write down the loss in his ledger. There was no need for him to take the loss; he was exempt by law, but, acting beyond the strict requirements of the law, he accepted a moral responsibility for the woman's loss and therefore reimbursed her at his own cost.[131]

If R. Chiyya's self-sacrifice in the name of morality is understandable, because he did, after all, cause an innocent party to lose money, what are we to make of the following incident reported in the Talmud?[132]

> Some porters broke a barrel of wine[133] belonging to Rabbah bar bar Chana.[134] Thereupon he seized their garments, and they went and complained to Rav. "Return them their garments," Rav ordered. "Is that the law?" Rabbah enquired. "Even so," Rav rejoined, "that thou mayest walk in the way of good men."[135]
>
> Their garments having been returned, they complained: "We are poor men who have worked all day and are in need. Are we to get nothing?" "Go and pay them," Rav

---

[130] V. *Choshen Mishpat* 306:6 and *Shach*, explanation 11; cf. *Remah* on 306:8, which deals with a scribe who makes an error.

[131] *Bava Kama* 99b.

[132] *Bava Metzia* 83a.

[133] Negligently, according to some commentators; accidentally, according to others. V. *Rashi*, ad loc.

[134] Another version has Rabbah son of R. Huna.

[135] *Mishlei* 2:20.

ordered. "Is that the law?" he [Rabbah] asked. "Even so,"
was Rav's reply, "and keep the path of the righteous."[136]

The fact that Rav relied on a Hagiographic verse demanding
"goodness" and "righteousness" clearly indicates that in absolute law the employer was justified in both not paying the
porters and in exacting compensation from them. Because
the porters were obviously needy, Rav made him forego
all his rights so that Rabbah ended up not only suffering a
loss because of the damage, but paying the very people who
caused it! Rav did not suggest, request or plead with Rabbah;
he ordered him to pay, confirming that his order was "the
law"—a demanding law on any level of morality.

Was this a unique ruling in one specific case, as has been
suggested, on the grounds that the employer was a leading
scholar, possibly a pupil of Rav from whom a higher moral
standard was demanded than from any other, or was this a
general ruling applicable to any person who wishes to act in
a highly moral fashion?[137]

If the ruling laid down was a general one, can the courts
coerce a litigant to act beyond the requirements of the law, or
is the acceptance of such a ruling really voluntary?[138]

The opinion that the court may coerce a litigant into
foregoing his legal rights is comparable, in one aspect, to that
of R. Pappa, that the repayment of a debt is a religious ob-

---

[136] Ibid. A similar incident but with a different dramatis personae is
related in the Talmud Yerushalmi, *Bava Metzia* 6:6. In this version,
the Judge (R. Yosei b. Chanina) took a more aggressive stand and
himself raised the question of wages—ordering the employer to
pay.

[137] V. Silberg, *Talmudic Law and the Modern State*, pp. 199-223; S. Shilo,
"*Lifnim Mishurat Hadin*," *Israel Law Review*, 13, no. 3, pp. 383-86.

[138] V. dispute in *Tur, Choshen Mishpat* 12:4 between Bach, who sanctions coercion and *Beit Yosef*, who does not; cf. *Ketubot* 49b et seq. R.
Yonatan coerced sons who had been given all their father's property to maintain the father, although legally they were not obliged
to do so (v. *Rashi* ad loc. 50a, s.v. "*v'asitinhu*").

ligation on the debtor and does not arise from any charge or right held by the creditor.[139] Both are concerned with duties, rather than rights. In the case of the debtor, the court is not primarily concerned with the amount due to the claimant, but with the obligation of the debtor—with his religio-moral obligation, with his performance of a religious precept. It is only as through a side effect—as a secondary result of the process—that the creditor receives his money.[140]

Similarly, when instructing a litigant to act beyond the strict requirements of the law, the court is not concerned with rights, but with religio-moral obligations—the duties resting on the obligated person.[141]

Those who do not believe that a man can be coerced to act above the call of law consider morality as the domain of obedience to the unenforceable.

---

[139] V. supra, p.149, note 20.

[140] Silberg, op. cit., p. 68.

[141] This idea has been used by Rabbi M. Miller of Gateshead to explain an incident reported in *Midrash Rabbah, Bereshit* 33:1 and Talmud Yerushalmi, *Bava Metzia* 2:5.

The Midrash relates that Alexander of Macedonia wished to understand the culture of one of the lands in his dominion and therefore attended court to see how justice was dispensed. There came before the king of that land two disputants. One claimed that he had bought a cheap field from the other and had found buried therein a diamond, which he felt rightfully belonged to the vendor, as the deal had been for the field only and not for the diamond. Conversely, the other claimed that the diamond rightfully belonged to the purchaser as he, the vendor, had sold the field and everything that was in it. The king, acting as judge, asked one party if he had a son and the other if he had a daughter. On receiving affirmative replies he suggested that the couple be married and the diamond given to them as a wedding present, thereby being shared by both families. Alexander was astounded. On perceiving his astonishment, the king asked the conqueror how such a case would have been decided in his country, to which Alexander replied: both disputants would have been killed and the king would have confiscated the money or item in dispute.

In that domain there is no law which inexorably determines our course of action, and yet we feel that we are not free to choose as we would. Obedience cannot legally be forced upon him. He is the enforcer of the law upon himself...[it is] the intermediate domain, which, so far as positive law is concerned, is a land of freedom of action, but in which the individual should feel that he is not wholly free....

But there is, regrettably, a widespread tendency to regard the fact that one *can* do a thing as meaning that one *may* do it. There can be no more fatal error than this. Between "can do" and "may do" ought to exist the whole realm which recognizes the sway of duty, fairness, sympathy, taste, and all the other things that make life beautiful and Society possible.[142]

More astonishing than the original judgment was Alexander's reply. Although a successful warrior, he was no uncivilized barbarian; he was a pupil of the philosopher Aristotle—much respected by Rambam—and he was an unusual warrior who considered it worthwhile watching the administration of a foreign system of justice.

How could such a man give the reply he did?

Rabbi Miller suggests that the system of jurisprudence in Alexander's native land may have been based on the rights, rather than the duties, of the citizen. His country may even have had a Welfare State, as we know it today, based on the rights of each citizen against his neighbor and the State. In the case before the judge, it was not the *rights* of the litigants that were stressed,but their *duties*; each felt he had a duty to concede the valuable diamond to the other. Alexander understood the effect of such moral attitudes on the machinery and institutions of a state based merely on rights; if allowed to spread they could ultimately challenge that machinery and those institutions, which as their king he was duty-bound to protect.

A Jewish Court would presumably rule that in law the diamond belonged to the purchaser (v. infra p. 231).

[142] S. Shilo, loc. cit. p. 387, quoting Lord Moulton; v. *Rashi, Yirmeyahu* 31:14 and *Bereshit* 29:25. The self-sacrificing morality of the Matriarch Rachel has stood her descendants in good stead.

EIGHT
Of Law and Illegality

THE APHORISM *In pari delicto potior est conditio possidetis*—in case of equal guilt the position of the possessor is the more powerful—describes a general principle which is basic to, among other things, the administration of British Civil Law. It indicates that a right of claim cannot be derived from an illegal act, because "he who wishes to invoke the law must have clean hands."

In a leading English case[1] some hundred and seventy-five years ago, a claim was entered for payment against a purchaser of bricks. The defendant claimed that the bricks did not conform to the size prescribed by law and it was, therefore, forbidden for the seller to sell them; consequently, he, the seller, could not now claim their price. This argument was accepted and the plaintiff's obviously equitable claim was dismissed.[2]

---

[1] Law vs. Hodgson (1809) 170 E.R. 1111.

[2] Contrast this with the case of Gremmaire vs. Le Clerc Bois Valon (1809) 170 E.R. 1110 heard on the same day, in which the former healed the latter, only to have his fee bill refused by the patient because Gremmaire, not being licensed to practice medicine in London, had acted illegally. In that case the Court upheld the plaintiff's claim and ordered the defendant to pay the full amount due, notwithstanding the illegality.

In a later case, a landlord rented an apartment to a woman who used it to entertain her lover. In the moral climate of that time, the couple's immorality was considered an illegality, and once it was established that the landlord knew the purpose for which the flat had been rented, he became a party to this immorality and the court would not hear his claim for unpaid rent.[3] In the more recent case of Bigos vs. Boustead,[4] Boustead, in order to avoid the Exchange Control Regulations then prevailing, gave Bigos value in England for which he was promised an equivalent value in Italy. This was not forthcoming, and he asked for the return of the value he had given. Acting on the principle that where both parties offend (as they had done by attempting to evade Exchange Control), the one who is in possession (Bigos) enjoys the advantage; although this conclusion was patently unsatisfactory and inequitable, the Court could not intervene to help the victim of an obvious improbity because of the illegal nature of the underlying transaction.[5]

Jewish Law, however, is directly opposed to such an approach. It will not allow an offender to use his collusion in an offense to take unfair advantage of his fellow, for that would only be adding to his original offense. Concerned not only with protecting the just, Jewish Law obliges the court to circumscribe the immoral gains of the unjust, and therefore does not inhibit the court from hearing a case which in itself

---

[3] Upfill vs. Wright (1911) K.B. 506.

[4] 1981 1. All E.R. 92.

[5] The amorality arising from the application of this principle is much attacked by leading jurists; see for example Mr. Justice Silberg's *Talmudic Law and the Modern State*, pp. 70-76, with particular reference to note 31. A more radical and equitable, if bizarre, approach was adopted in the case of the two litigious highwaymen, Everett and Williams, in 1725 (reported in *English and Empire Digest* [1970 reissue], vol. 3, case 4515). Both were subsequently hanged and their attorneys punished—one by banishment. Cf. Jewish legal approach, infra p. 194.

arises out of illegal activity.

Thus, in principle, Jewish Law will oblige a man to pay a prostitute her agreed fee although the liaison is illegal:[6] why should a dishonest fornicator indulge himself for free at the expense of another? The court will oblige him to pay the sum agreed upon, in order that he should not have the sin of dishonesty added to that of immorality.

On the subject of illegal activity there is a difference of opinion which seems to be fundamental and to affect any number of activities or transactions: this hinges on the question, what is the legal effect of an illegal act? Said Abbaye: "Any act which Divine Law forbids, if it has been done, has legal effect; for if you were to think that the act has no legal effect, why then is it punishable?"[7] Rava, however, said, "The act has no legal effect whatsoever, and the reason why one is punished with lashes on account of it is because he has transgressed a Divine Command."[8]

This dispute would seem to be relevant to the laws of interest;[9] if one does transgress, may one keep the interest wrongly charged? In fact, there is a Talmudic argument on

---

[6] *Choshen Mishpat* 87:25 note. The ruling is based on Rava's statement, *Bava Kama* 70b and *Bava Metzia* 91a, in the event of a son's committing incest with his mother; v. *Rivash, Responsa* 41; v. *Bach* on *Tur, Choshen Mishpat* 87:39 and *Shach* on *Choshen Mishpat* 87:58. If the liaison is one which carries the death penalty, as in Rava's example of incest, payment for the mother's service, although legally due, will not be exacted because of the overriding criminal law rule of "*Kam leih bi-d'rabbah mineih*" (lit., "he is sure of the large portion"), stipulating that in the event of a man's being liable to two penalties, he is released from the lesser penalty—in this case, payment. However, although payment is not exacted, the woman's rights under civil law remain, and if she takes possession of value equal to her fees, she will be allowed to retain it (*Rashi, Bava Metzia* 91a, s.v. "*Rava amar*"). V. *Ketzot Hachoshen* 28, ad init.

[7] I.e., what has been done is valid.

[8] *Temurah* 4b.

[9] Infra Chap. IX.

this law, and the Talmud[10] does try to establish that it is based on the dispute between Abbaye and Rava. However, the Talmud reaches the conclusion that the argument regarding interest is not really related to that dispute, and even Abbaye, who is of the view that an illegal act is valid, holds that prime interest may not legally be kept by the lender.[11] Rather, this argument specifically hinges on a point connected with that particular prohibition of interest.

Similarly, this question should also apply in the case of a creditor who illegally seizes a pledge—may he keep it? Here, even Rava admits that, although he has acted illegally, the Torah has revealed in this particular case that his illegal act is valid and he may keep the pledge.[12] Ultimately, the Talmud comes to the conclusion that there is no practical difference between the views; the several examples cited are shown to be specific exceptions to the rules postulated by Abbaye and Rava.[13]

It is in responsa literature that this point is further developed. Rosh[14] was presented with the following problem: A Jewish Community pronounced a ban invalidating any document not written in its entirety by the Town Scribe.

---

[10] *Temurah* 6a, ad fin.

[11] Although under civil law it does become the usurer's money(supra p. 187), cf. infra p. 218 regarding the penitent usurer.

[12] Subject to the charitable obligation of returning bedding at night to enable the debtor to sleep, and (say) a ploughshare by day to enable him to earn a living.

[13] There is a minority view quoted by *Rashi, Temurah* 6b, s.v. *"b'shinui,"* in which Rashi suggests that a practical difference between Abbaye and Rava will be whether a thief who changes the article stolen obtains a good title, and from then on only has to make monetary restitution without the obligation to return the stolen article itself. Abbaye would hold that notwithstanding the illegality of the theft, the thief obtains a good title, whereas Rava would say he does not. V. *Maharatz Chajes, Responsa* 56 for a novel elucidation of this point; cf. *Noda B'Yehudah* II, *Even Ha'ezer* 129 (p. 137).

[14] *Responsa* 7:4; (v. supra p. 147 for the importance of this legislation).

In due course he died, and a successor was appointed, at which time, without lifting the ban, the Community legislated that the incumbent Scribe had only to write the last line in order to validate the document. As the ban was in the form of an oath, and the oath had not been lifted, the Community, in its later legislation, seemed to be acting contrary to the oath. Were the documents written under the new regulations valid or not? In a responsum which has since formed the basis of many rulings, Rosh argues that the later documents are valid: the Community could have had the original oath lifted; although it did not do so, there was no "illegality." An oath which can be lifted is not comparable to a Divine Precept which cannot be moved.[15]

There are, however, Authorities who do consider that an act executed contrary to an oath is indeed invalid; a prohibition as a result of an oath or a ban has the same effect as a prohibition arising from the Torah. This view is built on a Talmudic ruling:

> R. Yosef said, "Since the Rabbis have laid down that he [a *yavam* for whose marriage or *chalitzah* a sister-in-law is waiting], may not sell [the estate of his deceased brother, which he inherits], his sale is invalid, even if he had already sold it."[16]

The basis of R. Yosef's ruling could be that a Rabbinical

---

[15] This responsum seems to contradict an earlier one by Rosh (5:4) in which he rules that for subsequent acts to be valid, the original ban must be lifted. V. *Chatam Sofer, Responsa, Choshen Mishpat* 104, who distinguishes between the two different cases. One is the case of the Scribe, in which, even after the first few documents are written under the new rule, the ban still stands for later documents and therefore the ban *remains* intact and there is *something* to be lifted. In the other case, which concerns the sale of seats, once the sale is executed there is nothing left on which the ban has an effect and therefore it cannot post facto be lifted; hence it remains inviolate and does invalidate the sale unless it had *previously* been lifted.

[16] V. *Devarim* 25:5-10; *Ketubot* 81b.

Ordinance has exactly the same effect as one written in the Torah and therefore would have the effect of invalidating any transaction which is executed in disobedience. If so, the ruling can be extended to any man-made prohibition, even to one arising out of an oath, and therefore any transaction contrary to an oath would be invalid.[17]

Others understand that R. Yosef bases his ruling on the principle *Hefker Beit Din*,[18] by which the Rabbis have the authority to dispossess an owner, and in this case exercise it to dispossess the *yavam*, so as to stop him selling his brother's property until the widow's entitlements are honored.[19] According to this view, R. Yosef's Talmudic ruling has no bearing on prohibitions arising out of individual commitments.

Problems arising out of oaths seem to have been fairly common. A typical case documented is one in which all the brothers of a childless deceased who could have been *yevamim*, swore oaths to their father that none would release the widow, who owned property upon which her late husband's family was dependent, without the father's consent. Eventually, the youngest brother was induced to perform the *chalitzah* ceremony, thereby releasing her. Ritva ruled that the release was indeed valid. "The *chalitzah* is valid; even if he has transgressed his oath, his transgression does not invalidate it [the *chalitzah*] at all."[20]

---

[17] *Mordechai, Shevuot*, ruling 784 (end of third chapter).

[18] Supra p. 74.

[19] *Radvaz, Responsa* 6:2068; v. R. *Yaakov MeLissa, Responsa* 46 quoting *Panim Meirot* 34.

[20] *Responsa* 149. Ritva gives no reason for his ruling. Dr. Gordon Weingarten suggests that his ratio decidendi is that of *Oneg Yom-Tov, Responsa* 3, who maintains that if it is an *action* which is required, as opposed to a *result*—evidenced by whether the action can validly be performed by a representative (and *chalitzah* cannot be performed by anyone other than the *yavam*)—and that action is properly performed, it cannot be invalidated by outside consideration. V. also R. Elchonon Wasserman, *Kovetz Hea'arot*, chap. 74.

There were cases in which men took oaths not to divorce their wives and were subsequently persuaded to divorce without having the oath lifted;[21] there were similar cases where prospective fathers-in-law took oaths to future sons-in-law that they would not disinherit their daughters, which they subsequently tried to do.[22]

What happens if one slaughters an animal on Shabbat, thereby desecrating the Shabbat? The law is: the animal is kosher, notwithstanding that the act of ritual slaughter on Shabbat was against the law.[23] Several distinctions are suggested by commentators, distinguishing this Mishnaic ruling and that of Rava, who hold that an illegal act is invalid. For example, this is a physical action successfully completed and cannot be invalidated. Or, Rava's ruling applies only where the prohibition concerned is one specific to that particular act (e.g., the prohibition of interest only affects money passing for that purpose); a blanket prohibition such as Shabbat, which prohibits many an act, has the effect of saying "you *may* not do this" and not "you *cannot* do this."[24] These distinctions are important in deciding whether a forced sale is valid.[25] After all, the purchaser who has forced the sale has transgressed the prohibition contained in the Decalogue, "you shall not covet."[26]

What would be the Law if both parties enter into an agreement to settle their disputes in non-Jewish Courts?[27]

---

[21] *Noda B'Yehudah* II, *Even Ha'ezer* 129.

[22] R. Akiva Eger, *Responsa* 129; R. Yaakov MeLissa, *Responsa* 46.

[23] *Mishnah, Chullin* 14a.

[24] *Noda B'Yehudah*, loc. cit. and II *Yoreh De'ah* 9; R. Akiva Eger, loc. cit.; R. Yaakov MeLissa, loc.cit.; *Kovetz He'arot*, loc.cit.; Rabbi M.A.Amiel, *Hamiddot Lecheker Hahalachah*, 2, *Middah* 11:22, pp. 15-16. Noda B'Yehudah and R. Akiva Eger both suggest that, contrary to the normal rules of Halachah, in this particular case the Halachah, exceptionally, follows Abbaye and not Rava.

[25] *Bava Batra* 47b.

[26] *Shemot* 20:14. V. *Chatam Sofer, Responsa, Choshen Mishpat* 104.

[27] V. supra p. 89 et seq.

Although they did agree between themselves at the time of (say) the loan, that it can be reclaimed either in religious or secular courts, nevertheless if they do go before the latter, they have transgressed a precept and therefore the condition is in fact against the requirements of the Torah. Even so, when one succeeds and extracts money through the secular courts, he is not a thief, for, as the condition concerns monetary matters and money can be relinquished,[28] the condition is a valid one; the litigant who is successful does not have to give back what the secular court awards him.[29]

Under Jewish Law, a debtor's person is not charged for a debt.[30] Can a debtor stipulate that such a charge be placed upon his person? The ruling: A Jew is not allowed to charge himself as a servant, nor is another Jew allowed to force a debtor to work for him, to imprison him, or to chastise him in any way.[31]

Under any system of jurisprudence, it is forbidden for a judge to take bribes; if he does, under Jewish Law the bribe must be refunded, even if it caused no perversion of justice. The judge's acquisition and possession of the bribe does not give him a legal right of retention, as it was taken against the Torah. Are witnesses caught by the same rule? The answer is no; there is no prohibition on witnesses from taking payment for giving evidence. The prohibition is against their giving false evidence, which is forbidden whether or not they receive payment. As the Torah has not banned the taking of the money per se, if they do so take, they may keep it, although their evidence is invalidated. Witnesses taking payment is different from a judge taking payment, which the Torah expressly forbids and which

---

[28] V. infra p. 219.

[29] *Birkei Yosef, Choshen Mishpat* 26:3, s.v. "*veli.*"

[30] Supra p. 153 note 27.

[31] *Choshen Mishpat* 97:15. V. *Rashba, Responsa* 1:1069. *Rosh, Responsa* 68:10; *Rivash, Responsa* 484. (Pain, humiliation and imprisonment are not merely monetary matters.)

therefore is, in itself, an illegal act.[32]

How would the Jewish judge deal with the following example of extreme illegality? A hires B to kill C (in modern parlance, A takes out a contract on C's life with B). B carries out his commission and C is duly done to death. A now refuses to pay B, and B sues in the Beit Din for his "fee." There are two questions: who is to be punished for the crime, and will B succeed in obtaining payment? Is there any distinction between this case and that of the incestuous prostitute who does receive payment for her illegal services?[33]

The basic law is covered by the Talmud in *Kiddushin*.[34]

> He who uses a deaf mute, idiot, or minor[35] to start a conflagration is not liable [for the damage caused] by the Law of Man, yet he is liable by the Law of Heaven.[36] But if he arranges it through a normal [sane] person, the latter [the agent (B)] is [legally] liable. Yet why so? Let us say that a man's agent (B) is treated as if it was he himself (A) who did the act [so that the principal (A) should be liable]?[37] There it is different, for there is no agent for wrongdoing, since we argue, "when the words of the master and the words of the pupil are in conflict, whose are to be obeyed?"

---

[32] *Netivot Hamishpat* 9:1. For further reading on this subject, v. Dr. Eliav Shochetman, *Ma'aseh Haba B'Averah* (Mossad Harav Kook, Jerusalem, 1981), who analyzes this *sugyah* (unit of argumentation) in depth.

[33] Supra p. 187.

[34] 42b.

[35] None of whom are of legal capacity.

[36] I.e., morally, even though not legally.

[37] Based on the general law of agency: an act by a person's agent is as if performed by the person himself (v. *Kiddushin* 41a et seq.). There are of course a number of exceptions to this rule; e.g., an act which needs personal performance such as wearing *tefillin* on one's own person or taking the *lulav* in one's own hands or the "giving of *chalitzah*"(v. supra note 20.) Performance of an illegal act through an agent is also one of the exceptions to the general rule, as explained in the text.

The answer to this rhetorical question is obvious; hence if A instructs B to do wrong, B is really acting on his own accord, for if working merely to carry out instructions, he would obey God's, as expressed in the Torah, and not those of A.

The metaphor could be understood to mean that, being obligated to listen to God's commands, B is in no position to enter into a contractual arrangement against them, with A;[38] or it could be understood to mean that A did not really enter into a valid contract, knowing that B could not keep it.[39]

The practical difference could well be where B is known (as in this case) as an assassin easily available for hire. A could not very well argue that he did not believe B would carry out his part of the bargain,[40] and in fact, on this point there is a dispute between two leading Authorities. "If the agent is known to engage in this activity [spying and reporting on fellow Jews], the principal who sent him is liable, and we do not invoke the rule that the Law of Agency does not operate in the case of an illegal act." So rules Remah[41] in a case which could lead to an informer being put to death[42] by the community. Shach, however, disputes this ruling of Remah.[43]

The question to be resolved is: in these circumstances is there a valid agency?[44] If so, however illegal the act, payment

---

[38] R. Akiva Eger, *Novellae, Bava Metzia* 10b.

[39] S'ma, *Choshen Mishpat* 182:1, para. 2.

[40] R. Akiva Eger, *Novellae,* loc. cit.

[41] *Choshen Mishpat* 388:15.

[42] *Sefer Zichron Yehudah, Responsum* 75.

[43] Cf. the parallel dispute between Remah and Shach, *Choshen Mishpat* 348:8; v. *Terumat Hadeshen, Responsum* 315.

[44] V. *Noda B'Yehudah* I, *Even Ha'ezer* 2 and II:110, which rules that today a Bill of Divorce sent via a messenger to a wife who does not want to be divorced is in fact invalid. Since the Synod of Mayence (approx. 1010 C.E.), led by Rabbenu Gershon Me'or Hagolah, it is forbidden under Ban for an Ashkenazic Jew (i.e., one of European

of the "fee" must be made, for in the case of partnership, in which each partner is de facto the agent of the other, R. Yosef Karo rules, "If one of the partners or managers deals in carcasses or prohibited foods, or similar, the profit must be divided,"[45] to which Remah adds his note, "and similarly if one partner stole or robbed, he must divide the proceeds with the other."[46] Certainly, according to Remah, the illegality of the acquisition does not overrule the equitable laws of partnership, which are those of quasi agency.

So much for transactions which are illegal under Jewish Law; what of those which are illegal under the Laws of the particular State in which the Jew lives, the State in which he has found refuge and sanctuary from persecution? Even in a Jewish State, the Jew welcomed a strong central authority; indeed, the Book of Ruth opens with a woeful expression, translated by the Talmud, "Woe! it was in the days of the Judges; woe! there was a famine in the land."[47] What caused these woeful expressions is explained in another place: "In those days [of the Judges] there was no King in Israel; every man did that which was right in his own eyes."[48]

After the destruction of the Jewish State, when the Jew could no longer look to a central Jewish authority, he learned

---

extraction) to divorce his wife against her will. Thus, this divorce is against that Ban; the messenger is doing wrong; therefore he ceases to be an agent and the giving of the Bill is invalid. *Ketzot Hachoshen* 182:2 disputes this ruling. In this responsum the Noda B'Yehudah also makes the point that one cannot be an agent of one party to harm the interests of another; as the wife does not wish to be divorced, no third party can act to her detriment. He defends this ruling in the second responsum quoted.

[45] *Choshen Mishpat* 176:12.

[46] Shach disputes this ruling. The point is similar to that of Everett and Williams (supra note 5).

[47] *Ruth* 1:1 as explained in *Megillah* 10b.

[48] *Shoftim* 17:6. For further development of this theme v. overview to *Megillat Ruth* (Art Scroll); v. supra p. 21.

quite early in his experience in exile that only a strong central temporal authority could ensure his own self-preservation and survival. Throughout the Diaspora he instinctively recognized that any semblance of unity for the Jewish people would be impossible if they were to be subject to the arbitrariness of the local officialdom of each small community in which they may find themselves. Furthermore, he realized that the very survival of the Jews as a people was predicated upon their ability to maintain communal autonomy, only possible by disassociating themselves from the endless shifting mercies of local officials. As a result, Jews were always in the forefront of the struggle to strengthen the power and authority of the King, recognizing that ultimately their welfare depended on the state rather than the city, on the empire rather than the province. History has shown that the Jews forged an alliance with the central figure in their respective countries and subjected themselves directly and exclusively to his authority,[49] praying for the welfare of the Sovereign of the Realm in which they resided.

This attitude must be reflected in the Jewish legal approach and indeed it is, with a clear Talmudic ruling. "All documents which are accepted in the secular courts [or registry], even if they are signed by non-Jews, are valid for Jewish courts, except for bills of divorce and of emancipation [of slaves]. R. Shimon says: 'these also are valid; they were only pronounced [to be invalid] when drawn up by an unauthorized person.'"[50] The Talmud queries this ruling, as, after all, the document has not been prepared in accordance with Jewish Law, to which Shmuel responds with the rule, "The Law of the State is Law."[51]

While this dictum may be politically convenient, what are

---

[49] Rabbi Dr. J. Schachter, *Dinei Yisrael*, vol. 8, p. 77.

[50] *Gittin* 10b, *Mishnah*. It must be stressed that ultimately the Halachah is not with R. Shimon. On the contrary, we are warned not to "alter the form fixed for a Bill of Divorce."

[51] *Gittin* 10b.

the legal sources? There are in fact several places in which the Scripture mentions the authority of the sovereign.

The Prophet Shmuel, in acceding to the demands of the Jewish People to anoint a King, describes the power of that King.

> This will be the manner of the King who shall reign over you. He shall take your sons for himself, for his Chariots and to be his horsemen, and some shall run before his Chariots. And he will appoint Captains over thousands and Captains over fifties and he will set them to plow his ground, to reap his harvest and to make his instruments of war and instruments of his Chariots. He will take your daughters to be confectioners and to be cooks and to be bakers. And he will take your fields and vineyards and your oliveyards, even the best of them, and give them to his servants, and he will take the tenth of your seeds, of your vineyards and give to his officers and his servants. And he will take your menservants and your maidservants and your goodliest young men and your asses and put them to work. He will take a tenth of your sheep; and you shall be his servants.[52]

So also in prayer does the Exilarch Nechemiah admit to the authority of the non-Jewish Sovereign in whose realm the Jews then lived.

> Behold we are servants this day, and for the land You gave unto our Forefathers to eat the fruit thereof and the good thereof, behold we are servants in it. And it yields much increase unto the Kings whom You have set over us because of our sins. Also they have dominion over our bodies and over our cattle at their pleasure and we are in distress.[53]

---

[52] *Shmuel* I, 8:11-17; v. *Mabit, Kiryat Sefer, Gezelah* chap. 5; v. Talmud Bavli, *Sanhedrin* 20b, that possibly the Prophet was deliberately painting a black picture so as to discourage the anointing of a King; v. infra p. 204.

[53] *Nechemiah* 9:36 & 37. V. also *Chatam Sofer, Responsa, Choshen Mishpat* 44 for another Biblical source.

Others who are not satisfied with these Biblical sources find other Halachic reasons why even the Torah accepts the Law of the State. In describing the Sovereign's power to confiscate land from a Jew for non-payment of taxes and then to sell that same land to another Jew who does pay the taxes, Rashbam explains Shmuel's dictum that "the Law of the State is Law" thus:

> All taxes and other obligations emanating from the lord of the State are Law, because all the subjects in that Kingdom accept it upon themselves willingly to keep the State's laws and judgments, which therefore become proper law.[54]

If this is indeed the underlying source, the state power would be limited only to laws for the common good of members of the state, not extending to discriminatory laws nor to laws concerned with religious ritual or personal affairs. Indeed there is a legally accepted maxim

> that while the Law of the State is Law, theft by the state is not, and the expression "Law of the State" means just that: Laws of the State setting out the organization of a system of jurisprudence, legal methods of preparing documents, activities such as planting forests, uprooting trees, digging canals, building bridges; all these are within the definition of Laws of the State, but what one local ruler decides on an ad hoc basis is theft by the State and has no legal validity.[55]

If the ruling power enacts laws which discriminate against individuals or minority groups, the Jews are not obliged by Jewish Law to recognize them.[56]

---

[54] *Bava Batra* 54b, s.v. *"veha'amar."* This is an extension of *Takkanot Hakahal.* V. supra p. 80.

[55] *Rashba, Responsa* 2:356.

[56] *Choshen Mishpat* 469:8. V. Rabbi Chaim Zuckerman, *Otzar Chaim* on *Shemot* 1:22, explaining that Pharaoh's decree to drown children had to be "all sons born," not just Jewish babies. V. also *Birkat Chaim*, vol. 2, p. 57, quoting Rabbi E. Falklash of Prague who offers an original interpretation of the verse in the Book of Esther (1:7) "And *the drinking* was according to the Law."

Another suggestion as to what gives State Law validity in the eyes of Jewish Law, is the fact that all the land in that particular state belongs to the Sovereign Authority and even land owned ostensibly by private individuals is held at the pleasure of that Authority.[57]

One point, rarely mentioned because it is so obvious, is that the Law of the State is only recognized in connection with commercial and financial matters, and it can in no way interfere with Jewish ritual or religious observances.[58] In fact, some scholars limit the application of this rule only to real estate,[59] but others hold, "We conduct ourselves according to the rules of the State, for all rules of the State in monetary matters are valid for us."[60]

Who is considered a King or a Sovereign Authority?

> These rules [the rights of the King] relate only to the King whose coinage is accepted in those lands, for the residents of those lands have agreed and accepted him and conduct themselves on the understanding that he is their Sovereign and they are his subjects. But if he is a ruler whose coinage is not accepted, he is [in law] as a bandit, an outlaw, and he and his men are like groups of armed robbers, and the rules they enact are not law.[61]

The principle that the Law of the State is the operative law only applies to those rules which the State mandates. Thus, if the State legislates that ownership of real estate can only be transferred by means of physical transfer of the title deeds, that becomes the only method for the Jewish Community as well. However, if the State, while recommending this method of transfer, also allows another method (for example, if it recognizes that ownership passes with the

---

[57] *Rosh, Nedarim* 3:11.

[58] *Tashbatz, Responsa* 1:158.

[59] V. *Beit Yosef, Tur, Choshen Mishpat* 369, ad fin.

[60] *Yad, Zechiyah Umattanah.* 1:15.

[61] *Yad, Gezelah* 5:18.

handing over of the purchase price), the Jewish Community may complete transactions by the alternative method. Should the circumstances be such that a litigant would win his case under a non-obligatory State Law but would lose it under Jewish Law, he is not allowed to take it before the secular courts; since the civil law is not obligatory, the transaction is not covered by the principle of *dina demalchuta*.[62]

Which prevails when State Law does not actually coincide with the Law of the Torah? An example of this type of problem is dealt with by Shmuel.[63] In his time, Jews did not complete the purchases of real estate among themselves merely by paying the money; the deal was actually completed when the documents of title were passed to the purchaser. This differed from the non-Jewish world, in which it was sufficient for the purchaser to hand the vendor the purchase consideration in order for the deal to be completed. What happens if a Jew buys land from a non-Jew? The non-Jew gives up his ownership as soon as he receives the money; the Jew does not consider himself the owner until he receives the documents. Shmuel rules that if a second Jew were to intervene and take possession of this land, however reprehensible his action may be, he is entitled to keep the land since, as far as Jewish Law is concerned, it is ownerless, although according to State Law it already belongs to the purchaser, as he has handed over the money.

A problem could face a Jew in the event of the government altering the currency of the land. For example, one Jew owes another a certain sum of old currency and as a result of the change must pay the same sum in the new currency, which in real terms may have more value. Is this considered usury? After all, in real terms the lender has received back

---

[62] *Bava Batra* 54b, Rashbam, s.v. *"amar;" Nimukei Yosef,* p. 58; *Shitah Mekubetzet, Bava Batra* 55a in the name of R. Yonah.

[63] *Bava Batra* 54b.

more than he loaned. Remah rules "and if the King decrees that all who have to repay debts repay in the new coinage, we must follow the decree of the King, for the Law of the State is the Law and there is no prohibition of usury nor of stealing [although the lender may be making a profit].[64]

What would be the Law if a man betrothed a woman with an article belonging to him under Jewish Law, but not under the Law of the State in which he lives. Conversely under the Law of the State, the article is his absolutely, whereas Jewish Law does not recognize his ownership, is the woman betrothed according to the Torah or not?[65]

In these previous circumstances, while there may be different conclusions, dependent upon which system of law is followed, there is, in fact, no direct conflict between them. The Torah never insists on what constitutes the completion of a transaction,[66] or what is the definition of money, or when ownership actually passes; if the State is prepared to lay down those definitions, it may well be that the Torah recognizes them because of the rules of *dina demalchuta dina*. Where, however, there is a conflict and the Law of the State contradicts that of the Torah, it is quite obvious that for the Jew, the Torah must prevail. Thus, even if the State accepts the testimony of women, minors or relatives, that testimony must remain invalid in Jewish Law.[67]

Cases of inheritance are often good examples of where problems arise as a result of conflicting laws. For example, under Jewish Law, a daughter does not inherit from her

---

[64] *Yoreh De'ah* 165:1, but v. *Shach*, ad loc., who casts doubt on this ruling.

[65] This problem can arise under a legal system which never gives a thief a good title to a stolen object (v. supra p. 77). V. *Beit Shmuel, Even Ha'ezer* 28:3; *Avnei Miluim*, ad loc., s.v. *"od katav habeit Shmuel"*; cf. *Chatam Sofer, Responsa, Yoreh De'ah* 314; *Binyan Tzion Responsa*, 2:15.

[66] *Sha'arei Yosher* 3:3.

[67] *Shach, Choshen Mishpat* 73:39.

father if she has a brother or brothers,[68] but a father can, if he wishes, take advantage of the Rabbinical innovation that the wishes of a dying man are to be honored, and leave all or part of his estate to a daughter.[69] What happens if, instead of expressing his wishes in the form of a donation mortis causa acceptable under Jewish law, he executes a will valid under the law of the land in which the property concerned is situated? This will may in fact be worded in the form of a "bequest" that is effective only after death. Although this is the standard form in many countries, it is not acceptable in Jewish Law, which holds that with death a person loses all his rights in property and is therefore in no position to arrange any disposal to be effective after death.[70] Does the fact that this document is valid under the Law of the State give it validity in Jewish Law because of the principle that "the Law of the State is Law"?[71]

What would the Law be if one Jew rented a residential dwelling to another for a period of three years, at the expiry of which, the tenant then invoked a Rent Control Act, giving him security of tenure? The original agreement is valid under Jewish Law, but is overruled by a State Law; which prevails?[72]

---

[68] A daughter is entitled to be maintained out of her late father's estate and to receive one tenth as a dowry, an entitlement which holds good against her brothers.

[69] V. supra p. 68.

[70] *Bava Batra* 152a, ruling of Shmuel; v. *Rashbam*, ad loc., s.v. *"lo"*; v. *Choshen Mishpat* 258:1.

[71] V. Rabbi H. B. Padwa (of London), *Cheshev Ha'efod* II, 106 & 107; v. Rabbi E. Schlessinger (also of London), *Notes on the Subject of Wills*; v. *Remah, Choshen Mishpat* 369:11 ad fin. that the Rabbinic legislation that a widower inherits from his wife prevails over State Law or custom; v. R. Shlomo (Hyman of New York), *Novellae*, part II, letter 8, on the subject of a wife inheriting from her husband under local law.

[72] V. Rav Moshe Feinstein, *Iggerot Moshe, Choshen Mishpat* 72, who rules that as the Rent Control Act was in existence when the tenancy was negotiated, the tenant may take advantage of it, as both parties were aware of it and the landlord knew it could be used against

A problem arose in the Middle Ages when a community which lived within the walls of a ghetto wished to build gates to close it off. Several Jewish families who lived outside the ghetto, but who used its religious facilities, protested. Under Jewish Law, these latter had the right of ready access and therefore a power of veto over the proposed new gates. According to Rashba,[73] however, this power was lost because the State had granted authority to build the walls, and it is this authority which is paramount.[74]

---

him. Unfortunately, he does not address himself to the academically more interesting problem: what is the law if a Rent Control Act is newly enacted after the lease had already been negotiated?

[73] *Responsa* 2:134.

[74] The Sassover Rebbe (Rabbi Simcha Rubin), of London, told of an incident in prewar Hungary: A Jewish liquor merchant sold his stock of *chametz* to a non-Jew over the Pesach Festival (for more on this particular subject v. Rabbi S. J. Zevin, *Hamo'adim B'Halachah*, *Pesach* 4, who devotes an entire chapter to it). Unfortunately, the schedule of goods attached to the Bill of Sale grossly undervalued the goods. This became known to the merchant's competitors, who endeavored to put him out of business by persuading the non-Jew to take possession of the goods after Pesach, paying for them with money that they would provide. The non-Jew brought a civil action in the Hungarian courts demanding delivery, to which the Jewish merchant replied with the claim that the sale was not a valid one—it was merely a religious ritual and the purchaser was, in equity, obliged to drop his claim to the goods. He was successful in his defense and the Court ordered the goods to be left with him. This immediately created a problem under Jewish Law: If the sale was not a real one, the goods were *chametz* which had been in the ownership and possession of a Jew over Pesach, and therefore to derive any benefit from them was prohibited. The Halachic Authorities to whom the question was put ruled that in Jewish Law the sale was valid—indeed, had the merchant been sued in the Beit Din, he would have been unsuccessful; the sale was sufficiently valid to take the *chametz* out of his ownership over Pesach and therefore it was consequently not prohibited, notwithstanding the Civil Court's ruling. The detailed responsa, which are unfortunately not available, would be of great interest, and would help define the relation-

Thus far, reference to State, King and Government have been to non-Jewish states, Kings and Governments; what of a Jewish State in the Land of Israel or a Jewish ruler with autonomy in a land of exile?

Some Authorities are of the view that a Jewish King in the Land of Israel has no special rights whatsoever. He is bound by the Torah as is any other Jew, for "Israel is our heritage from our forefathers and it belongs equally to the King and to the subjects"[75]—the Land of Israel does not belong exclusively to the King. Others dispute this; they hold that as the purpose of giving the King or Sovereign Authority extra-legal powers is to protect the state, its citizens and its institutions, Jewish Kings in Israel have the same authority as non-Jewish Kings in their own lands.[76] This reasoning could also apply to non-Jewish Kings or governments who temporarily happen to rule in the Land of Israel.

Normally, a Jewish ruler in a land of exile had his rights and powers conferred upon him by the government of that land; this made him part of that government, and therefore the principle of *dina demalchuta* applied to him without reservation.[77]

With the advent of the State of Israel and its continual expansion through Jewish immigration from all corners of the Diaspora, the problems of legal dualism have increased in number and scope and have expanded to include within their boundaries the Civil Law of the State of Israel, as in many aspects, particularly of personal law concerning marriage and divorce, it is based on the rules of the Torah. How then

---

ship between Jewish and State Law. (Cf. similar problems quoted by R. Zevin, ibid.)

[75] *Rashba,* loc. cit., quoting Rabbis of France; v. *Tosafot, Sanhedrin* 20b, s.v. *"melech."*

[76] Ibid. V. *Chatam Sofer, Responsa, Choshen Mishpat* 44.

[77] *Rashba, Responsa* 1:637. For further reading on the subject of the "Jewish King", v. Rav Zvi Hirsch Chajes, *Torat Nevi'im,* chap. 6, *Hora'at Sha'ah* and chap. 7, *Din Melech.*

shall the State look at a marriage between two Jews, valid in accordance with Jewish Law[78] but not according to the law of the land in which the ceremony was performed? The Supreme Court of Israel held

> for the limited purpose of giving validity to such a marriage, it is proper to prefer to the Foreign National Law (Lex Patriae) of the parties at the time of their marriage—which only recognizes marriages celebrated in a special form— the other National Law which the parties then had, which has continued to be their Law up to the present, that is, Jewish Law.

In explaining why Jewish Law must be so regarded as the National Law of the Jews, the judge[79] went on to say:

> The very moment that we admit—as we are obliged to admit—the continued existence of the Jews in all generations and in all lands of their dispersion as a separate people, we must test the nature of Jewish Law by the historic relationship of the Jewish people to this Law. We shall then conclude that the Jewish people indeed treated Jewish Law throughout their existence and their dispersion as their special property, as part of the treasure of their culture. It follows that this Law served in the past as the National Law of the Jews and even today possesses this national character in respect of Jews wherever they may be.

Thus, the judge ruled that the marriage was valid, for the parties thereto were not bound merely by the laws of the land in which they lived, but also by the laws of the Torah which the Jewish people maintain and under those laws the marriage had been validly performed.

At this stage, no problems arise, for there is no direct conflict between the two Laws. The Israeli Court was not

---

[78] Proper *chuppah* and *kiddushin* before competent witnesses, but not registered with the Civil Authorities.

[79] Mr. Justice Agranat in Skornick vs. Skornick (1954) 8 P.D. 141.

faced with any contradiction; it was not bound by the civil laws of the country of origin of the couple concerned.

But what if there is a conflict? If, for example, a ceremony valid in the country of origin but invalid under the laws of the Torah is performed? This has happened in cases where Jews have married non-Jewesses and vice versa. Notwithstanding political, moral and humane considerations, the answer is—indeed must be—that for the Jew wherever he is, Jewish Law is the dominant factor and no Jewish Court, whether religious or secular, can bear to recognize such a marriage.[80]

---

[80] V. the Judgment of Mr. Justice Silberg; Miriam Streit vs. Chief Rabbinate of Israel, P.D. 18, p. 598-627, analyzed by Mr. Justice Elon, *Chakikah Datit*, p. 105 et seq.

NINE
Prohibited Transactions

PART FROM THE GENERAL laws which demand honest and upright conduct, the Torah lays down two prohibitions specifically related to monetary transactions: the prohibitions of usury and of extortion—and it is that of usury which is by far the more severe.

In current usage, the word "usury" denotes "the practice of lending money at exorbitant interest, especially at higher interest than is allowed by law."[1] Jewish Law, under the rule of the Torah, bans the charging and paying of *any* amount of interest between two Jews, however reasonable or normal the rate charged would be considered in the commercial world. There are five prohibitions specifically dealing with interest,[2] and two different terms are used. "You shall not give him [your fellow Jew] your money upon interest, nor

---

[1] *Concise Oxford Dictionary.*

[2] *Yad, Malveh V'loveh* 4:2. These are to be found in: *Shemot* 22:24; *Vayikra* 25:37 (twice mentioned in the same verse) *Devarim* 23:20 & 21. To these must be added the general prohibition of "put not a stumbling block before the blind" (*Vayikra* 19:14), for the parties involved are helping one another to transgress the Biblical Command.

lend him your victuals for augmentation."[3] The word used to denote interest is *Neshech*, which comes from the Hebrew root meaning "to bite," while the word to denote augmentation is *Ribit*, "interest," and is derived from the root meaning "to increase." There is in fact no legal difference between these two terms, for as Rava says, "You will not find *Neshech* without *Ribit* and not *Ribit* without *Neshech*."[4]

The different names given to interest denote its dual effect. *Neshech* emphasizes the damage done to the borrower: like the bite of a poisonous snake, which initially feels like no more than a minor sting but remorselessly leads the victim to his destruction, so interest, which seems at the time unimportant, inflates the loan and increases the debt until the borrower is overwhelmed.[5] In fact, in one of its exhortations the Torah instructs, "Do not take from him interest or augmentation; but fear your God, that your brother *may live with you*."[6]

This verse also explains why the second effect denoted by the word *Ribit*—that of the lender's enrichment—is undesirable: Does a God-fearing man have so little faith that he cannot accommodate a friend in a time of need[7] without thinking of his own profit? Does he feel that he must go to extremes to provide for his future? Has he no trust in Divine Providence? Such conduct is a denial of the Lord God of Israel.[8]

In one of its five warnings, the Torah uses the plural

---

[3] *Vayikra* 25:37.

[4] *Bava Metzia* 60b.

[5] *Kli Yakar, Vayikra* 25:37; *Midrash Rabbah, Shemot* 31:6; *Sefer Hachinnuch*, mitzvah 343.

[6] *Vayikra* 25:36.

[7] Originally, loans were made as a favor, to assist a person in need, as money itself was not a commodity dealt in, but merely a means of acquiring the necessities of life. V. infra the changes in approach as money itself became a commodity dealt in by "financiers."

[8] *Kli Yakar*, loc. cit.; *Malbim, Vayikra* 25:24.

form,[9] and from this our Rabbis deduce that all involved in an interest-bearing transaction transgress—the lender, the borrower, the witnesses and even the scribe who writes the document; although the lender is the most culpable, all are guilty.[10] That being so, usury differs from all other civil wrong-doings in that it is not open to the victim—the borrower—to consent to suffer the loss of money represented by the interest, and while deprivation by consent is neither theft nor tort, interest by consent remains prohibited.[11] Again, unlike ordinary theft, in which, in the first instance, the article or money stolen does not become the property of the thief, interest paid does become the property of the usurer as soon as he receives it. He owns it absolutely, subject to the religious injunction, "and your brother shall live with you,"[12] from which the Talmud derives the rule that primary interest is returnable and the courts must exact it.[13] A practical difference is that should a thief die with stolen property in his possession, his heirs must return it,[14] while if a usurer dies with unreturned interest in his possession, his heirs are under no such obligation,[15] other than possibly to restore honor to their father's memory.

Rambam himself, the first comprehensive codifier of

---

9 *Shemot* 22:24.

10 *Yad*, loc. cit., based on *Bava Metzia* 75b.

11 V. *Ramban, Devarim* 23:20. There are differences of opinion as to whether, after the Court has ruled that interest paid must be returned, the borrower can then forgive; Rambam holds that after the Court has ruled, the returnable money becomes an ordinary civil, and therefore forgivable, debt. V. *Yad*, op. cit., 13.

12 *Vayikra* 25:36.

13 *Bava Metzia* 71b.

14 *Yad, Gezelah V'avedah* 2:1.

15 *Yad, Malveh V'loveh* 4:3. Because the interest illegally taken becomes the absolute property of the lender, he is able to use it to betroth a wife. *Ritva, Novellae, Kiddushin* 6b; v. *Avnei Miluim* 28:22.(V. supra p. 76).

Jewish Law, included the Laws of Usury in the section of his *Yad Hachazakah* dealing with Civil Jurisprudence. However, two of his distinguished successors, R. Yaakov b. Asher, in his *Tur* and R. Yosef Karo in his *Codes*, chose to include them in the section of their works—which they called *Yoreh De'ah*[16]— dealing with religious and ritualistic precepts, laws of what is permitted and what is prohibited, and not in the section dealing with Civil Law, *Choshen Mishpat*.[17]

Usury is defined by R. Nachman:

> The general principle of usury is: all payment for waiting for one's money is forbidden.[18]

For legal purposes, usury is divided into two categories: prearranged and agreed interest, which is prohibited by the Torah; and secondary interest,[19] prohibited by the Rabbis. Because of the dual description—"interest" and "augmentation"—in order to be classed as primary interest prohibited by the Torah, the payment or benefit must be one which enriches the recipient and deprives the giver.

Although interest is only considered to be primary if it is paid by the borrower, after the loan has been granted,[20] to or on behalf of the lender and not to any procuring agent,[21] it does not necessarily have to be in the form of money.

> Similarly, someone who loans to his fellow on the condition that he [the lender] may live on the borrower's property free of rent until the loan is repaid, or that he have the property for less than the market value...or that he take a pledge and use its produce free of charge while the loan is

---

[16] Lit., "Teach Knowledge" (*Yeshayahu* 28:9).
[17] V. opening few words of *Tur, Yoreh De'ah* 160, and comment by *Bach*.
[18] *Bava Metzia* 63b.
[19] Known as *Avak Ribit*; lit., the "dust" of *Ribit*. (V. infra p. 211.)
[20] *Remah*, Yoreh De'ah 161:1, and *Tur*, ad loc.
[21] *Remah*, Yoreh De'ah 160:16.

extant—this is primary interest forbidden by the Torah for which the Court will exact restitution.[22]

Because of the severity of the Torah prohibition against usury, the Rabbis took it upon themselves, as a precaution, to ban any payment or transaction which contains either a hint of interest or unearned profit—defining such interest as *Avak Ribit*.[23] Thus, where, for example, the Torah banned only interest on loans, the Rabbis extended the ban to interest on delayed or early payment of purchase money.[24]

Similarly, the Rabbis prohibited the loan of goods by weight, the fear being that, at the time of repayment the value of the goods would have increased and, in monetary terms, the lender would be making a profit.[25]

As Biblical usury must be of a kind which shows a profit to the recipient and a loss to the payer, it follows that if the borrower has an empty building which he does not let, it would not be primary usury for him to allow his creditor to use it free of charge during the incidence of the loan, for while the lender is indeed receiving a profit, it is costing the borrower nothing. However, the Rabbis also forbade this type of arrangement.[26]

It is also forbidden to give interest in advance. For example, intent on borrowing money from a certain person, the hopeful borrower must not send his potential benefactor gifts in order to induce him to make the loan. Similarly, even

---

[22] *Yad*, op. cit., 6:1. Based on *Mishnah* 64b. There is much discussion on the various types of pledges. V. *Mishnah, Bava Metzia* 65b et seq., *Yad*, op. cit., 6:7-8 and *Ravad, Yoreh De'ah* 172:1-6.

[23] V. supra, note 19.

[24] *Tur*, ibid.; *Yoreh De'ah* 161:1; *Yad*, op. cit. 8:1. V. *Rashi, Temurah* 6b, s.v. "*avak*."

[25] *Mishnah Bava Metzia* 74b. This law, colloquially known as that of "*Se'ah* [a measurement] for a *Se'ah*," has a number of important exceptions—circumstances in which the Rabbis did not legislate. For a detailed exposition v. *Rosh, Responsa*, 108:15.

[26] *Bava Metzia* 64b.

after a loan has been satisfied, it is prohibited by the Rabbis for the borrower to send any token of appreciation, however spontaneous.[27] So concerned were the Rabbis to distance their people from any hint of usury, that they even forbade a borrower to go out of his way to greet his creditor more effusively than was his normal practice.[28]

The Rabbis did not confine their legislation to money owing as a result of loans; they also forbade any demands for excess payment arising out of sale or purchase. It is forbidden, for example, to stipulate to the buyer, "For immediate payment you can have the goods for a hundred shekel, whereas if you delay payment until the end of the season, I shall require one hundred and twenty shekel."[29] If, however, the same transaction is expressed differently, in the form of a discount—"The price with payment due at the end of the season is one hundred and twenty shekel, but I offer twenty shekel as a cash discount for immediate payment"—it is indeed within the law.[30]

A problem arose in connection with a penalty for late payment. A loaned B money for a certain period, the loan being evidenced by a document. In order to make sure that B repaid on time, the document stipulated that for late payment there would be a fixed penalty payable to a nominee of the lender.

Rashba[31] considered this to be secondary interest, but Ritva strongly disagreed:[32]

> I am very surprised by [Rashba's] responsum, as, several years ago, I noted that he expressed the opposite view. Nevertheless, whichever way he ruled, my view is that there is no question of interest in this case, as there is no

27 *Yoreh De'ah* 160:6.
28 *Yad,* op. cit., 5:12.
29 *Mishnah, Bava Metzia* 65a.
30 *Yad,* op. cit., 8:1.
31 *Responsa* 1:651.
32 *Responsa* 35; v. *Bava Metzia* 66a & infra p. 243 et seq. on the matter of penalties in Jewish Law.

payment [to the lender] for *waiting for his money*. On the contrary, had the debtor paid on time, there would have been no additional payment. He was obliged to pay the penalty only because he did not pay on the due date, at which time he would have paid only the initial amount of the loan.

A further notable Rabbinic extension of the prohibition of taking interest relates to contracts of partnership. Any arrangement by which one partner finances a business and the other manages it, with losses to be borne by the managing partner only, while the profits are shared between them, is illegal. Even an agreement whereby both parties share losses is prohibited, unless the managing partner is remunerated for his efforts over and above his share of the profits.[33]

Summed up briefly, the Rabbis prohibited any transaction in which the lender is "close to a profit and far from a loss."[34]

The difference in law between primary and secondary interest is that primary interest, once paid, can be reclaimed through the courts, whereas secondary interest, once paid, remains the property of the recipient.[35]

As the Torah specifically prohibits interest from "your brother,"[36] the question arises, can a charitable institution receive interest from, or pay interest to, a Jewish borrower or lender; is such an institution within the definition of "your brother"? Both Rosh[37] and Ritva[38] distinguish between *Hekdesh*—charity endowed for the use and maintenance of the Temple—and charitable institutions such as burial societies,

---

[33] *Yad*, op. cit., 5:9.

[34] *Mishnah, Bava Metzia* 68a & 70b; *Yad*, op. cit., 5:9 and 8:12; *Yoreh De'ah* 177:1.

[35] Ruling of R. Eliezer, *Bava Metzia* 61b, which has become the Halachah.

[36] *Devarim* 23:20.

[37] *Responsa* 13:8, 13:10 & 13:17.

[38] *Responsa* 118.

Jewish schools, and benevolent funds. The Temple and its funds are not within the definition of "your brother," and therefore the Treasurers may, in the first instance, arrange to earn (or pay) primary interest, whereas charitable institutions which are for the benefit of Jewish people are considered within that definition. However, as we find that the Talmud permits the guardian of minor orphans to invest their money to earn secondary interest,[39] so charitable institutions are permitted to loan their money in order to earn secondary interest, normally prohibited to individuals.

This leads on to a contemporary problem: What is the legal status, in Jewish Law, of a Limited Liability Company? Is it identified with its shareholders and treated merely as a group of people using a common name—in which case it would be forbidden to take interest—or is it treated as a separate entity, a creation, albeit artificial, in its own right, obviously not subject to the laws of the Torah?[40]

Even under British Law, which pioneered the creation of "Chartered Companies" in the seventeenth century and which has been periodically updated by detailed Companies' Acts, the matter remained in some doubt until 1897, at which time Salomon vs. Salomon & Co., Limited, was heard in the House of Lords.[41]

Salomon formed the company for the purpose of continuing his boot business, which he sold to the company. Part of the consideration for the business remained unpaid, and for this Salomon accepted a debenture on the company which gave him a charge over its assets. Subsequently, the company wound up, and there were insufficient assets to pay Salomon and all the other creditors. The creditors claimed that Salomon and the company were one and the same; therefore the company could

---

[39] *Bava Metzia* 70a.

[40] The same problem arises with regard to *chametz* on Pesach. A Jew may not keep any; may a limited company with Jewish shareholders?

[41] *Appeal Court* (Law Reports) 22.

not owe him the money secured by the debenture and, that being so, the assets should be applied towards paying them—the other creditors. The lower courts accepted this plea, but on appeal their decision was reversed by the House of Lords, which held that as soon as the company was incorporated, it became, in the eyes of the law, a separate and independent entity from Salomon, and was in no way his agent. "The company is at Law a different person altogether from the subscribers to the Memorandum; and although it may be that after incorporation the business is precisely the same as it was before, and the same persons are managers and the same hands receive the profits, the company is not in Law the agent of the subscribers or trustee for them."[42]

Does Jewish Law accept this? Many are the eminent scholars who have expressed opinions, some negative, some positive, all citing earlier Authorities and claiming support for their views from earlier rulings. Currently the debate continues.[43]

---

[42] Per Lord McNaghten.

[43] V. *Noam*, which was a regularly published forum for the clarification of Halachic problems, where this problem is dealt with in vol. 2, pp. 31-37; vol. 3, pp. 195-203 (a responsum from Rabbi I. Wasserman); vol. 4, pp. 251-57 and on p. 14 of the appendix. The majority of the contributors support the view expressed by Lord McNaghten. On the subject of whether there is a legal distinction between communally owned property (and company property would be considered communal property) and partnership property (which belongs to the partners personally), v. Dr. Yedidya Cohen, "The Kibbutz as a Legal Entity," in *Jewish Law and Current Legal Problems* (Library of Jewish Law, August 1983); Dayan Dr. M. S. Lew, *The Humanity of Jewish Law*, p. 125.

R. Elchonon Wasserman (not to be confused with the author of the responsum in *Noam*) reads into a commentary of Rashbam (*Bava Batra* 126b, ad init., s.v. *"lo asa"*) that Rashbam holds that the undivided estate of a deceased is not partnership property, but a separate estate or entity of its own (in which case presumably the managers may use its funds to earn interest, and on Pesach do not have to dispose of *Chametz* left by the deceased) (*Kovetz Shiurim, Bava Batra* 404). V. Rabbi H. B. Padwa, *Cheshev Ha'efod*, I:53, on the question of bank interest.

Today the problem is largely overcome by adopting the accepted stratagem of the *Heter Iska*.[44]

It is well known that in recent generations people have devised a permissible method of taking interest by using the *Heter Iska*, as will be explained. At first glance this is surprising, for we find not the slightest hint in the Torah allowing us to circumvent the prohibition of interest, nor has the foundation and legal basis of this circumvention been explained to us by our Sages.

The answer to this is that our wise men found the basis of this circumvention by considering the reasons for the prohibition in the first place, and decided that the foundation for the prohibition is the precept "and your brother shall live with you."[45] At the time when the Torah was given, the basis of the Jews' life and commerce was agrarian; agriculture was the source and support of their wealth, for he who had large crops was considered a rich man. Money itself was not the basis of their activities, and when money was loaned it was not for the purposes of business and commerce, but for the purposes of personal expenditure—for the poor man to buy bread and clothes which he could not afford from the yield of his land and his work. Therefore it is obvious that the poor man could not afford to pay interest, while the wealthy lender would not feel the loss if he did lend money without interest: as he did not use his money for business, he would suffer no deprivation. However, in the Middle Ages, by which time Israel had lost its share in the land and could keep itself alive only by commerce, the prohibition became onerous, for by then money had become the Jews' basis of business; it became a business commodity both to the lender and to the borrower which they both needed in order "to live." Therefore, our wise men believed, in these circumstances the Torah would not dogmatically forbid interest, and so they advised as to how the prohibition could be circumvented.[46]

---

[44] Lit., permission (to take interest) through a business transaction.
[45] *Vayikra* 25:36.
[46] R. Baruch Halevi Epstein; *Torah Temimah*, ad loc., note 192.

The legal basis of the circumvention is set out in the *Terumat Hadeshen.*[47] The author prefaces his ruling by expressing the fear that this circumvention may cause the words of the Torah to seem "like a jest and be treated with derision," but that nevertheless "the just will walk in them."[48]

Under the *Heter Iska*, the loan document is drawn up in the form of a partnership agreement. To avoid the trap of interest, the lender must share in the risk, and for taking the risk, his share of the partnership profit shall be no less than the stated percentage on the money advanced. At this stage, of course, the lender is indeed at risk, and therefore a clause is inserted to the effect that his risk is limited only to theft or accident, whereas if the borrower is negligent, then he, the borrower, must alone bear the loss. The onus of disproving negligence is laid, by agreement, on the borrower, who must produce witnesses to satisfy the lender that he has in fact not been negligent, and the agreement stipulates the caliber of the required witnesses—for example, two senior Rabbis of the town. Obviously, it is impossible for the borrower to obtain this testimony, and therefore, in practice, he will have to bear the total loss and the lender is thus protected. The deed, which also contains provision for the borrower to receive a nominal sum as remuneration for his efforts, is attested by two ordinary witnesses, in the normal way.[49]

A document, not a *Heter Iska*, which blatantly contains an

---

[47] Responsum 302.

[48] *Hosea* 14:10. The whole verse reads, "Whoever is wise, let him understand these things: whoever is prudent, let him know them; for the ways of the Lord are right and the just shall walk in them; the transgressors shall fall therein." *Terumat Hadeshen*'s comments are relevant, not merely to this particular innovation, but to any legal device designed to avoid what is considered to be too onerous for the general public. It is important to comprehend that these devices are within the Law; they make use of the rules of the Torah itself in order to arrive at an acceptable solution. In no way do they attempt to alter or "reform" (Heaven forbid) the Torah.

[49] V. *Yoreh De'ah* 167:1 and 177:2.

interest clause, is of course illegal; nevertheless, while it cannot be used to claim the interest, it can be used to claim the principal.[50] After all, the borrower was also a party to the sin; why should he profit from his wrongdoing?

While it is the duty of an errant lender to return any interest he may have received, the borrower is advised not to accept it. Our Rabbis wished to encourage sinners to repent, and understood that it would be virtually impossible for a man practiced in usury to give up profits he has made over the years, and so they rule:

> If, as the result of repentance, [the lender] voluntarily returns the interest, if it is one fixed amount, it is accepted, but if not, and most of his business and income was from interest, [returned interest] is not accepted from him, in order to ease the way of repentance for him; any borrower who does accept it from him displeases the Sages of Israel.[51]

The second piece of *d'Oraita* legislation framed specifically for monetary transactions is that which prohibits "extortion": "And if you sell ought or buy ought from his hand, you shall not be extortionate to one another."[52]

In fact, extortion by means of knowingly overcharging (in the case of selling to an innocent buyer) or knowingly underpaying (in the case of buying from an innocent seller) is included in the general prohibition of stealing, for it is taking money or making a profit to which one is not entitled.[53]

---

[50] *Bava Metzia* 72a, a point of dispute between R. Meir and his colleagues. There are differences of opinion on what R. Meir's ruling actually is. V. *Tosafot*, loc. cit. Although the witnesses have also sinned, their testimony is not void: They are not themselves considered "dishonest," as they have not attempted personal gain (v. supra p. 101).

[51] *Yoreh De'ah* 161:7 (v. supra p. 70).

[52] *Vayikra* 25:14. The Hebrew word for extortion is *Ona'ah*.

[53] *Bava Metzia* 61a: The Talmud explains why the Torah makes specific mention of extortion.

The basis of this Commandment is obvious. It is not right that people should profit through lying and cheating; each man should profit through his genuine and honest efforts and gain that with which the Lord has graced him. This rule is of benefit to everyone, for as he must not cheat others, so others may not cheat him; even if he feels he would gain the advantage, being cleverer than is adversary, nevertheless, who knows whether his children would be as successful—they in turn may be victims. Therefore, this is of great benefit to society, and God created the earth for men to dwell in society.[54]

While it is forbidden to both the buyer and the seller to cheat one another, overcharging is not in itself forbidden, as is usury. If the victim is aware of the advantage being taken of him, yet nevertheless consents, the transaction becomes perfectly legal and valid.[55]

There is a general overriding rule that in monetary matters other than usury, the parties may enter by consent into a transaction which the Torah in the first instance forbids. For example, when a man marries he undertakes three basic obligations towards his wife: to feed her, to clothe her, and to honor her conjugal rights. These three obligations are laid upon every husband by the Torah and are inherent in every Jewish marriage. What would the Law be if the husband stipulates with his future wife that she marry him on condition that he be absolved from these three obligations? R. Meir holds that as the act of betrothal was a valid one and the stipulations were against the Torah, they fail. R. Yehudah, while agreeing with the basic proposition that any stipulation which is against the command of the Torah must fail, does add the words, "in respect of monetary matters, the stipulation is valid."[56] This is taken to mean that according to R. Yehudah (and that is the Halachah), the new husband has

---

[54] Sefer Hachinnuch, mitzvah 337.
[55] Choshen Mishpat 227:21.
[56] Ketubot 56a.

freed himself of the obligation to feed and clothe his wife as she has consented to those stipulations, but he remains obliged to honor her conjugal rights, as these are not "monetary matters."[57]

It may well be that the validity of this type of stipulation depends on its wording. The *Shemittah* year brings with its close a release of debts; in normal circumstances creditors may not pursue debtors for outstanding loans.[58] What if, at the time the loan is granted, the parties stipulate that there will be no release in the coming *Shemittah* year? The Talmud distinguishes: If the condition is that "the Sabbatical year *does not* cancel the debt," then the Sabbatical year *does* cancel it, as this stipulation conflicts with a law prescribed by the Torah. If, however, the condition is "that *you do not* cancel the debt due to me in the Sabbatical year"—meaning, that you do not take advantage of the release of *Shemittah*—it becomes a condition between the parties in connection with a monetary matter, and is valid.[59]

Shmuel, in the Talmud,[60] makes the same distinction in connection with a stipulation regarding extortion: "If the stipulation is that there *be* no complaint of an unfair deal in this transaction," it must fail if the price is unfair, whereas "a condition that *you* will not make a complaint against me of an unfair deal in this transaction," will stand. However, in the event, this is not the final ruling; it is possible that the victim does not know exactly what is involved, and therefore, his agreement to the stipulation is not a valid self-imposed obligation. However, if amounts are mentioned, the condition will stand.[61]

---

[57] *Yad, Ishut* 6:10; *Even Ha'ezer* 69:6.

[58] V. supra p. 72.

[59] *Makkot* 3b. V. *Choshen Mishpat* 67:9: "The condition is valid, for all it means is that the borrower obligates himself to pay money in circumstances in which the Torah has released him from doing so."

[60] *Makkot* 3b.

[61] *Choshen Mishpat*, 67:21; v. *S'ma*, ad loc.; *Aruch Hashulchan, Choshen Mishpat* 227:22.

In a straight case of sale there are three levels of pro-hibited profit: less than one-sixth discrepancy between the asking price and the market price; exactly one-sixth discre-pancy; more than one-sixth discrepancy.[62]

After a Talmudic discussion as to how the one-sixth is calculated, the ruling is that there are two relevant calcula-tions: firstly, on the simple value of the object, and secondly, on the value of the money passing. Each calculation is equally valid in determining the legal consequences.

A simple example of the first calculation would be in the event of the article's having a market value of six coins. A sale price of seven coins would be unfair on the buyer, while that of five coins would be unfair on the vendor; in each case the discrepancy is just one-sixth.

An example of the second calculation would be, where the article is only worth five coins but the agreed sale price is six coins. In terms of the value of the article, the discrepancy is one-fifth; in terms of the money passing, the discre-pancy is only one-sixth. Conversely, if the vendor is duped and is offered six coins for a seven-coin article, he has suffered a loss of one coin in seven, which is less than the prescribed one-sixth, but he has suffered a loss of one-sixth based on the agreed price.[63] If the discrepancy is less than one-sixth, the sale is a valid one and no restitution is required; it is considered that the victim will forego his legal rights for so small an amount.

Interestingly, although generally a minor has no legal capacity and therefore cannot forgive a debt,[64] nevertheless, if he is old enough to enter into commercial transactions, he would be treated as having foregone his claim if the amount involved is less than the one-sixth, the reason being that if this were not so, it would be impossible to do business with him.[65]

---

[62] *Bava Metzia* 50b.
[63] *Choshen Mishpat* 227:2.
[64] V. infra p. 229.
[65] *Choshen Mishpat* 235:3 and *S'ma*, ad loc.

If the discrepancy is exactly one-sixth, the transaction stands and cannot be voided, but the excess profit must be restored to the victim.[66]

If the difference exceeds one-sixth, the victim may void the transaction, but not the perpetrator, should the victim wish to continue with it.[67]

This last ruling is not strictly a "legal" one, for if the transaction is void, it should be open to both parties to cancel it—not merely to the victim. It is, in fact, only on moral or ethical grounds that the right of avoidance has been taken away from the perpetrator "in order that the sinner should not gain,"[68] for presumably he would only want to withdraw if the price changed, now enabling him to make a higher legal profit than his original illegal one.

If the buyer is the aggrieved party—that is, he feels he has been overcharged—there is a time limit within which he must register his protest in order to void the transaction; this is normally just long enough to give him time to show the article he has bought to an expert, in order to ascertain whether or not he paid a fair price. As the vendor does not have the article in his possession, no time limit is placed on his right of protest; any time he realizes that he has undercharged, he may demand that the transaction be revoked.[69]

Not only do the Laws of *Ona'ah* apply to direct buying and selling, but also to cases of renting. "Rent is nothing more than a sale for a period"; the only difference is that there is no time limit to refute a transaction.[70]

Among transactions which are exempted, at least from the consequence of the laws of *Ona'ah*, are transactions involving land or documents. Because the Torah, in describing

---

[66] *Choshen Mishpat* 227:2 & 3.
[67] Ibid., 4.
[68] *S'ma*, ad loc.
[69] *Choshen Mishpat* 227:7 & 8.
[70] Ibid., 35. V. *Terumat Hadeshen* 318 for a fuller discussion.

a purchase, uses the words, "Or buy ought from his hand,"[71] the Rabbis understood that this law only affects something of value which can pass from "hand to hand," thus excluding land or anything built on land, which cannot be passed from hand to hand. Similarly, documents are also excluded because, while they represent value, having no actual value themselves they differ from articles bought "from his hand."

Some Authorities hold that, nevertheless, the prohibition does apply[72] and it is wrong to overcharge or underpay; what does not apply is the remedy—restitution in the event of the difference being just one-sixth and avoidance of the entire transaction if the discrepancy is greater. The reasoning behind this rule is that it is difficult to determine what is a fair price for land and buildings; to one who requires it in that particular position, land can be worth much more than to others.[73] In the same way, documents representing debts have no fixed value; there is no standard discount, as each case is quite distinct, the value of the document and the underlying debt depending on the general financial situation, credit rating and honesty of the debtor concerned.[74]

Many Authorities, however, do hold that even in those cases to which the laws of *Ona'ah* do not apply, there is a limit to the amount that may be charged—no more than double the accepted value. For example, a transaction involving the sale of land normally considered worth five hundred coins per acre, at something in excess of one thousand coins per acre, can be set aside.[75]

Although the Torah uses the word "companion," implying that *Ona'ah* is only prohibited between man and man, and not between man and charity, nevertheless this applies

---

[71] V. supra note 52.

[72] *Ramban* quoted by *Sefer Hachinnuch*, mitzvah 337.

[73] *Bava Kama* 14b: "Land is worth all money."

[74] *Aruch Hashulchan, Choshen Mishpat* 227:34.

[75] *Choshen Mishpat* 227:29, commentary of *Remah* and *S'ma* 50 & 51.

only to the Temple charities—not to contemporary charitable institutions such as educational funds, benevolent funds, and burial societies.[76]

Any transaction which is a quasi purchase comes within the orbit of these rules; for example, brothers who divide up property inherited from their father, or partners who divide partnership property on dissolution of the partnership, must be careful that the values upon which the division is based are fair, and that any differences do not exceed the legal limits laid down by law. If, for example, property is over-valued by more than one-sixth, and is given to one heir or one partner as part of his share, he can in principle undo the transaction and demand a reapportionment.[77]

Closely resembling the prohibition of Ona'ah, which is Biblical, is the Rabbinical prohibition of profiteering.[78] The major difference between the two laws is that the law of Ona'ah can be set aside by mutual agreement,[79] while that of profiteering cannot; it is a Rabbinic enactment which over-rides the consent of the parties concerned. If the seller tells the buyer what the article cost him, but that he wants to make a one hundred per cent profit, and the buyer agrees, the seller has not transgressed the law of Ona'ah; neverthe-less he is prohibited by Rabbinic enactment from making a profit of more than one-sixth in essential commodities.[80] The

---

[76] S'ma, ad loc. 49; see supra p. 213, debate re Usury.

[77] V. Aruch Hashulchan, Choshen Mishpat 227:38 et seq. There are several differences of opinion among Authorities regarding the detailed application of this rule.

[78] Hafka'at She'arim: lit., raising the price of a commodity beyond the accepted level, or beyond that fixed by a competent Authority.

[79] Supra p. 219.

[80] Meiri, Beit Habechirah, Bava Metzia 51b; this law seems to be one of first instance only, unlike that of Ona'ah; none of the Authorities demand the return of the excess profit or the avoidance of the transaction in the event of profiteering.

basis of the Rabbinic prohibition is a desire to see that the Jewish people live in accordance with the Biblical precept of "Your Brother shall live with you,"[81] which the Rabbis interpreted as "Let the other man also live."[82]

The Talmud goes so far as to equate the Rabbinic prohibition of profiteering with the Biblical injunction prohibiting usury.

> Our Rabbis taught: Concerning those who hoard food-stuffs,[83] lend money on usury, reduce the measures, and raise prices, Scripture says "Saying: when will the new moon be gone that we may sell grain [the months passing and the stores being depleted, allowing us to sell at higher prices] and the Sabbath [*Shemittah*] that we may set forth grain? [when only *we* will have produce to sell]...."[84] Concerning these it is written in the Scripture, "the Lord hath sworn by the Pride of Yaakov,[85] surely I will never forget any of their works."[86]

Generally, middlemen were discouraged in dealing with essential commodities such as bread, meat, fish, wine, or oil.[87] "It is forbidden to *deal in* essential commodities in Israel. It is best that each farmer brings to the market the crops from his own barn and sells them directly to the public in order that they should be sold cheaply,"[88] and it

---

[81] *Vayikra* 25:36.

[82] S'ma, *Choshen Mishpat* 131:25, commentary 43.

[83] To sell it later when prices have risen, or to "corner the market."

[84] *Amos* 8:5.

[85] His Holy name, which is the Pride of Yaakov.

[86] Ibid., 7; *Bava Batra* 90b; v. *Megillah* 17b that the Blessing for the crops was placed in ninth place in the *Amidah* because it is in the ninth Psalm (v. *Rashi* and note explaining how it is the ninth) that the Psalmist promises vengeance on those "who lie in wait to catch the poor: those who ensnare the poor when they draw them into their net." See a similar theme in Talmud Yerushalmi, *Berachot* 2:4.

[87] *Aruch Hashulchan, Choshen Mishpat* 231:20.

[88] *Choshen Mishpat* 231:23

was the duty of the Beit Din to control wholesalers who dealt in those commodities to see that they did not raise their prices excessively.[89] The legal limit of profit allowed to the wholesaler by the Talmud is one-fifth of the net price, which equals one-sixth of the gross price; in other words, something that cost one hundred coins could be sold for one hundred and twenty. The twenty coins profit would be one-fifth of the original one hundred, and one-sixth of the ultimate one hundred and twenty.[90] If the writ of the Halachic Authority was not accepted by all traders in any particular trade, the regulation was dropped so as not to discriminate against the obedient trader.[91]

Apart from Talmudic legislation, it was open to any community to legislate controls as part of the general powers of Communal Legislation,[92] provided they did not conflict with the rules and controls instituted by the State in which the community found itself.[93]

An early example of a Beit Din interfering in order to reduce prices is the ruling of R. Shimon b. Gamliel, that a mother who over a period of years has given birth to (say) five children and is thus obliged to offer five sacrifices, need offer one sacrifice only to cover them all. By doing this, he succeeded in bringing down the price of a pair of doves from one gold coin to half a silver coin.[94]

This precedent was followed some sixteen hundred years later when the fishmongers of Nikolsburg, Moravia,

---

[89] Ibid., 20.

[90] *Bava Batra* 90b.

[91] *Choshen Mishpat* 227:20; S'ma commentary 38, quoting *Tur*.

[92] V. supra p. 83; *Bava Batra* 8b. "The townspeople are also at liberty to fix weights and measures, prices, and wages, and to inflict penalties for the infringement of their rules"; *Choshen Mishpat* 227:27.

[93] *Aruch Hashulchan*, ad loc. 27 on the effect of the laws of the State (*Dina demalchuta*); v. supra p. 196 .

[94] One-fiftieth of the original price; *Mishnah Keritot* 8a. V. *Rashi, s.v. "nichnas."*

greatly raised the price of fish, having seen that the Jews were not deterred by high prices from buying fish for the Sabbath. The Nikolsburg community enacted a rule which prohibited all members from buying fish for a period of two months.[95] On occasions "control" legislation may be removed as a matter of public policy; R. Yehudah ben Beteira specifically allowed wine to be dealt with by wholesalers acting as middlemen, in the hope that this would indeed drive up prices—in order to keep the people sober and respectable.[96]

---

[95] *Tzemach Tzedek, Responsa* 28; v. *Mishnah Ta'anit* 15b, "We do not commence a series of fast days on a Thursday so as not to raise the prices," for on the Thursday it would be necessary to purchase for a post-fast meal in addition to the usual Shabbat requirements. Shopkeepers, not being aware of the new series of fasts, would conclude that the additional purchases presaged a shortage and would therefore raise their prices in anticipation of a rush to buy; v. *Magen Avraham* 242:1.

[96] *Bava Batra* 90b.

TEN
Knowledge, Intention, and Consent

I N JEWISH LEGAL IDIOM, the three English concepts which form the title of this chapter are all normally expressed by just one Hebrew word— **Da'at.** No matter how perfectly formalized a transaction may be, it will not be valid unless that form is supported by knowledge, intention, and consent—by *Da'at.* Conversely, *Da'at* without form cannot normally have any legal effect.[1]

---

[1] Rosh, discussing the gemara *Rosh Hashanah* 17b, explains that the first of the Thirteen Divine Attributes of Mercy signifies that the Almighty does not punish for *intention* to commit even so severe a sin as idolatry—only a *deed* is punished. An exception to the rule that intention itself has no legal effect is the law of *Pigul*, which invalidates a sacrifice should the officiating priest have (and express—*Tosafot, Bava Metzia* 43b, s.v. *"hachoshev"*) the intention of eating his portion at an improper time. There is a controversy in connection with the Law of Bailment as to whether a bailee is liable for all accidents (as a thief) from the moment he expresses his intention to make use of the bailment, although in fact he never touches it. Beit Shammai maintains he becomes forthwith responsible, whereas Beit Hillel (and that is the Halachah) rules that the bailee is not responsible until he actually makes use of the bailment for his own purposes, i.e., steals it (*Mishnah, Bava Metzia* 43b). There are cases where form may be dispensed with; v. note 44 & infra p. 239.

The act of a person who does not know what he is doing has no legal validity. Thus a sale or a purchase completed by someone who is drunk would be valid unless he had reached "the stage of Lot's drunkenness."[2] The fact that a man was drunk at the time he entered into a transaction does not allow him to annul it, unless he can demonstrate that he was totally unaware of what he was doing.[3] Neither a madman[4] nor a minor[5] is deemed to know what he is doing and is therefore deprived of legal capacity, with the result that, however formally correct his action may be, it has no legal validity. The law covering minors was, however, modified by Rabbinic Legislation, which recognizes transactions in personal property entered into by an intelligent minor who appears to understand what he is doing and who has no guardian to act for him. This legislation was required in order to help a capable minor sustain himself, if necessary.[6]

Both parties to any given transaction must be aware that it is being carried out. For example: A deposits an article with B and indicates to B that he actually wishes to sell it. B, at the time, refuses the offer, but subsequently changes his mind. No unilateral act of acquisition carried out by B can be valid until he makes A aware of his change of mind and of the fact that he does intend acquiring the article. Should A and B find

---

[2] *Bereshit* 19:33. The fear of drunkenness and therefore legal incapacity is one of the reasons why a bride and groom are obliged to fast on their wedding day (v. *Even Ha'ezer* 61:5 and *Ba'er Heitev*, ad loc.).

[3] *Eruvin* 65a; *Choshen Mishpat* 235:22.

[4] *Ketubot* 20a; v. supra p. 117 for discussion of the case of a person who suffered periods of sanity interspersed with periods of insanity. He sold property, subsequently claiming to have sold during a period of insanity and thereby attempting to avoid the sale.

[5] *Yad, Mechirah* 29:1.

[6] Ibid. and 6, 7 & 8. V. *Torah Temimah, Shemot* 25:2, commentary 1. The Biblical source disqualifying a minor is different from that which disqualifies a madman, because a minor may indeed be intelligent and understanding.

themselves together in a place remote from the article and agree that B should acquire it, immediately on that agreement being reached it becomes B's without the necessity of any further formal act— because it is situated in his property.[7]

This is known in Talmudic parlance as **Kinyan Chatzer**.[8] The form of this act of transfer would be for the disponer, be he a donor or a vendor, to arrange for the article to be placed in the house, garden, courtyard, or any similar property belonging to, and under the control of, the donee or purchaser. In the case of a gift, the donee's knowledge is not required, whereas, of course, in the case of a sale the purchaser's knowledge is. In either case, as soon as the article is placed on or in the disponee's property, it becomes his.[9] In fact, this mode of acquisition—executed with the disponee's knowledge—is not particularly original; there is no reason to distinguish between putting an item into his hand or giving it to his agent, and putting an item into his locked house, which for this purpose can be considered either an extension of his hand or as his agent.[10] The originality of this rule (and that is indeed why the Talmud cites Biblical sources), lies in the fact that it is effective and valid, in the case of a gift, without the owner's (donee's) knowledge.[11]

Nevertheless, this power of acquisition bestowed upon property can in no way exceed that of its owner; if he is not able, or does not wish, to make the acquisition, his property cannot do it for him. The following case illustrates this limitation.

If, after A sells a field to B, hidden treasure is found

---

[7] *Aruch Hashulchan, Choshen Mishpat* 189:2.

[8] Lit., "Acquisition by Courtyard."

[9] *Choshen Mishpat* 243:20; v. 268:3 regarding lost property and 275:28 regarding ownerless property.

[10] *Bava Metzia* 10b. (v. infra p. 240).

[11] *Chatam Sofer, Responsa, Yoreh De'ah* 310 & 316.

buried there, to whom does it belong?[12] The vendor will claim that he sold only the field and not the hidden treasure, whereas the buyer will claim that he purchased the field and everything in it. The buyer will prevail because *Kinyan Chatzer* can be effective without the owner's knowledge only in cases where, had the owner been present, he would have performed the act of acquisition. In this particular case, because he did not know the treasure was there, he himself would never have executed the required formal act of acquisition, and therefore the field cannot act in his place.[13]

On the same principle: If a proselyte dies[14] in a Jewish lodging house, the property left in his room will belong to the landlord, as the landlord's house acquires the now-ownerless property on the landlord's behalf. If subsequently, the landlord gives away one of the dead man's garments, and if the recipient opens the lining and finds hidden gold pieces, to whom do they belong? The landlord will naturally claim that his house acquired the gold pieces on his behalf. He will fail in law; as he himself would not have taken possession of the gold pieces, not knowing of their existence, so his house would not have taken possession on his behalf.

Similarly, if a Jew buys lead for roofing his house from a non-Jew, and then changes his mind and sells it to a fellow Jew, who finds that intermixed with the lead is valuable gold, the Jewish vendor has no claim against his purchaser; at the time when he acquired the lead, he did not know there was gold mixed with it and so he could not have acquired it;

---

[12] V. supra p. 183, note 141, the case attended by Alexander the Great, which was, of course, not being heard by a Jewish judge.

[13] *Mordechai, Bava Metzia* 258 & 259. V. *Tosafot, Bava Metzia* 26a, s.v. "deshatich."

[14] According to Jewish Law, a proselyte can have no heir unless he had children after his conversion; his non-Jewish relatives, including sons born before conversion, do not inherit his property, and all his former family connections are considered as ended.

it never became his, and it remains with the present owner.[15] His lack of knowledge that gold was present is fatal to his case.[16]

An action committed deliberately is not valid in the eyes of the law unless the intention is also that it have legal consequences; it must be intended to achieve its objective. This requirement is to be found in every branch of the Torah. To be guilty of murder, one must intend to commit murder; hence, if A raised his sword with the intention of killing a horse but instead killed its rider; or even if he aimed a blow at a part of the rider's body where a blow of that nature would not cause death, and accidentally hit a more delicate part, he is not guilty of murder. Without the intent to kill, there can be no crime of murder.[17] R. Shimon rules that even if A had intended murdering a different person but in the event actually killed B, he would not be executed for murder.[18]

One basic rule in tort is that a man is always responsible for damage he does (and therefore liable to pay full compensation), whether he acts willfully or inadvertently, whether awake or asleep.[19] From this decisive statement, it would appear that intention or the lack of it is totally irrelevant in cases of tort, but this is in fact not so. In case of intentional bodily injury, the law provides compensation not only for the immediate injury, but also for attendant damages: compensation for the pain suffered, payment for the services of a physician, compensation for time lost, and compensation

---

[15] *Mordechai,* loc. cit.

[16] V. supra p. 220; a victim of extortion who does not know the amount he has lost cannot forgive it, as he has no knowledge of what he is forgiving. Cf. *Mishnah Ketubot* 8:2 and commentary of *Tosafot Yom Tov.*

[17] *Sanhedrin* 79a. This is an argument between R. Shimon and R. Yehuda; cf. *Beitzah* 23b regarding intention on Shabbat.

[18] Ibid. As to whether the final ruling is in accordance with R. Shimon is a matter of argument; *Yad, Rotzeach* 4:1.

[19] *Mishnah, Bava Kama* 26a.

for incidental indignities.[20] However, if the injury was caused unintentionally, the perpetrator would be charged only for the immediate injury, and not under the four attendant subsidiary headings of compensation. Thus, if one had a stone in his lap and, not being aware of it, stood up so that the stone fell and injured another; or if one intended to throw an object a short distance, but actually threw it further and injured a passerby, the victim would be entitled to compensation only for immediate injury, but not for pain, cost of medical treatment, time lost, or indignity suffered.[21] So too, in matters of religion: If, for example, one intentionally plucks flowers on the Sabbath under the misapprehension that this is permissible, thereby inadvertently desecrating the Sabbath, he is obliged to bring a Penitential Offering. However, if he intends picking up a bunch of cut flowers, but in error plucks some uncut flowers, he is exempt from the Penitential Offering, as his action is considered unwitting.[22]

It is therefore not surprising that in mercantile law, the rule is:

> All formal acts of acquisition require the intention of the acquirer to acquire and the disponer to dispose; thus, if one "draws," "lifts,"[23] or actually takes possession, but has no intention to acquire, there is no acquisition. An act without intention is worthless; for by what legal means

---

[20] Ibid. 83b.

[21] Ibid. 26b.

[22] The word used is *mitasek* (lit., preoccupied); other Authorities hold that he is exempt from a Penitential Offering because of the requirement of "purposive work" (*Melechet Machshevet*), which is unique to the Sabbath. According to them, Sabbath laws are not governed by the general rule of *Mitasek*. V. *Rashi, Keritot* 19a, s.v. "*mibaya lei*"; v. *Tosafot, Shevuot* 19a, s.v. "*prat l'mitasek;*" v. R. *Akiva Eger, Responsa* I:8.

[23] Symbolic acts of acquisition.

does the ownership of the article or property change?[24]

In Talmudic literature, we find the terms **Gemirat Hada'at** and **Semichut Hada'at**. These two terms describe the two aspects of intention which are of fundamental importance in the law of conveyance, the former term indicating firm resolve or finality of intention, and the latter indicating confident reliance. Thus, the disponer must have the firm intention to dispose, while the purchaser must have the confident reliance that he will acquire. No form of acquisition would be effective if these two aspects of intention were not present, and it may well be that form is necessary only as testimony to the intentions of both parties.[25]

So, if one makes a furrow or performs any other acts usually construed to be acts of possession on a field, but

---

[24] *Aruch Hashulchan, Choshen Mishpat* 189:2. It is important to distinguish between acquisition by purchase and acquisition by gift. In the latter case, the recipient's intention to acquire may not in fact be necessary. V. infra. p. 240.

[25] Rabbi Dr. I. Herzog, *The Main Institutions of Jewish Law*, vol. 1, p. 63; vol. 2, p. 107; cf. Rabbi Elchonon Wasserman, *Kovetz Shiurim, Bava Batra*, 430; v. *Yad, Malveh V'loveh* 11:11 and *Kesef Mishneh*, ad loc.: if a transaction is governed by Rabbinic legislation of which one party is unaware, the law will be enforced upon him, as it is his religious obligation to obey the Rabbinical edict. Nevertheless, under civil law he is not bound by it, as, not knowing of the edict, he could not have contracted to be bound by it. The practical difference between his being bound by civil or by religious law would arise if he were to die before carrying out the legislated requirement; under civil law his heirs inherit his estate subject to any unfulfilled obligations and are therefore obliged to honor them; whereas under religious law, as they were not parties to the transaction, the obligation on the deceased, which was a personal one—to obey the Rabbis—dies with him.

Intention to consecrate property for Temple service needs no form, nor indeed even expression. A firm intention is binding (*Yad, Ma'aseh Hakorbanot* 14:12, based on *Shemot* 35:22); v. *Remah, Yoreh De'ah* 258:13, as to whether this rule covers charitable donations today (v. supra p. 213).

thinking that the field is his own, does not do it with intention, and this field belonged to a proselyte[26] who has died, he does not acquire the field. However, if one intended to perform an act of acquisition, as such, on a field that he thought had belonged to the dead proselyte A, but afterwards discovered that it had actually belonged to proselyte B, who had also died, he would have acquired the field. In both cases, there was no bar to his becoming the owner, and in both cases he performed the necessary act, but in the former there was no "confident reliance" and therefore no animus acquirendi, whereas in the latter both were present, albeit in error.[27] A symbolic transfer—such as a *Kinyan Sudar*, which is effected by the transfer of a scarf or some similar item—is in itself only evidence of the intention of the parties, and the Talmud discusses[28] the question of when exactly a transaction is considered to be completed. One view is that as long as discussions continue, it is incomplete, notwithstanding the formal act; but the moment the subject of the discussion is changed, the transaction is treated as finalized. Another view is that the transaction is only finalized when the session itself breaks up.

> It appears that it is only when a "form" is used, that the Rabbis argue. For [in this case] there has been no acquisition by the acquirer from the disponer, and each is still in possession of his own as before, as the exchange of a kerchief does not finalize a transaction; therefore, each party still believes he can change his mind, either as long as the meeting is in session or at least as long as this same transaction is being discussed. But if one acquires with real possession, or with a document, the transaction is completed immediately....[29]

---

[26] V. supra, note 14.
[27] *Yevamot* 52b.
[28] *Bava Batra* 114a.
[29] *Ritva, Novellae,* ad loc.

There is a Talmudic argument on the case of a man who sold the fruit of a date tree during the winter, before the tree had even blossomed. R. Huna says that either party may withdraw from the sale before the fruit appears; but after the fruits have come into existence they may no longer withdraw; for he holds that the form of transfer that was executed before the fruit came into existence takes effect as soon as it does come into existence. R. Nachman, however, is of the view that either party may withdraw even after the fruit has come into existence, because in his opinion no transfer is effective unless the object sold is actually in existence at the time of the sale.[30] The ultimate ruling is in fact in accordance with R. Nachman's views, that a man is not able to transfer possession of any item that is not yet in existence, and this principle applies whether the transfer is by way of sale, by way of gift inter vivos, or by way of gift mortis causa.[31]

Even if the item is in existence but is not yet in the ownership and possession of the transferor, no transaction can be binding. Thus, if a form of transfer is entered into whereby one transfers a certain field "when I buy it," the transaction is ineffective.[32]

Some are of the opinion that the ratio decidendi behind this basic rule is that, as the object concerned is not currently available for transfer, the transferor does not really have the finality of intention and the transferee does not have the confident reliance necessary to make the transaction binding. In Talmudic language, there is a lack of Da'at.[33]

---

[30] Yevamot 93a.

[31] Choshen Mishpat 209:4. This rule also applies to gifts to the Temple. One cannot consecrate something which is not yet in existence. However, one can take a binding oath to consecrate it once it does exist. (Yad, Arachin 6:26 & 31-33).

[32] Choshen Mishpat 209:5.

[33] Nimukei Yosef on Bava Metzia 66b. There is a dispute as to whether, if the husband of a pregnant woman gives an undertaking to

In fact, the Talmud rules quite clearly that if one says to another "what I am to inherit from my father is sold to you" or "what my net is to bring up[34] is sold to you," it is as if "he said nothing."[35] The reason is clearly given, that in these cases the buyer places no reliance on the words of the seller.

The Talmud then goes on to distinguish these two cases from cases where, for example, one says, "what I am to inherit from my father today is sold to you," or "what my net is to bring up today is sold to you," in both of which his words are valid and the sale is effective. The distinction is that by adding the word "today" the seller in the first instance indicates that his father is dying and he requires the money for the purpose of giving him a decent burial, and in the second instance he indicates that he depends for his livelihood on that day's catch; and it is because of these pressing reasons that the Rabbis declared the sales to be binding, although, in fact, in strict law, they are not.[36]

It is with these guidelines that the *Or Hachaim*[37] explains the transaction in the course of which the Patriarch Yaakov purchased the birthright from his brother Esau.[38] As the birthright carries with it rights in futuro which are not yet in existence—such as the right to an additional share of the paternal inheritance—how could a sale be effective? The answer is that Yaakov deliberately used the words, "Sell me *this day* your birthright"—you are making the sale because you require food to sustain you today; therefore, the transaction is effective, as in the case of a

---

another that, in the event of the child's being male, the other will be appointed to perform the rite of circumcision, this undertaking is binding (*Rosh, Responsa* 102:10).

34 I.e., any animals, birds or fishes that may be caught in my net or snare.

35 His words are of no consequence. *Bava Metzia* 16a.

36 *Rashi*, ad loc. V. *Shitah Mekubetzet*.

37 *Bereshit* 25:31.

38 Ibid., 29-34.

poor man who sells his anticipated catch for his day's sustenance.[39]

Can one make a valid gift to an unborn child? The ultimate ruling in the Talmud is that one cannot, except in the case of one's own child, "because a man is favorably disposed towards his son [or daughter]" and so he wholeheartedly transfers ownership to the unborn child. Obviously, in the case of a stranger, however, this principle is inapplicable.[40]

This ruling is understandable if the ratio decidendi for invalidating transfers to an unrelated unborn child is because the transferor as yet does not have absolute intention; the exception—that to his own child the transfer is valid—would cover any transfer whether inter vivos or mortis causa, but could not, of course, include a child not yet conceived. But, there are Authorities who do not accept that intent or lack of it is the ratio decidendi; they are of the view that an unborn child can in no way acquire ownership or other rights until it is born, in which case the question arises, why should one's own child be different? And to this the answer is, that in fact this is an extra-legal Rabbinic enactment relevant only to a donation mortis causa: in order that on his deathbed the father should not be disturbed by the fact that he is unable to provide for this unborn child of his to which he is "favorably disposed," the Rabbis order that such gifts be recognized and effective in law.[41]

So fundamental are the intentions of the parties to a transaction, that, in exceptional cases, the Rabbis abolished the need for any form of transfer, ordaining that the transaction be treated as completed on the basis of the intentions of the parties.

---

[39] V. also *Ketzot Hachoshen* 278:13 ad fin. Some explain that that was the reason Yaakov added the oath, in order to confirm the intention (v. *Or Hachaim, Bereshit* 25:31).

[40] *Bava Batra* 142b.

[41] *Nimukei Yosef*, ad loc.

R. Chanina said: If a person arranges for the marriage of his eldest son to take place in a house belonging to him [which is empty and in which the father has placed no symbol of title], he, the son, acquires ownership. But this is only in the case of his eldest son and only when he is marrying a spinster and only when she is his first wife and only when he is the first son whom the father is marrying off.[42]

In such cases, the father's joy is so great that he willingly and wholeheartedly gives away the house to his son; therefore there does exist the finality of intention. Conversely, because the son who is about to be married sees that the house is empty and he has nowhere else to live with his bride, he places confident reliance on this gift from his father;[43] therefore, the Rabbis understood that neither party needs any further form of completion.[44]

If the intention of the recipient is an essential part of a legal transfer, how is it that there are any number of instances in which it is bypassed—for example, acquisition by

---

[42] *Bava Batra* 144a.

[43] *Tosafot*, ad loc., s.v. *"k'hilchata."*

[44] This is one of three enactments which the Rabbis arbitrarily introduced as if they were *"Halachah L'Moshe MiSinai."* (V. p. supra 29; *Ran* on *Gittin* 14a).

Another is the rule of *Ma'amad Sheloshtan*, which stipulates that if A, B, and C are together and A instructs B: "Give the money you owe me to C," the transfer is binding without any other formal act and A is no longer the owner of that money. Here the Rabbis did away with the necessity of form as a matter of convenience. V. *Gittin* 14a and *Tosafot*, s.v. *"k'hilchata."* (v. supra p.69).

The third enactment is that when a dying man gives his entire estate to his wife, she does not become the legal owner, but is merely the administratrix, acting as trustee for the children, who are the rightful heirs. (*Bava Batra* 131b; v. chap. VI on the subject of Equity). V. *Bava Metzia* 49a, quoted by *Tosafot, Ketubot* 102a, s.v. *"alibba,"* that a "small gift" also needs no form of transfer. (v. supra p. 108).

"courtyard," acquisition by a minor, or even by an unborn child?

The answer lies in two other principles of Jewish Law: "A right can be acquired for a person in his absence" and "The donor's intention bestows a right to property on another."

How do we know that a right can be acquired for a person in his absence? "And you shall take one prince of every Tribe to divide the Land for inheritance";[45] by being present and participating in the division of the conquered land of Canaan, the princes acquired rights of ownership for their fellow tribesmen although the beneficiaries themselves were not present. As the division was a fair one and was made with the underlying intention that it should be to the advantage of their people, the acts of the princes were valid even if, in the event, some individuals were displeased.[46] Some Authorities are of the view that this rule is merely an extension of the general rules of agency—a constructive agency, "For we can testify that he, the principal, really wishes him to act as his agent."[47] This of course solves the problem as to how a courtyard can act for its owner; it is treated either as an extension of himself or as his agent, for he would be competent to appoint an agent. However, in the case of a minor or unborn child, who are incapable in law (or fact) of appointing an agent, how can this principle operate? It may well be that the underlying principle is indeed one of agency—not of the general rule of agency, which is irrelevant to a minor, but of a specific type of agency, established by the Torah to include minors who also received a share in the Land, and from this we derive the rule that a right can be acquired on behalf of minors.[48]

Other Authorities differ, and are of the view that the

---

[45] *Bemidbar* 34:18.
[46] *Kiddushin* 42a.
[47] *Rashi, Bava Metzia* 12a, s.v. "*gabi matanah.*"
[48] *Ketzot Hachoshen* 105:1.

ability to acquire a right on behalf of a minor or unborn child is in fact of Rabbinical origin and not from the Torah itself.[49]

The general principle does explain how it is legally possible for a finder to pick up a lost article on behalf of his fellow without the other's knowledge, making it ab initio the other's property,[50] notwithstanding that the beneficiary is a minor or, even according to some Authorities, an unborn child. It also convincingly explains the point already made, that if a Proselyte dies in the house of a fellow Jew, his evident property belongs to the householder, whereas hidden property of which the householder could not be aware does not, as he would never have taken possession himself or appointed an agent.[51]

But these examples involve an original act of acquisition by someone of something. What if one wishes to make a gift to a third person without his knowledge, or to a minor or unborn child, who in fact, and in law, are considered to have no knowledge or intention? To cover this type of case, we have the second principle, that the donor's intention bestows a right to property on another,[52] and many take the view that this principle is from Torah itself.[53]

---

[49] *Ramban, Novellae, Bava Metzia* 71b. Those of this view consider that, as all Israel already owned a share in the Land, the distribution was not a new acquisition, but merely a matter of organization as to who actually takes what.

[50] *Bava Metzia* 8a; cf. op. cit. 10a. But v. *Aruch Hashulchan, Choshen Mishpat* 269:1.

[51] Supra p. 231.

[52] *Da'at Acheret Makneh Oto* (lit., another's intention bestows it upon him). As to why this principle cannot be applied to validate a betrothal by a minor male of an adult female on the grounds that "she bestows herself upon him," v. *Noda B'Yehudah* II, *Even Ha'ezer* 54 (p. 52); cf. *Ran, Nedarim* 30a, s.v. *"v'ishah."*

[53] *Tosafot, Kiddushin* 19a, s.v. *"omer;" Ran,* ad loc. V. *Machanei Efraim, Zechiah U'matanah* 4. No Authority known to the author quotes any source; presumably it is a *sevarah* (v. supra p. 32). V. *Ketzot Hachoshen* 235:4 and 275:4.

As this mode of transfer depends entirely on the transferor, the capacity or intention of the transferee is irrelevant. Thus, whereas in order to use a courtyard to acquire hitherto ownerless property, the courtyard must be under the control of the owner, either by means of fencing or by his own controlling presence, this is not necessary if another deposits a gift there.[54] Ownerless property, if not under the control of the owner of the courtyard, remains ownerless, and any other person may take it, whereas a gift remains in the ownership of the donor until it becomes the property of the recipient; thus there is no moment during which it is ownerless.

The intention of the donor is so powerful that it can compensate for the defective intention of the donee. For example, A makes a gift of his field to B; B goes to that field and ploughs it, which in itself is an act of taking possession, but he does so thinking it is his own field and, therefore, of course, he has no intention of taking possession. As he has performed the correct act and it is A's intention that by this very act the field should become B's, B's intention is irrelevant and the field becomes his.[55] It is this intention of A which distinguishes this case from that cited above,[56] in which one ploughs the field of a deceased proselyte who has no heirs, thinking it is his own; in that case he does not become the owner, for as the field is ownerless, there is no other person's intention which can overcome the defect in his own.[57] It may well be that this rule only holds good in the case of a gift, in which there is merely unilateral deprivation; as B is not called upon to give anything in exchange, he would certainly want the field irrespective of the fact that he has made a mistake. However, in the case of a sale by A to B, B must knowingly undertake the deprivation of owing, and subsequently paying,

---

[54] *Bava Metzia* 11b. V. *Remah, Choshen Mishpat* 243:21.
[55] *Nimukei Yosef* on *Bava Batra* 41a.
[56] Supra, note 26.
[57] *Nimukei Yosef,* loc. cit.

the purchase price, and for this it is necessary to have proper intent.[58]

Contracts or forms of disposal and acquisition can only be binding if the parties to them regard them as binding—that is, there is a finality of intention on the part of the disponer and confident reliance on the part of the acquirer. If either side does not regard the transaction as binding, it is not. A case is reported[59] in which a woman sent A to buy an estate on her behalf from B, who happened to be her relative. B, the vendor, stipulated with A, the agent, that should he, B, come into funds, the buyer, who was his relative, should allow him to buy back the property. A replied saying, "You and the woman are as close as brothers"—meaning, "I am sure she will return the property to you and is not determined to keep it." When the court heard this case, it ruled that A had not acquired the property on behalf of his principal, as he had only given B a vague undertaking, and because B did not rely on that undertaking he did not have the finality of intention of transferring.[60]

It follows, therefore, that if one obligates himself to an unreasonable penalty in the event of default which he does not really intend to pay, his commitment is not enforceable in law, and for this type of agreement the Talmud uses the word *Asmachta*. The root of the word is obviously *Samach*, which means "support", or in this connotation, "reliance." Some take this to mean that he who undertakes to pay the penalty is so sure or reliant on the conditions being fulfilled, that he does not for one moment imagine that he will be called upon to pay it.[61] Others interpret the word to denote

---

[58] *Netivot Hamishpat* 200:14.
[59] *Bava Metzia* 67a.
[60] This is Rambam's interpretation of the Gemara; *Yad, Mechirah* 11:12, but v. *Lechem Mishneh*, ad loc.
[61] *Rashbam, Bava Batra* 168a, s.v. *"asmachta."*

that the penalty is an exaggeration on the proposer's part, which he uses to bolster his words so that the other party should rely on what he says.[62]

The classic example is to be found in a mishnah:[63]

> In the case where a debtor paid part of his debt and the bond was deposited with a trustee whom the borrower instructed: "If I do not pay the balance between now and a certain date, give the creditor the bond." If that date was reached and he did not pay, R. Yosei said: The Trustee should give it;[64] R. Yehudah said he should not give it.

R. Yosei is of the opinion that although the undertaking to repay the full debt, despite the fact that some part will have been paid twice, was given in the hope and expectation that it would never have to be honored, it is, nevertheless, legally binding. R. Yehudah considers that it was obvious that the borrower never intended to repay the full debt after he had already paid part of it, and his undertaking therefore was only in the nature of an expression of good faith, an attempt to show that it was his earnest hope and intention to pay the balance before the due date. In the event, the Halachah follows the view of R. Yehudah; the condition fails, as there was no finality of intention on the part of the borrower to, in fact, penalize himself.[65]

It is this factor which distinguishes between this particular case and the case where a man undertakes a gratuitous obligation. For example, if A writes out an I.O.U. in which he states that he owes B a sum of money, and presents that document to B, he is obliged to pay when requested to do so, although A, B, and any witnesses there may have been are

---

[62] Tosafot, Bava Batra 168a, s.v. "amar."

[63] Bava Batra 168a.

[64] To the creditor, who can consequently claim payment of the full debt, including that part already paid.

[65] Choshen Mishpat 55:1 and note 207:11.

fully aware that in fact A did not owe B that money.[66] As A has made no conditions, he has clearly intended to obligate himself to pay that sum of money to B, and the liability on him is now what it would have been had he indeed borrowed that money from B; so much so that, if the document or the handing over is properly attested by acceptable witnesses, it lays a charge[67] on all A's property which holds good against any subsequent purchaser.[68]

It is for this reason, too, that the Torah obliges a guarantor to honor his guarantee.[69] He knows that the lender's reliance on his guarantee was an inducement to make the loan and—not being a cheat, and being flattered that the lender accepts his guarantee—he does, at the time of the commitment, truly intend to honor it and to accept the obligation of guarantor upon himself.[70]

Because it is accepted that no person intends or wishes to pay a penalty, if it should happen that A and B strike a bargain, agreeing to do a deal, and as an act of good faith, A, the buyer, deposits money with B, stipulating that if he withdraws from the transaction his deposit is forfeited to B, while B, also to show good faith, stipulates that if he, the vendor, withdraws, he will return to A double the amount deposited with him, neither stipulation is binding as both are for penalties which, in fact, neither party intends to suffer.[71]

---

[66] Chosen Mishpat 40:1.
[67] V. supra p. 146 et seq.
[68] Choshen Mishpat 40:2.
[69] Bereshit 43:9; Mishlei 6:1 & 2; ibid. 20:16. V. Bava Batra 173b.
[70] Aruch Hashulchan 129:1. V. Rashbam, Bava Batra 173b, s.v. "gamar," who adds that "it is as if the guarantor appoints the lender as his agent [to advance the money]."
[71] Choshen Mishpat 207:11, based on Bava Metzia 48b. This is the view quoted by Remah in his note. R. Yosef Karo rules that only B escapes his commitment. A, however, loses his deposit, as having put B in possession of the money, he cannot claim lack of intent. (V. Tur, ad loc. 15.)

Normally, people engaged in financial transactions may make whatever conditions they wish; the classical example of a conditional transaction is found in the Torah itself, when Moshe struck a bargain with the Tribes of Reuven and Gad, and half the Tribe of Menashe. They requested to be allowed to settle in Trans-Jordan and not to take a share in the Land of Canaan over the river. Moshe agreed on the condition that the eligible fighting men among these tribes cross over with their brethren, the bulk of the Israelites, and help them conquer the Land of Canaan.[72] It was only because they honored this condition that they were, indeed, allowed to remain in Transjordan. That and similar conditions differ from those of *Asmachta* in that in the former circumstances the parties want the result and intend to honor the condition, whereas in cases of *Asmachta*, the parties obligated do not really want the event which obligates them to occur, and do not really intend to be bound to the penalties.[73]

Yet we do find that agreed penalties are payable: If one leases a field from its owner on a percentage basis and neglects it, the court will assess how much it ought to have produced, and the lessee must pay the landlord that amount, for thus he obligates himself: "Should I neglect the field and not cultivate it, I will pay of the best."[74] The Talmud itself takes the point and explains that in the case of the lessee there was no exaggeration; the landlord had suffered a loss through the lessee's neglect (his agreed percentage) and it is only fair that he be compensated, whereas in cases of *Asmachta*, the penalties are unwarranted or excessive. Indeed, if the stipulation would be that in the event of the lessee's not working the field he would pay an exaggerated amount of

---

[72] *Bemidbar* 32.

[73] *Nimukei Yosef* on *Bava Batra* at p. 130 ad fin., quoting *Ritva*; a conditional oath to give charity in the event of any stated occurrence is not considered an *Asmachta*, and is therefore binding. (*Mordechai, Bava Kama, 4:45*).

[74] I.e., the estimate is of the maximum that field could produce.

damages, it would fail as, being an excessive penalty, not warranted by the loss caused, it is an *Asmachta*.[75]

It may happen that in a betrothal agreement between families, a clause is inserted to the effect that if either party retracts and does not proceed with the proposed marriage, that party shall pay an agreed sum to the other. While prima facie the penalty stipulated may appear to be extravagant and therefore an *Asmachta*, nevertheless, many Authorities consider it to be legally effective and the parties bound on the grounds that it is an attempt to compensate the "wronged" party for the humiliation suffered in so personal and delicate a matter.[76]

Are gambling debts enforceable in Jewish Law?[77]

On the one hand, as no player wishes to lose, nor does he believe he is going to lose, he does not have "the finality of intention" to obligate himself to pay if indeed he does lose.[78]

On the other hand, in order to have the opportunity to win on some occasions, every player must accept that his opponent will win on others, and it may well be, therefore, that on the occasions he loses he does indeed intend to honor his obligation, in which case there is the required "finality of intention."[79] According to the view that gambling debts are

---

[75] *Mishnah, Bava Metzia* 104a, and Talmudic discussions 104a. V. *Choshen Mishpat* 328:2; v. *Rashba, Responsa* 1:933; v. Rabbi S. J. Zevin, *L'Or Hahalachah*, who discusses the case of Shylock in *The Merchant of Venice* in the light of Jewish Law. He quotes a magazine article in which the writer puts forward the view that as a "pound of flesh" for non-payment of a debt is excessive, the agreement is void on the grounds of *Asmachta*. British law follows the same principle in distinguishing between liquidated damages and "penalty" damages which are extravagant.

[76] *Choshen Mishpat* 207:16; v. *Aruch Hashulchan, Choshen Mishpat* 207:48; v. infra p. 251.

[77] Under British Statute Law, gambling debts are not recoverable, although under Common Law, they would have been.

[78] *Sanhedrin* 24b.

[79] This is a dispute between Rami bar Chama and R. Sheshet.

not enforceable, gamblers would be disqualified from giving evidence in a Jewish Court, for by claiming his winnings and making the loser pay him, the gambler is taking money which is not his; therefore in law he is looked upon as a thief, with ensuing consequences. As the ruling is that gambling debts must be paid and the gambler is not a thief, why then does the Mishnah[80] disqualify him from giving evidence? The answer[81] is that the Rabbis only disqualify *professional* gamblers from giving evidence; they contribute nothing to the development and betterment of society and are, therefore, not to be treated as responsible citizens.

Interestingly, there are those who distinguish between playing with cash stakes—which, being on the gambling table in front of all players, may be considered as being transferred from loser to winner as the games are being played—and gambling on credit, where the loser later has to bring the money required to pay the winner. In the latter case, at the time of play there has not been sufficient intention or reliance, making the transaction an *Asmachta* and not binding.[82] Presumably, according to that view, gamblers who play on credit are disqualified by the Torah from giving evidence, as when they claim, and subsequently take, their winnings, they are in fact stealing money to which they are not entitled.

Because the validity of a transaction depends on the determined intention of both parties, a sale agreed upon and even concluded by a form of transfer is ineffective unless the price has been agreed in advance. Unless the buyer knows what he is paying and the seller knows the amount he is receiving, there can be no finality of intention, although if the article being sold is of the type that has a fixed and known price, the sale would be effective, as it is assumed

---

[80] Ibid.

[81] *Choshen Mishpat* 34:16, based on the Talmudic debate.

[82] *Remah, Choshen Mishpat,* 207:13.

both parties are aware of the amount involved.[83] Presumably, in the same way as the value changing hands must be determined, so must the item which is the subject of the transaction; and therefore, if one were to offer all the contents of his house without specifying them, or the unspecified contents of a box or a bag, there can be no reliance by the buyer; he just does not know what he is buying—the box could contain gold or brick.[84] A transaction of this nature closely resembles a game of chance played by gamblers.[85] It must also follow that if the ultimate transaction differs materially from that which was in the mind of either of the parties, it would be void; the criterion of whether the difference is material is: would normal people consider this the same transaction as envisaged, or would they consider it a different one?[86] For this reason, a wrong price either way which differs from the fair price by more than one-sixth is considered oppressive[87] and the sale is void. The figure of one-sixth is arrived at by the Rabbis on the premise that a difference of less than one-sixth would not be considered material by most people. Thus, if the price is too high, it is the buyer's intention to pay a fair price which is thwarted; conversely, if the price is too low, it is the seller's intention to achieve a fair price which is defeated.

Normally, if a transaction is entered into for a specific purpose, that purpose must be expressed; unexpressed conditions have no validity in law. For example, if one sells all his property, telling neighbors, friends, and all who hear him, that he intends emigrating to Israel, that sale is irrevo-

---

[83] *Yad, Mechirah* 4:11 & 12.
[84] Ibid. 21:3. V. *Maggid Mishneh*, ad loc.: "These are sensible words, but I have found no Talmudic source from which this rule can be inferred."
[85] Rambam's own comparison.
[86] *Choshen Mishpat* 232:6.
[87] V. supra p. 221.

cable, even though it transpires that unforeseen circumstances, even a force majeure, prevent the hoped-for *aliyah*.[88] Although all concerned may have understood that this was the vendor's intention and purpose in selling his property, nevertheless, as he did not make his *aliyah* a stipulation of the sale at the time of the sale, he cannot reverse the transaction; an unexpressed stipulation is not valid, and unless he does so expressly stipulate, it is possible that despite his announced intention, the vendor is, in fact, selling his property for other reasons, which he does not wish to reveal.[89]

If, however, the unstated purpose of, or stipulation to, a transaction is obvious and understood by both parties, it does become an integral part of the transaction, and if it fails, would void the transaction. For example, if it is understood that a farmer was buying a particular bull to harness to a plough or to service his cows and the bull is found to be dangerous, the transaction is void, although the farmer did not expressly state the purpose for which he was buying it.[90] Only if the purpose of the purchase was not clear would the vendor have any right to insist that the sale is valid.[91]

However, not every defect invalidates a sale; if, while not being as perfect as the buyer would wish, the article has only a defect which does not affect the use to which it is to be put, the sale will stand. If, for example, one buys a servant and subsequently discovers that the servant has an unpleasant wart on the back of his neck, the buyer cannot rescind the sale; unpleasant as the sight of it may be, the wart does not affect the servant's performance. If, however, he has boils or infections on his hand, the buyer may rescind on the grounds that the servant's performance is impeded by his defect, be-

---

[88] *Kiddushin* 49b. *Rashba, Novellae,* ad loc.; cf. *Ketubot* 97a, incident concerning R. Pappa.

[89] *Rosh, Responsa* 34:1.

[90] *Choshen Mishpat* 232:23.

[91] Ibid.; v. R. *Yaakov MeLissa, Responsa* 63 & note 9.

cause he cannot, with those hands, be allowed to handle food to be eaten by others.[92]

If it should happen that a man lying on a sickbed and thought by all, including himself, to be dying, gives away all his property to another without retaining anything for himself, it follows that if he does happily recover, the gift is null.[93]

In a similar vein, if a man receives news that his only son, who is abroad, has died, and thereupon writes over all his property to another in what would normally be a valid method of making a gift, that gift is defeated should it transpire that the son was in fact alive.[94] It is obvious that the gift was made by the donor, under the misapprehension that he was now without a primary heir, for the purpose of arranging the succession.

At the turn of the fourteenth century there arose a famous dispute. Shimon agreed to the betrothal of his son to a daughter of Reuven. Agreement was reached between the fathers as to when the nuptials would take place, and to underline this agreement each accepted upon himself that if his side retracted from the agreement and did not proceed with the marriage, he would pay an agreed penalty to the other. Before the set date was reached, another daughter of Reuven, a sister of the bride, left the ranks of Jewry and became an apostate. On hearing of this, Shimon withdrew from the agreement and would not allow his son to marry his betrothed. The date set for the wedding therefore passed, and Reuven demanded the agreed penalty.[95] Shimon refused to pay, claiming that it had obviously not been his intention to ally his family in marriage to one which was now disgraced.

The dispute came before Rosh, who in a long and detailed responsum[96] setting out the guidelines, ruled in favor of Shi-

---

[92] *Yad*, op. cit. 15:12 and 13.
[93] *Bava Batra* 146b.
[94] Ibid.
[95] V. supra p. 247; this is not *Asmachta*.
[96] 34:1.

mon: although it had never been expressed, the court accepts that it was an implicit condition of the agreement that neither family should in the interim be thus humiliated.

In the time of the Temple, people often consecrated their property by dedicating it for use in, or on behalf of, the Temple.[97] What if today, when, regrettably, the Temple does not exist, one uses the old formula, "I make this *Hekdesh*" (*Hekdesh* which cannot actually be used in or for the Temple must be destroyed). Do we take his words literally, so that the item would have to be buried or dropped irretrievably into the sea, or do we interpret his words generally, to give a more practical result? The answer is: since we no longer have the Temple, unqualified consecration of property means consecration for the purposes of the synagogue or for the benefit of the poor.[98] Unless it is expressly stated to the contrary, we interpret the donor's intention to be in favor of one of the "holy" charitable institutions in his vicinity.

The legal point is similar to the one in dispute in the Talmud in the case where one man said to another, "You and my donkey should become possessed of my property."[99] R. Hamnuna rules that the gift fails entirely; R. Sheshet rules that the human donee takes all; R. Nachman, in between the two, rules that the human donee takes half. The matter is one

---

[97] Made the item *Hekdesh*, lit., something consecrated. Consecration requires no formal act; it is achieved by the owner's merely making a statement such as "This item is consecrated," because "Dedication to the Almighty is [in law] equivalent to delivery to a mortal" (*Kiddushin* 28b). One rationale given for this is that as "The earth is the Lord's, and the fullness thereof" (*Tehillim* 24:1), He, so to speak, acquires any gift made to Him, through the legal machinery of *Kinyan Chatzer* (supra p. 230), as the universe is His estate (*Beit Habechirah, Kiddushin*, ad loc.).

[98] *Ri Migash, Novellae, Bava Batra* 102b. V. *Rashba, Responsa* 1:618 and 5:135, which notes that nowadays a debtor cannot defeat his creditors by consecrating his property.

[99] *Bava Batra* 143a.

of interpretation. The donor knew full well that a donkey cannot acquire property; did he therefore mean that as the donkey cannot acquire his half, his friend should also not get *his* half (the view of R. Hamnuna); or, conversely, knowing that a donkey cannot acquire property, did he really intend it *all* for his friend (R. Sheshet); or, did he in fact not tie the two gifts together, intending each to be a separate one, the fate of the gift to the man in no way connected with the fate of the gift to the animal (R. Nachman)? In the event, the ruling is in accordance with the view of R. Nachman, in that we understand that his intention is to make a gift to his friend, but only of half his property. Similarly, in the case of *Hekdesh*, we say the donor's intention is to make a gift to a beneficiary which has characteristics of "holiness."

What if we are satisfied that there is a finality of intention to make a gift, but we have no indication as to who is the beneficiary? A man traveling abroad, away from his family, sent home lengths of silk, without saying to which members of the family they should be given. The finality of intention to make a gift is obvious, because he took the trouble to send the silk, but there is no indication for whom he intended it.

The Talmud quotes the ruling of R. Ammi,[100] that those lengths which are suited by color or texture to males, belong to his sons (presumably equally), while those suitable to females, belong to the females—unmarried daughters being first in the order of precedence, as a father wishes them to look elegant so as to be attractive to potential suitors. The next in his order of priorities are his daughters-in-law, because a father feels obliged to share his sons' burden of clothing their wives. Conversely, he feels little obligation towards his married daughters, as the burden of clothing them falls on his sons-in-law—previously strangers—and therefore his

---

[100] *Bava Batra* 143b.

married daughters are only third in his order of priorities. Interestingly, the Talmud does not mention the donor's wife; some Authorities are of the view that if he had left his wife at home and sent lengths of silk suitable for women without specifying the recipient, they were all intended for his wife, for whom he has prime responsibility; others hold that the order of priorities is as set out by the Talmud (his wife taking none of the lengths) notwithstanding that he has left his wife at home.[101]

A similar case of doubt as to the donor's intention arose when a man on his deathbed said to those around him, "Let my estate be given to Toviah," and then died. A man named Toviah came to claim the estate. "Behold," said R. Yochanan, "Toviah has come, the estate must be given to this man"—this notwithstanding that the deceased had not made clear which Toviah he had intended. Had he said "Toviah" and a Rabbi Toviah come forward, he would not be entitled, as the deceased had not said "Rabbi Toviah." If, however, the testator was on very familiar terms with the Rabbi, the estate will be given to him, since the omission of the title would have been due to the intimacy between the two men. What if two Toviahs appeared claiming the estate? If one was a neighbor of the deceased, and the other a scholar associated with him, the scholar is to be given precedence, as a testator is assumed to be more favorably disposed towards a scholar than towards others. This is specially so when he feels death approaching and would wish to obtain merit and Heavenly reward by benefiting a scholar. Again, if one of the Toviahs is a relative, and the other a scholar, the scholar is, for the same reason, given precedence. What is the position where one is a neighbor and the other a relative and they are equal in scholar-

---

[101] *Ritva, Novellae,* ad loc. V. *Tur, Choshen Mishpat* 247:1. It is difficult to comprehend why daughters-in-law have priority in his mind over his wife. It has been suggested that by sending the silks via a messenger, he indicates that they are not for his wife, for whom he would rather bring gifts personally.

ship? To this the Talmud replies with the Scriptural verse, "...better is a neighbor that is near than a brother that is far off."[102] If both claimants are relatives, and both are neighbors, and they are of equal scholarship, the Talmud rules that the decision is left to the discretion[103] of the judges.[104]

What is clear from all these cases is that once there is finality of intention to make a gift, it does not fail out of uncertainty as to who the beneficiary is; it is up to the courts to decide as best they can.[105]

---

[102] *Mishlei* 27:10.

[103] *Ketubot* 85b. There is a difference of opinion as to how this discretion is to be exercised. One view is that the judges must investigate all the circumstances and try to understand the mind of the donor, to determine which of the claimants he preferred. Others rule that this discretion may be exercised arbitrarily and by their decision the judges themselves make a gift to the claimant they prefer. V. *Rashi* and *Tosafot*, s.v. "*shudah.*" (v. supra p. 137).

[104] *Rif* quotes this and other cases of doubtful intention alongside his rulings on *Bava Batra* 143 (v. supra p. 253).

[105] As illustrated by the Talmud in *Bava Batra* 143a & b, these problems often arise in cases of bequests. For example, a man leaves a son and daughter, and, using the Hebrew plural "*banim*", meaning "sons," he bequeaths his property to "my sons"; either the plural form or the gender is wrong. The Talmud rules that the son takes all, as the Torah itself uses a plural form when talking about an only son. V. *Divrei Chaim, Responsa I, Choshen Mishpat* 38, which rules that if a neutral term such as "my children" (or *Kinde* in Yiddish/German) is used, the testator intends his daughter also to inherit. There is a problem in this, for the Torah makes only the son the heir, and not the daughter; normally this can be overcome by treating the bequest as a gift, not an inheritance, which means it is not in conflict with the Torah. In the particular case before the *Divrei Chaim*, the testator used the words, "all my children should be equal," implying equal heirs; this, he ruled, conflicts with the Torah and the bequest to the daughter must fail. What if the testator leaves a son and grandson and says, "My sons should have my property"; are grandsons considered as sons? Not in ordinary language, rules the Talmud (loc. cit.) V. *Rosh, Responsa,* 85:3 which deals with a case in which a testator left property to "the orphans

In a case where the extent of the gift is in doubt, for example, a testator asks that the contents of a room holding one hundred barrels should be given to a beneficiary, and in the event, we find he leaves no rooms holding that number, the nearest being one which holds, say, one hundred and twenty barrels, the beneficiary will be given the contents of the larger room.[106] This ruling is based on the inference that a donor makes a gift in a "liberal spirit,"[107] a principle which does not of course apply to a vendor who sells for valuable consideration.[108]

It would, at first glance, have seemed unnecessary to include the word "consent" in the title to this chapter; after all, if there is no consent to any particular transaction, there can be no intent on its consummation. Certainly, without some measure of consent, the transaction would, indeed, be void; but what if there is a grudging consent—say, a consent obtained by duress?

> R. Huna said: If a man consents to sell something through fear of physical violence,[109] the sale is valid. Why so? Because whenever a man sells, it is under compulsion [presumably he is short of money] and even so the sale is valid. But should we not differentiate between self-generated compulsion [such as the need of money] and external com-

---

of my sister." *Rosh* rules that the word "orphans" "includes minors and adults, male and female."

[106] *Choshen Mishpat* 253:14.

[107] *Bava Batra* 71a.

[108] Ibid. V. *Bava Batra* 65a et seq. and 78a & b for discussions and rulings in connection with sales. For problems arising because of doubt and ambiguity in communal enactments and provisions for taxation, see (inter alia) *Responsa, Rashba* 3:397; 3:407 & 408; *Rosh* 6:19; *Ritva* 157.

[109] Lit., if they hang him and he sells. V. supra p. 187 regarding the legal effect of the purchaser's transgressions of the scriptural injunction "Thou shalt not covet."

pulsion [such as physical violence]?[110]

After debate, the Talmud comes to the conclusion[111] that it is reasonable to suppose that under the applied pressure the reluctant vendor really did make up his mind to sell (e.g. a field); there was a finality of intention; for, as he receives the value of the field, he loses nothing, while at the same time he gains by freeing himself from the suffering being inflicted upon him.[112] In other words, the intent and form of the sale were complete and legal, notwithstanding the way in which they were obtained.[113]

In accepting this rule, Rava tries to limit it, saying that it applies only if the vendor is forced to sell *a* field, that is, he is called upon merely to sell one of his fields and is allowed to choose which. In such a case, it assumed that the sale is not unwelcome to him and, therefore, he intends it to be effective, whereas if he is forced to sell *this* field, that is, one which his torturers specify and which perhaps he particularly wishes to keep for himself, the sale is not valid. However, the Talmud does not accept Rava's limitation and rules that in all cases a sale would be valid. For,

> the betrothal of a woman is analogous to the buying of *this field*,[114] and yet Amemar[115] has laid down that if a woman consents to betroth herself under pressure of physical violence, the betrothal is indeed valid. Mar, b. R. Ashi, however said: In the case of the woman, the betrothal is certainly

---

[110] *Bava Batra* 47b. V. infra p. 258. The distinction is between a "grudging" sale (where money is required) and a "forced" sale (by threat of torture). Under British Common Law, duress invalidates a transaction; under Equity even subtle pressure is sufficient to invalidate it. (Geldart, *Elements of English Law*, p. 35).

[111] *Bava Batra* 48a.

[112] *Rashba*, ad loc., s.v. "*elah*."

[113] V. chap. VIII, note 24.

[114] Because the woman may be regarded as giving herself to the betrother, who is intent on her alone.

[115] The name of an *Amora*, whose ruling in this case is accepted as law.

not valid; he treated the woman cavalierly,[116] and therefore the Rabbis treat him cavalierly and nullify his betrothal.[117]

Even Mar, b. R. Ashi, agrees that according to the rules of
Jewish Civil Law the betrothal is a valid one; it is only by
using supralegal powers that the Rabbis can annul it.

In view of the clear-cut law that a sale under duress is
valid—and the duress need not necessarily be one of physical
violence, but can be any form of threat or blackmail[118]—what
can a vendor who really does not want to sell do in order to
protect his position? He must, if he is able, make a declaration[119]
that the sale is made under duress and that he intends to reclaim the item sold as soon as possible. In their attestation, the
witnesses before whom the declaration is made must themselves
testify, in the case of a sale, that they were aware of the circumstances and were aware of the compulsion.[120]

So far only the position of the vendor has been discussed;
what if a purchaser is obliged to purchase under duress?
Rules Remah: A purchase made under duress is invalid,[121] for
as most sales are made as a result of compulsion, albeit self-
generated because of shortage of money, there is an established principle concerning sale as a result of compulsion,
whereas that principle has never been applied in any form in
the case of a purchase.[122]

---

[116] Lit., "not as it beseems."

[117] *Bava Batra* 48a & b on the understanding that all betrothals in Israel
are on the basis that the Rabbis concur. V. *Aruch Hashulchan, Even
Ha'ezer* 42:2.

[118] *Yad, Mechirah* 10:4, which also quotes an example of commercial
blackmail.

[119] *Moda'ah*—lit., notification.

[120] *Bava Batra* 40b. Otherwise any vendor can "protect" himself by
making such a declaration.

[121] *Choshen Mishpat* 205:12, note.

[122] *Aruch Hashulchan*, loc. cit., para. 3, which also deals with the contro-
versial case of a man who is coerced to marry a certain woman. V.
Maggid Mishneh, Yad Ishut 4:1. V. *Chatam Sofer, Responsa, Even Ha'ezer* 112.

What if coercion is applied to force one to make a gift or waive a right, and the reluctant donor does execute the form of gift or waiver? If the witnesses to the gift or waiver were aware of the compulsion, the gift is invalid even if the donor does not protest; after all, unlike a forced sale where, apart from freeing himself from the discomfort of the torture, he does receive value, in the case of a gift or waiver he receives nothing. If the witnesses are not aware of the circumstances, the donor should make a declaration, for as the gift or waiver does not depend on consideration, but merely on the intention of the donor, any caveat in his intention invalidates it.[123]

The cases of sales or gifts referred to above are those in which the predatory buyer or donee has, from the outset, indicated his intention to acquire the item concerned and only takes possession after the form of transfer has been executed. What if he first steals the article so that it enters his possession entirely illegally and then offers to buy it, giving the vendor no choice? Rambam rules that in such circumstances the sale is totally invalid, and it is not even necessary for the vendor to make any declaration in order to avoid it.[124]

It must be remarked that while in Jewish Civil Law—be it in the Law of Property or in the Law of Tort[125] — duress in itself is not an excuse, it *is* in criminal and religious law. To be punishable under those laws, the perpetrator must act willfully, and willfulness is obviously excluded if he is acting under duress.

---

[123] Yad, Mechirah 10:3. V. *Tosafot, Bava Batra* 48a, s.v. *"amar."* For a forced purchase at less than full value v. *Radvaz, Responsa* 1:55. For a forced *Hefker* (renunciation) v. Talmud Yerushalmi, *Sukkah* 4:2 and commentaries; v. *Maharit, Responsa, Choshen Mishpat* 4, who deals with a case of one who forcibly had himself treated as an heir to an estate, which under Jewish law he was not.

[124] *Yad,* op. cit. 5. V. *Kesef Mishneh,* loc. cit., which tries to find a Talmudic source for this ruling.

[125] V. supra p. 232. A man is responsible for the damage he does even under the "duress of sleep." (V. *Berachot* 4b.)

The All-Merciful absolves any person who acts under pressure, as it is written, "but unto the damsel, thou shalt do nothing."[126]

Similarly, duress by force majeure such as sickness relieves a man of any punishment should he, for example, consume prohibited food.[127] Even the forgetfulness of old age is considered duress.

> Be careful to respect an old man who has forgotten his knowledge through no fault of his own [through illness, or weariness from fighting for sustenance]. For it was said: "Not only the unbroken Tablets [the second set] of the Decalogue, but also the fragments of the earlier Tablets [the set broken by Moshe][128] were placed in the Holy Ark."[129]

There is a basic law that if one enjoys any food or drink, even that taken for medicinal purposes, he is obliged to recite the appropriate benedictions before and after partaking. It is understandable, therefore, that Remah adds the note, "But if he is forced to eat or drink, although his palate benefits, nevertheless, he does not make any benedictions, seeing he partook under duress."[130] In fact, this ruling is questioned by a number of commentators who find difficulty in distinguishing that case from the case of a sick man who has to eat on the Day of Atonement. Although also under duress (of ill health), he is nevertheless obliged to recite all the appropriate benedictions.[131]

One suggested distinction supporting Remah is to be

---

[126] *Avodah Zarah* 54a, quoting *Devarim* 22:26, the law of a betrothed maiden who is raped in isolated countryside.

[127] *Yad, Yesodei HaTorah* 5:6. However, he may not engage in adultery or even lesser indecency to save his life (ibid. 9, based on *Sanhedrin* 75a).

[128] *Shemot* 32:19.

[129] *Berachot* 8b.

[130] *Orach Chaim* 204:8.

[131] *Magen Avraham,* ad loc.

found in the Talmud itself, quoted above,[132] which distinguishes between self-generated coercion and external coercion, the former being considered far less duress than the latter; being forced to eat is an external coercion, while eating on the Day of Atonement because of ill-health is self-generated or internal coercion. Thus, in the former case no benedictions are due because the eating is under the highest form of duress, while in the latter case the duress is of a lesser degree—the eating is not entirely against the sick man's will and, therefore, it follows that he is obliged to recite the appropriate benedictions.[133]

In leaving this subject, it is worth noting that the first request in our thrice-daily prayers is for *Da'at*, for without knowledge there can be little comprehension, little capacity to recognize that which requires recognition, to distinguish that which requires distinction.[134] Increased knowledge brings with it a desire to repent one's misdemeanors, and following repentance comes atonement, bringing in its wake salvation, health, and blessing.[135]

---

[132] Note 110.

[133] *Oneg Yom Tov, Responsa* 13. V. *Aruch Hashulchan, Orach Chaim* 204:19, which makes another distinction; cf. *Chatam Sofer, Responsa, Orach Chaim* 202; cf. *Or Same'ach* on *Yad*, op. cit.

[134] Talmud Yerushalmi, *Berachot* 5:2.

[135] V. *Megillah* 17b.

Brief Historical Overview

RULINGS IN JEWISH LAW, based as they are on earlier Authorities and Precedents, depend to a great degree on the status and persuasiveness of those Authorities and Precedents, and unlike other systems, the earlier those Authorities flourished and the earlier those Precedents were established, the greater their status and the more powerful their persuasiveness. This results from the fact that the Torah has been transmitted: "Each great sage and Righteous Man received [the teachings of the Torah] from [an earlier] great sage and righteous man, each Head of an Academy and his school having received them from [an earlier] Head of an Academy and his school, as far back as the men of the Great Assembly who received them from the Prophets, of blessed memory all."[1] The Divine revelation at Sinai was the original source, and the closer in time to that source a scholar flourished, the more magisterial are his rulings. This does not mean that scholars of each and every generation are necessarily bound by decisions made in generations immediately preceding their own; it does mean that the chain of transmission is, broadly speaking, divided into six definable periods, and judg-

---

[1] *Ravad*, Prologue to *Sefer Hakabbalah.*

ments rendered by scholars of a later period are subject to, and must be in accordance with, accepted rulings issued in any earlier one of those defined periods.

In researching Jewish law, it is, therefore, important to be acquainted with those periods and, when studying the works of any scholar, to be able to identify the period to which he belongs.[2]

Therefore, against the name of every scholar of whom a brief biography is given, appears a numeral indicating in which of the six definable periods he lived and worked.

Period 1—Scripture: Creation to c. 3440 (320 B.C.E.)

The first period in Jewish history is obviously that covered by Scripture: from Creation to the completion of the Book of Chronicles by Nechemiah,[3] circa 3440 in the Jewish calendar (320 B.C.E.). This period saw the Exodus from Egypt and the establishment of a Jewish Nation, the Divine revelation at Sinai, the entry into the Land of Israel, the creation of the Jewish State and the establishment of a Royal House. This period saw both the establishment and destruction of the First Temple, established in great splendor, only to be ruined when the political fabric of the Jewish State was destroyed, as had been prophesied by the Prophets who were active during a long period of national decadence. It was during this period that the nation split into two kingdoms, Judea and Israel. The Ten Tribes which comprised the larger kingdom Israel, were driven into exile during this time, to be swallowed up and disappear among other nations, the people losing their Jewish identity. The smaller kingdom Judea, lasted longer, its decline dating from the establishment of Babylonian domination in the reign of King Yehoyakim in 3320

---

[2] The present tense is often used in Talmudic scholarship as, by their works, long-deceased scholars live on.

[3] V. *Bava Batra* 15a.

(440 B.C.E.), culminating with the final destruction of the
Temple eighteen years later. Then began the seventy years
of exile foretold by the Prophet, Yirmeyahu,[4] towards the
end of which occurred the incidents related in the Book of
Esther, which gave rise to the Festival of Purim.[5]

The fact that the destruction was spread over eighteen
years, and that the exile took place in stages, helped keep the
chain of tradition alive in Babylonia, so that when the new
exiles arrived they were still able to meet scholars who had
been taken there earlier.[6] This was the foundation of the
Babylonian community that ultimately established the Yeshivahs which for many hundreds of years were the power-
houses of Jewish scholarship and which laid the building blocks
of the Talmud and of Talmudic study as we have them today.

During this Scriptural period, the seventy years of the
first exile ended; Ezra and Nechemiah and their colleagues
led those willing to follow back to their own land, under a
mandate given to them by Darius II (son of Artaxerxes and
Esther), where eventually they completed the building of
the Second Temple, in 3410 (350 B.C.E.) It was with the re-
settlement that the spirit of prophecy was lost to Israel, and
the chain of tradition gradually entered into its second identifiable period under the leadership of the *Anshei Knesset
Hagedolah*, members of the Great Assembly or Synod.

Period 2—Anshei Knesset Hagedolah, Zugot and Tan-
naim: c. 3450 (310 B.C.E.)–3960 (200 C.E.)

This period, which began some forty or fifty years after
the construction of the Second Temple, after the passing of
the last of the Prophets, and which ended circa 3960 (200
C.E.), can itself be divided into **four** distinct eras.

---

4   *Yirmeyahu* 29:10.
5   V. supra p. 31.
6   *Sanhedrin* 38a; *Rashi*, ad loc., s.v. "*shehikdim*."

The first covers some 130 years during which time Israel was under the leadership of the *Anshei Knesset Hagedolah*, leaders who felt it their duty to ensure that the text of Scripture and the traditions of the Oral Law were passed on in scrupulously correct form. For this purpose, and to formalize the order of prayer, they gathered in synod, and they derived their title from these vital activities.[7]

The Great Assembly was, of course, based in Jerusalem, and once the Temple was rebuilt, they returned to the Hall of Hewed Stone in the Temple precinct,[8] the traditional home of the Sanhedrin. At the same time, however, because a large, well-established, well-organized Jewish community had elected to remain in Babylonia, that country too was a center of Jewish study. Little is known to us of the early Babylonian scholars of this and subsequent periods, because they accepted the writ of the Eretz Yisrael scholars. Indeed, the Mishnah itself, which climaxed the entire period, having been redacted in Eretz Yisrael Yeshivahs, heirs to the Eretz Yisrael tradition, does not make mention of any contemporary or earlier Babylonian scholars.[9]

During most of this era, Persia was mistress of much of the civilized world, and the Jews, whether in Eretz Yisrael or Babylonia, lived under the tolerant rule of the Persian kings. Towards the end of the era, Alexander the Great of Macedonia, himself a disciple of the Greek Philosopher Aristotle,[10] conquered most of the Persian Empire and brought Eretz Yisrael into his domain. Fortunately, out of deference to the then leader of the small Jewish Nation, which after all only occupied an area of some 1,200 square miles in the vicinity of Jerusalem,

---

[7] V. *Megillah* 17b; *Berachot* 33a; *Nedarim* 37b; *Kiddushin* 30a; c.f. Talmud Yerushalmi, *Megillah* 3:7, "They brought back *Hagadol*—the great and mighty and revered God" (from the *Amidah*).

[8] V. supra p. 15.

[9] V. Rabbi A. Miller, *Exalted People*, paras. 488-500.

[10] V. supra Chap. VII, note 141.

he agreed to spare Jerusalem itself and to establish friendly relations with the Jewish Nation.[11] The leader of the Jewish People at that time who so impressed the conqueror, was Shimon Hatzaddik (the Just), the incumbent High Priest, accepted as having been the last leader of the era of the Great Assembly.

The second era in this period lasted some 270 years, during which Jewish scholarship in Eretz Yisrael was, after a transitionary period, dominated by a group lead by the "Zugot," literally translated as "Pairs." As the term implies, the supreme leadership was divided between two men, one who held the title Nasi (President), the other his slightly junior colleague, with the title of Av Beit Din (Head or Senior Judge of the Sanhedrin).[12] These Zugot and their predecessors are listed in their first chapter of Avot; indeed, it is in that chapter that we find the first quotations from individual scholars, beginning with a collective quote from the Men of the Great Assembly.

In the wider world, the hegemony of empire was beginning to disintegrate. On the death of Alexander the Great, his dominions were divided among four of his generals: Ptolemy took the kingdom of Egypt; Selucid that of Syria; Antigonos, Asia Minor; and Philip, Macedonia. Originally, Judea, as the Eretz Yisrael kingdom was known, came under the dominion of Ptolemy of Egypt, but subsequently fell to the Selucid Dynasty of Syria, which attempted to suppress Judaism and substitute Hellenism as the national culture or religion. It was during this era that the Hasmonean revolt against the then Selucid ruler, Antiochus Epiphanes, succeeded, and circa 3620 (140 B.C.E.) the Hasmonean Dynasty was founded amid popular acclaim—a dynasty which lasted until Herod the Idumean assassinated all remaining members of the family and usurped the throne some one hundred years before the destruction of the Second Temple.

---

[11] *Yoma* 69a.

[12] *Chagigah* 16b.

The successful Hasmonean revolt is, of course, commemorated by the Festival of Chanukkah—the Festival of Lights. But, unknown at the time, these lights also marked the beginning of the ascendancy of the Roman Empire. Initially Rome maintained friendly relations with Judea, lasting some thirty years, but thereafter embarked upon a relentless course of subjugation that culminated in the conquest of Judea and the destruction of the Second Temple in 3830 (70 B.C.E.).

During this time there existed a large, prosperous and well-organized community in Alexandria, Egypt. A community of scholars whose scholarship was based on the Greek translation of the Torah known as the Septuagint, which celebrated the Festival of Pharos in honor of the completion of that work, it has left us little, other than the works of Philo Judeas. Successful as that community was in its own time, it is not part of the chain of Torah transmission.

In contrast to their brethren in Judea, the Babylonian Jews lived under a benign sovereign power, ruled by their own exilarchs, all descended from the Royal House of David. Far from the troubles, turmoil, and oppressions of the Mother Country, Babylonian Jewry lived peaceful and uneventful lives, and those so inclined were able to concentrate on the study of the Torah, remaining faithful to its traditions. It was from Babylon that there arose at this time a leader who was to infuse new vigor and life into the community in Judea and to lead the Jewish people into the next link in the Torah chain—that of the early *Tannaim*, the **third** era of this period.

The fact that Hillel himself was a Babylonian who, because of his erudition, succeeded to the post of *Nasi*, does indicate the degree of scholarship there was among Babylonian Jewry. Hillel himself was the founder of a dynasty which lasted until 4135 (375 C.E.), of which, except for a short break at the time of the destruction of the Temple, son succeeded father to the office of *Nasi*, the last of whom was a descendant who bore his name—Hillel; a dynasty which played a pivotal role in the transmission of the Torah and which, by virtue of its descent (albeit through the female line) from the Royal House of David, acted for a number of generations as both the spiritual and political leaders of the people of Judea, long after it had lost the right to call itself a State.

In contrast to their predecessors, Hillel, Shammai (his colleague), and their respective disciples are the first to be quoted extensively in the Mishnah and the Talmud, and one may be permitted to wonder why; had there been no intellectual Talmudic activity hitherto? "You ask: Why did the early scholars apparently leave so much to the later ones?" writes R. Sherrira Gaon in his famous *Iggeret* "That is not so." In detail he explains that the early generations had more knowledge than the later ones, and if there were doubts they were resolved by a vote in the Sanhedrin. Because of the unanimous acceptance of the ultimate decisions, they became binding law and there was no necessity to report the surrounding debate. Later, as the standard of scholarship declined during periods of harassment and oppression, when the Sanhedrin could not convene in formal session, problems remained unresolved. It was no longer possible to hand down comprehensive decisions to later generations and so the debate itself and the doubts discussed were reported to enable later generations to resolve their own problems.

The era of early *Tannaim*, during which Judea was under the domination of an often cruel and capricious Rome, ended with the destruction of the Second Temple in 3830 (70 C.E.), when the fourth and final era of this period began, that of the later *Tannaim*.

It is these *Tannaim* who are most featured in the Talmud, as it is their work which forms the basis of our Mishnah. Seeing scholarship decline, knowing of the persecutions, of the deaths[13] of 24,000 eminent scholars, R. Yehudah Hanasi decided

---

[13] R. Sherira Gaon uses the word "*Shmad*" (persecution) in reporting on the deaths of these scholars, pupils of R. Akiva. Today the period of the counting of the Omer (between Pesach and Shavuot) is kept as a period of mourning because of this tragedy.

to formalize the Oral Law. Hitherto, teachings were handed down by word of mouth from teacher to pupil, each teacher using his own favored idiom. Gathering the wealth of material available to him, R. Yehudah Hanasi, or Rabi, as he is known, together with his colleagues, redacted[14] and edited a fixed text—the Mishnah we know today—the Mishnah which forms the basis of our Talmud.

This, Rabi was able to do because of the tranquillity Judea enjoyed in his own time due, in no small measure, to his warm friendship with the then Roman Emperor, known in the Talmud as Antoninus, but usually identified as Marcus Aurelius.

The fact that a number of Rabi's closest colleagues and greatest disciples[15] had traveled up from Babylon to study with or under him indicates that in that country too, Jewish scholarship flourished, although from the Mishnah there is no hint of this, as no Babylonian scholar is quoted. Indeed, the fact that Rabi, in all his eminence, was subject in Jewish eyes to the authority of the exilarch, indicates that the Baby-

---

[14] Whether the Mishnah was actually committed to writing for general publication, or only for private use, or whether it was not committed to writing at all until a later date, Rabi merely formalizing the oral transmission, is a matter of dispute among scholars. R. Sherira himself sometimes uses a word meaning "edited" or "redacted" and sometimes a word meaning "wrote."

[15] E.g., R. Natan Habavli; R. Chiyya and his sons; R. Abba Ayyevu, known as Rav. V. *Magen Avot Tashbatz* (*Avot* 2:1), who explains that the title "Rabbi" was given to a Judean scholar, while that of "Rav" to a Babylonian scholar. Sometimes the same person is known as Rav and sometimes Rabbi, indicating that originally he was a Babylonian scholar who subsequently emigrated to Judea. (The title of "Rabban" was given to the *Nasi*.) There is a familiar saying (R. Sherira Gaon), "Greater than the title Rav is the title Rabbi; greater than the title Rabbi is Rabban; greater than the title Rabban is his own unadorned name" (e.g., Hillel, the founder of the dynasty, who bore no title).

lonian community was extremely well-established and organized.[16]

The scholars of this period, the "*Tannaim*," knew the entire Oral Law by heart. It was with the redaction of the Mishnah that this second period in the chain of transmission of the Torah came to an end; the Mishnah could now easily be committed to writing, and no longer did scholars qualify for the formal title of *Tanna*. No later scholar dared differ from a decision of a *Tanna* unless he, the later scholar, could find support from the views expressed by another *Tanna*; the authority of the Mishnah on all succeeding generations is absolute.[17]

Period 3—Amoraim and Rabbanan Savorai: c. 3960 (200 C.E.)–4350 (590 C.E.)

The next identifiable period is that which began after the redaction of the Mishnah and lasted for some 400 years until the completion of the Babylonian Talmud (including those tractates known as the minor tractates), around the year 4350 (590 C.E.). The first three hundred of those years were dominated by scholars known as *Amoraim*, which can be translated as "interpreters"—interpreters of the Mishnah. It was their function to understand every nuance of earlier rulings, to reconcile apparent contradictions, to know which of the conflicting views quoted in a Mishnah prevailed as the Halachah, and to apply those rulings to problems which arose in their own day. It is the recorded debates, arguments, and rulings of the *Amoraim* which make up the Gemara. The word "Gemara" can be translated as "tradition" or "memorizing of verbal teachings,"[18] a word chosen to indicate that it was still studied orally, in contrast to the Mishnah which had

---

[16] *Horayot* 11b.; v. supra p. 267.
[17] V. *Kesef Mishneh, Yad, Mamrim* 2:1.
[18] Jastrow Dictionary.

by that time been committed to writing.

While this period was dominated by the great Yeshivahs of Babylonia at Neharde'a, Sura, later at Pumpedita, and for a short while in Masa Mechesia, nevertheless there was considerable scholastic activity in Israel, at least during the first 150 years of the period, during which time Yeshivahs flourished in Caesarea and Tiberias.

The foundations of the Jerusalem Talmud were laid in the Yeshivah of Tiberias with its final redaction around the year 4110 (340 C.E.) in Sepphoris. The formalization of the Babylonian Talmud began fifty years later in a process which lasted some one hundred years, with the work on the major tractates being completed in 4260 (500 C.E.). With the Gemara arranged in systematized order, including only those which the editors considered authentic teachings, the verbal transmission of the Oral Law came to an end. From then on, no scholar was authorized to insert or in any way materially alter any Talmudic teaching; indeed even the authority to legislate for the Jewish people as a whole ceased at that time.[19] Thus no later scholar may in any way dispute a ruling by any Authority quoted in the Gemara unless he can find support from other Authorities quoted in it or in equal works, such as the Yerushalmi, *Sifrei* or *Sifra*.

It was during this period that Christianity became the official religion of what was becoming the decadent Roman Empire. The Jews of Eretz Yisrael, as well as others living within the boundaries of that Empire, suffered considerable persecution, which was one of the major causes of the decline of Eretz Yisrael as a Jewish center. Before the final collapse of the Western Roman Empire, Eretz Yisrael had been one of the battlegrounds between the old Roman Empire and a new Persian Empire under its energetic Sassanid kings, and it became a despoiled and ravaged land. The fourth century saw the last flickers of the flame of Jewish life and

---

[19] *Bava Metzia* 86a; *Rashi*, s.v. "*sof*"; v. Soncino Talmud, p. 493, note 6.

learning in Eretz Yisrael, a flame not to be lit again for many centuries. Consequently, the Eretz Yisrael Rabbis of that era became masters of homily, for they saw it as their duty to encourage with welcome words of hope and conciliation a people who were too weighed down by care to have much heart for the intricate study of the Mishnah and the Talmud.[20]

At the beginning of the Amoraic period, Babylonian Jewry suffered too, at the hands of the Magi, priests of the Zoroastrian religion, which at that time was being revived with the establishment of the new Persian empire. Fortunately, this was only for a short while, and within a few years the Jews of Babylonia were able to resume their normal lives, during which time the community prospered and Jewish scholarship flourished, a happy situation which lasted for some two hundred years until Jezdegerd II ascended the Persian throne. He initiated a period of persecution which lasted some fifty years, after which time Talmudic scholarship once again flourished. The Babylonian Talmud owes its preeminence today to the scholars of that later period, who were fully aware of the achievements of their predecessors, both in Eretz Yisrael (as incorporated in the Jerusalem Talmud), and in Babylonia (as they themselves received the tradition). Left in peace to concentrate on their studies, they were able to produce a work which has proved over the generations to be the lifeline of the Jewish people.[21]

This period saw the expansion of the Diaspora, with the establishment of new communities in what is now Turkey, and in Greece, Spain, and Northern Africa, all of which looked to the great Yeshivahs of Babylonia for their spiritual guidance, a state of affairs which was the main feature of the next period.

---

[20] Halpern, *History of Our People: Post Biblical Times*, chap. VIII.
[21] V. supra p. 23.

There was a short transitionary period between the closing of the Talmud and the first identifiable post-Talmudic era, which was bridged by scholars known as the *Rabbanan Savorai*. This title signifies that it was their function to apply logic and reasoning to understand and transmit Talmudic rulings, differing from their predecessors, the Amoraim, whose scholarship allowed them to amend existing text and create new Rabbinical laws.

Period 4—Geonim: 4350 (590 C.E.)–4798 (1038 C.E.)

During this period, the word "*Gaon*" was not used as an adjective, as it is today to describe an outstanding scholar, but was a formal title bestowed on the Principals of the two Great Yeshivahs of Sura and Pumbedita.[22] It was a period which lasted almost 450 years until midway through the eleventh century, during much of which these two Yeshivahs served as the central sources of Torah scholarship for most of the growing Diaspora, with the final arbiters of the Law being the two *Geonim* who led them. Halachic problems were sent to Babylonia to be considered by the eminent scholars in the Yeshivahs who, under the guidance of their *Gaon*, would write the appropriate responsum, the letter then being signed by the *Gaon* himself. In turn, the far-flung communities of the Diaspora felt the responsibility of supporting the Yeshivahs financially. The Jewish community in Babylonia itself was governed by a triumvirate led by the Exilarch (a descendant of the Royal House of David who acted as lay and political leader) and the two *Geonim* of the Yeshivahs, an arrangement which often gave rise to tension and conflict.

However, as the communities of the Diaspora grew, and more and more eminent scholars left Babylonia for these

---

[22] Early in this period there was a Yeshivah in Peroz Shavor (Neharde'a) which was active for about 60 years.

communities,[23] the influence of the two Yeshivahs and their *Geonim* declined, as, correspondingly, did the financial support they received from the Diaspora. The Gaonic era is considered to have ended with the death of R. Hai Gaon in 4798 (1038 C.E.), although the two Yeshivahs remained open, first independently and then jointly, in Baghdad, for a further 150 years, still granting their heads the title of *Gaon*.

It is a matter of debate as to whether a Geonic ruling is binding on later generations in the same way as rulings of the *Tannaim* were binding on the *Amoraim*, and those of the *Amoraim* binding on the *Geonim*.[24]

Period 5—Rishonim: 4790 (1038 C.E.)–c. 5160 (1400 C.E.)

This period, which may be defined as the period of the *Rishonim* (translated as "early" scholars or commentators), lasted for four centuries, during which time there was no single central authority, and centers of learning sprang up and thrived, only to disappear, at various times in different places. It would not be an exaggeration to say that Talmudic study in our own day can only flourish because of the academic activity of the scholars of those four centuries. This period produced the great commentators whose explanations are basic to our understanding of Scripture, Mishnah, Gemara and Midrash; scholars who adjudicated on the disputes between earlier Authorities, thereby giving us the basis for our Halachah; scholars who gathered these decisions and codified them, giving us our first systematized codes of conduct; scholars who were poets from whom we have much of our current liturgy; scholars who wrote histories, and scholars who were philosophers and moralists.

---

[23] V. foreword to *Sefer Ha'itim*, para. 1, regarding Talmud study in Spain; *Ravad, Sefer Hakabbalah*, chap. VII, reporting the incident of the four captives.

[24] V. *Rosh, Sanhedrin* 4:6; cf. *Choshen Mishpat* 25:1, note.

Because of the relatively wide geographic spread and lack of easy communication, there were differences in tradition, emphasis, and methodological approach. Hence, Jewish scholarship of that period can be divided into four major geographical areas.

First is that of the Sephardic lands (i.e., places settled by the Jews of Spain and their descendants, and others who followed the Halachic ruling of the Rambam) which include the small settlements in Eretz Yisrael itself, the remnants of the Babylonian or Iraqi settlements, the communities of Egypt and of other North African countries—Morocco, Algeria, and Tunisia. Perhaps the most important center of the Sephardic tradition of those times was that of Moorish Spain. There, under the rule of benevolent and liberal Moorish Caliphs, the Jews enjoyed "golden years" during which scholarship flourished, as it did for an even longer period in the much smaller sister communities of Portugal. In both countries, the Jews eventually suffered under Christian rule, although in Portugal their lot was somewhat better, as its rulers shielded them from some of the great excesses of fanatical clergymen. Unfortunately, by the end of the fifteenth century, Jewish communities had ceased to exist in either of these countries.

The second geographical area of major importance during this period was that of northern France, consisting in the main of what is now known as Île-de-France and Alsace-Lorraine, together with southwestern Germany, although there were important scholars as far north as York in England and as far south as Vienna in Austria. This area was the cradle of the Ashkenazic tradition as western Jewry knows it today.

The third geographical area was that of Provence in southern France, which had close connections with the communities south of the Pyrenees and was thus dominated by the Sephardic tradition of Moorish Spain.

The fourth major geographical area of Jewish settlement was that of Italy, the communities there being among the oldest of the Diaspora. Torah scholarship in fact arrived at the Ashkenazic areas of Europe from the early Italian settlements, and the deep analytical approach adopted by the group of scholars whose work appears on virtually every page of our Talmud as *Tosafot* was developed from the methodology and approach of the early Italian Yeshivahs.[25]

A Halachic ruling of a *Rishon* carries great weight; indeed there are views that a *Rishon* has the competence to overrule the decision of a *Gaon* of the previous period,[26] but so vast was the output of scholastic literature during the Rishonic period and so diverse were the methods, approaches, and conclusions, that had it not been for the work of the great codifiers of the fourteenth and sixteenth centuries, it would have been virtually impossible today to arrive at a clear Halachic decision on any number of disputed problems. Indeed, in our own contemporary times, matters would have been complicated by the discoveries in great libraries (such as those at the Vatican or the Bodleian) of hitherto unknown manuscripts recording interpretations and writings by eminent *Rishonim* which were lost to scholars of intervening generations.

The earliest comprehensive codifier was R. Moshe b. Maimon, known as Maimonides or Rambam, who lived in the twelfth century. His codification is known as the *Mishneh Torah* (Repetition or Précis of the Torah) or as the *Yad Hachazakah* (Mighty Hand), the Hebrew word *Yad* having the numerical value of fourteen, which is the number of separate books which comprise the work. It is one of the pillars upon which Halachah is founded, but as many of Rambam's sources were disputed and his conclusions contested by scholars of his own and immediately succeeding generations, it was not accepted as entirely binding. Thus there was consid-

---

[25] Rabbi N. S. Greenspan, *Pilpulah shel Torah*, chap. 12, ad fin.
[26] V. supra p. 273 et seq.

erable judicial discretion for the next two centuries until R. Yaakov b. Asher published his Halachic compendium, *Arba'ah Turim* (Four Rows).[27] In this he codified the rules of the Jewish faith that were relevant to his times (and ours), omitting those of, for example, Levitical Cleanliness or Sacrificial Ritual which had lapsed through historical circumstances. R. Yaakov, as the son of Rosh, was of course educated in the Franco-German tradition, but, like his father, fled Germany, first settling in Barcelona and subsequently in Toledo, in which cities he came into contact with scholars of the Sephardic tradition.

Unlike Rambam, R. Yaakov quotes his sources together with interpretations offered by earlier scholars. More than any of his predecessors, he cites opinions of earlier adjudicators and codifiers; virtually all opinions available to him from the Geonic period through to the earlier centuries of the Rishonic period, whether they be Sephardic or Ashkenazic, are mentioned, as are the numerous customs of which he was aware.

By the time the Rishonic period came to an end in the last quarter of the fourteenth century, the *Tur* (as this work is known) was accepted as an authoritative Code, bringing some order to the mass of Halachic literature produced during the Rishonic period. Its importance and preeminence was enhanced by the decision of R. Yosef Karo to base his own magnum opus, *Beit Yosef*, around it.

Period 6—Acharonim: 5280 (1480 C.E.) to Present Day

To contrast them with their predecessors, great scholars of this period, which includes contemporary times, are known as *Acharonim*, "latter" ones. By the beginning of this period,

---

[27] V. *Shemot* 28:17 et seq.

at the end of the fifteenth century, Talmudic scholarship had declined in the Sephardic lands while continuing to flourish in the new communities of central and eastern Europe, which were the successors of the Franco-German settlements destroyed by the expulsions of the thirteenth and fourteenth centuries. Early in this period, R. Yosef Karo published his Halachic compendium, the *Shulchan Aruch* (Prepared Table), otherwise known as the *Codes*. The fact that this work was a digest of the *Beit Yosef*, in which a detailed examination of the source of every law was made, and the fact that the author's ultimate adjudication was based on the majority opinions of three giants of Halachah—Rif, Rambam, and the Rosh—gave it an unchallenged role as the code par excellance of Jewish Law. Although the author was a Sephardi steeped in Sephardic tradition, the amendments of Remah in his notes, which quote the differing rulings of the Ashkenazic tradition, served to complete the work, to make it universally acceptable to all the people of Israel in whatever communities they may find themselves.

It is true that eminent scholars differ with the conclusions of the author on a number of issues, and that many segments of the Jewish people follow these dissenting views; nevertheless, in its entirety it remains the Code of Law of all the Jewish people; certainly no serious contemporary scholar would dream of challenging any ruling found therein, unless it were one which had already been challenged by one of the great scholars who were active early in that period of the *Acharonim*.[28]

Through the intervening centuries, great scholars have arisen whose works have been accepted as authoritative, and while in theory a modern-day scholar could differ, in practice the rulings of these giants of Halachah have been accepted as Law.

---

[28] V. Rabbi Yonatan Eibishitz, *Urim v'Tumim Kitzur Takfo Kohen*, p. 96.

Perhaps the best way to sum up our relationship with our predecessors is by using a Talmudic metaphor: "If the earlier scholars were as angels, we are men; but if the earlier scholars were men, we are like asses,"[29] which a contemporary preacher interpreted thus: "If we consider our predecessors to be angels, we may be treated as reasonable men; but if we consider them to have been men no wiser than us, we deserve to be treated as asses."

---

[29] *Shabbat* 112b; cf. *Eruvin* 53a, which compares the intellectual powers of earlier and later generations.

Biographical and Bibliographical Notes

The figures in brackets after names refer to the historical periods discussed in "Brief Historical Overview."
R. stands for Rav or Rabbi; b. stands for *ben* (son of).

R. ABBA [3]: Third generation (c. 300 C.E.) Babylonian *Amora*. Eventually settled in Eretz Yisrael, although occasionally traveled back to Babylonia on business.

R. ABBA b. ABBA: See AVUHA DE SHMUEL.

ABBAYE [3]: R. Nachmeni b. Keilil; fourth-generation Babylonian *Amora* (c. 340 C.E.) who headed the Yeshivah at Pumbedita for thirteen years. Many of his debates with his colleague (and successor) Rava are reported in the Babylonian Talmud, which cites them as masterpieces of incisive analytical reasoning (*Bava Batra* 134a).

R. AKIVA [2]: Acknowledged head of the third generation of *Tannaim* (c. 120 C.E.), he began the task of organizing the entire Oral Law, laying the foundation of the Mishnah and other contemporary Talmudic compilations. An ardent nationalist, he gave unstinted support to the Bar Kochba uprising (132-135 C.E.), ultimately suffering martyrdom after its collapse.

AMEMAR [3]: Babylonian *Amora* of the sixth generation (c. 400 C.E.). A native of Neharde'a, he eventually became the spiritual head of that town (*Berachot* 12a) and possibly of the nearby town of Mechuza (*Shabbat* 95a), presumably acting as Rosh Yeshivah in both places.

R. MOSHE AVIGDOR AMIEL [6]: Born in 1883, he first studied in Telshe Yeshivah, and subsequently under R. Chaim Soloveitchik and R. Chaim Ozer Grodzinsky. In 1920, he was appointed Rabbi in Antwerp where he became one of the leaders of Religious Zionism and established a network of educational institutions. In 1936 he was called to be Chief Rabbi of Tel Aviv, where he continued his educational work, establishing inter alia the Yeshivah High School *Hayishuv Hechadash*, which was renamed in his honor, after his death in 1946.

ARUCH HASHULCHAN [6]: Updated Code of Law by R. Yechiel Mechil Halevi Epstein (d. 1908). Ordered and numbered the same way as the *Shulchan Aruch* itself, it includes problems arising, and rulings laid down, after that work was completed, often giving legal justification for accepted practice. The author was the father of the Torah Temimah.

ARUCH L'NER: See R. YAAKOV ETTLINGER.

R. ASHI [3]: Leading *Amora* of the sixth generation and head of the Babylonian Yeshivah of Masa Mechesia. A scholar of great wealth, he combined Torah and secular greatness (*Gittin* 59a) and succeeded in attracting to his Yeshivah the most eminent scholars of his day. With their assistance he began (c. 4110) the arduous task of compiling and redacting the Babylonian Talmud in the form we have it today.

R. AVIAH [3]: Babylonian *Amora* of the fourth generation (c. 350 C.E.). R. Aviah spent some time in Eretz Yisrael studying under the leading Eretz Yisrael *Amoraim* of the period.

AVNEI MILUIM: See KETZOT HACHOSHEN.

AVRAHAM AVINU [1]: Abraham, our father, first of the three founding Patriarchs of the Jewish race (1800 B.C.E.).

AVTALYON [2]: Descended from proselytes who traced their lineage to Sennacherib, King of Assyria (*Gittin* 57b), he and his colleague Shemayah rose to the highest rank, becoming one of the five *Zugot* who succeeded to the leadership of the people after the dissolution of the Great Assembly (c. 50 B.C.E.).

AVUHA de SHMUEL [3]: Father of Shmuel, Talmudic appellation of R. Abba b. Abba, a first-generation Babylonian *Amora* who studied in Eretz Yisrael under Rabi, but who returned to Neharde'a to become one of the spiritual leaders of Babylonian Jewry.

R. AYYEVU: See RAV.

R. CHAIM YOSEF DAVID AZULAI: See CHIDAH.

BACH [6]: Acronym of *Bayit Chadash*, the title of one of the two major commentaries on the *Tur* (the other being the *Beit Yosef* of R. Yosef Karo), the magnum opus of R. Yoel Sirkes, Rabbi of Krakow until his death in 1640. The Bach was also the author of numerous glosses of textual corrections of the Talmud, *Tur*, Codes, and other major works.

R. BANA'AH [2-3]: Rosh Yeshivah in Tiberias who lived at the end of the Tannaic and beginning of the Amoraic periods. He is quoted in late Tannaic compilations.

BARAITA D'RABBI YISHMAEL [2]: Collection of 13 hermeneutical principles collocated by R. Yishmael b. Elisha.

BE'ER HAMAYIM [6]: Responsa of R. Rafael Yaakov b. Avraham Menashe (1762-1832), of the Rabbis of Salonika.

BEIT HABECHIRAH: See MEIRI.

BEIT HILLEL [2]: Early *Tannaim*, disciples of Hillel the Elder. Parties to many disputations with their contemporaries of the

School of Shammai, they eventually prevailed and their rulings became the Halachah.

BEIT SHAMMAI [2]: Disciples of Shammai, early *Tannaim*, often in dispute with the disciples of Hillel.

BEIT YOSEF: See R. YOSEF KARO.

BERTINORO [6]: R. Ovadiah of Bertinoro, Italy. Of the first generation of *Acharonim* (c. 1450-1510), his commentary on the Mishnah has become the standard work, and rarely is a *Mishnayot* published without it. R. Ovadiah, after a long journey lasting some three years, settled in Jerusalem and did much to improve the quality of spiritual life in the holy city.

BINYAN TZION: See R. YAAKOV ETTLINGER.

BIRKAT CHAIM: See OTZER CHAIM.

BIRKEI YOSEF: See CHIDA.

RABBI B. BLAU [6]: Currently Rav of the Stamford Hill Beth Hamedrash, London.

BOAZ [1]: Descended from the first Prince of the Tribe of Yehudah (Judah), he married Ruth the Moabitess and became the great-grandfather of King David.

RABBI ZVI HIRSCH CHAJES [6]: (1805-1855) Rabbi of Kalish. Widely respected as a great Talmudic Authority whose scientific and philosophical scholarship were also recognized. Apart from Halachic responsa, he wrote extensively on methodology, philosophy, and Jewish history.

R. CHANANEL: See RACH.

R. CHANINA [3]: Babylonian *Amora* of the first generation. He settled in Eretz Yisrael where he became a distinguished disciple of Rabbi, in turn becoming the mentor of the leading Eretz Yisrael *Amoraim* of the next generation.

CHATAM SOFER [6]: Title given to the writings of R. Moshe Sofer, Rabbi of Pressburg, Hungary, from 1806 until his death in 1839. The Chatam Sofer spearheaded the battle against reform and innovation in Judaism and was recognized as the leader of Orthodox Jewry in southeastern Europe. Most of his voluminous writings were published posthumously by his family.

CHAVAT YA'IR [6]: Collected responsa of R. Chaim Ya'ir Bacharach (1638-1702), a leading German Talmudic scholar who possessed considerable scientific knowledge coupled with mystical inclinations.

CHAZON ISH [6]: Title under which R. Avraham Yeshayah Karelitz (1878-1953), published his writings. The recognized leading Halachic Authority of his day, he settled in Bnei Brak prior to the outbreak of World War II. The practical application of his vast scholarship was of great help to religious kibbutzim and other agricultural settlements wishing to adhere to the agricultural laws of the Torah.

CHELKAT MECHOKEK [6]: Major commentary on Code *Even Ha'ezer* by R. Moshe Lina (1605?-1658). A contemporary and colleague of R. Heschel of Krakow, and of Shach, he served as Rabbi of Slonim, *Av Beit Din* of Vilna, and finally as Rabbi of Brisk, all in Lithuania.

CHIDA [6]: Acronym of the name of R. Chaim Yosef David Azulai. Born in Jerusalem (1724) to a family of Spanish origin, he spent most of his active years traveling as an emissary of the impoverished communities of Eretz Yisrael. His last mission ended in Livorno, Italy, in 1778, and he remained in that city until his death in 1806. He was a prolific writer and authored books on a variety of subjects of Jewish interest, including Halachah, mysticism, religious devotion, biography, and Jewish folk stories.

R. CHISDA [3]: Babylonian *Amora* of the second and third generations. Out of his personal wealth he rebuilt the Yeshivah of Sura, which had previously relocated to Masa Mechesia, serving as Rosh Yeshivah for ten years until his death in 309.

R. CHIYYA [2]: A late *Tanna* of the transitional generation. Of Babylonian origin, he emigrated to Eretz Yisrael where he became both a close disciple and collaborator of Rabi. He himself compiled *Tosefta* on the entire Talmud which have become intermingled with the *Baraita*, a similar compilation by his pupil R. Oshayah.

DAVID HAMELECH [1]: King David, first King of Israel to come from the tribe of Judah. He conquered the Philistines, captured Jerusalem and made plans for the building of the Temple, a task accomplished by his son King Solomon. Musician and poet, he authored the Book of Psalms.

DIVREI CHAIM [6]: Collection of the responsa of R. Chaim Halberstam, Rabbi of Sanz (Nowy Sacz), Galicia (d. 1876). A recognized Halachic authority, he was also the founder of an important Chassidic dynasty.

DUBNER MAGGID [6]: R. Yaakov Kranz (1741-1804), a renowned preacher who invariably produced an appropriate parable to illustrate the point he was currently making. As well as holding different pulpits at various times he traveled extensively in Poland and Germany, preaching to large and appreciative audiences.

R. AKIVA EGER [6]: (1761-1837), Rabbi of Posen (Germany); renowned for great scholarship coupled with exemplary piety and humility. His notes and novellae on the Talmud and his collected responsa are much studied in the Yeshivahs of Lithuanian origin. Indeed, R. Akiva Eger is considered a pioneer of the contemporary analytical approach to dialectic.

R. YONATAN EIBISHITZ [6]: Prominent eighteenth-century Talmudist, Kabbalist and preacher (c. 1690-1764). A child prodigy, his first appointment was as Rosh Yeshivah of Prague, in which role he was numbered among the leading Rabbis who pronounced excommunication on the Shabbetaian sect. In 1741, by which time he had become Dayan of Prague, he was appointed Rav of Metz a post he held until his election in 1750 as Rabbi of the "Three Communities"—Altona, Hamburg, and Wandsbeck. Unfortunately his remaining years were blighted by the accusation that he himself was a secret Shabbetaian—an accusation which led to a well-documented controversy involving many of the leading scholars of the day.

ELAZAR THE PRIEST [1]: Biblical figure, second High Priest of the Jewish nation. He assisted Joshua in dividing the conquered land of Canaan among the victorious Israelite tribes.

R. ELAZAR (b. AZARYAH) [2]: Third-generation *Tanna*, a member of the Yeshivah at Yavneh which provided the spiritual leadership of Israel after the destruction of the Second Temple (70 C.E.). As a young man he was elevated to the Presidency of the Sanhedrin and the Yeshivah when Rabban Gamliel II was deposed, subsequently sharing that office with him when Rabban Gamliel was reinstated.

R. ELAZAR (b. PEDAT) [3]: Eretz Yisrael *Amora* of the second generation (normally quoted in the Talmud without his father's name). He was the most distinguished disciple of R. Yochanan in the Yeshivah at Tiberias, subsequently succeeding him as Principal.

R. ELIEZER b. HURKANOS [2]: Second generation *Tanna* (normally quoted in the Talmud simply as "R. Eliezer," although occasionally as "R. Eliezer the Great"), who flourished before and after the destruction of the Second Temple (70 C.E.). A distinguished disciple of Rabban Yochanan b. Zakkai, he himself was the principle mentor of R. Akiva.

ELIMELECH [1]: Biblical figure, father-in-law of Ruth the Moabitess.

ELIYAHU (OF PARIS) [5]: Early Tosafist, contemporary of Rabbenu Tam (c. 1150).

ELIYAHU HANAVI (ELIJAH THE PROPHET) [1]: Zealous prophet during the antinomian reign of King Ahab and Queen Jezebel. Scripture relates that he did not die a death, but ascended to Heaven in a fiery chariot. Traditionally his return is eagerly awaited, as it will be to herald the arrival of the Messianic age.

R. ELIYAHU MENACHEM OF LONDON [5]: Tosafist also known as Elijah Magister, Chief Rabbi of England c. 1255.

ESTHER [1]: Heroine of the Purim story (c. 370 B.C.E.) related in the Scriptural book which bears her name. Empress of the Persian Empire which succeeded the Babylonian one of Nebuchadnezzar, it was her son Darius II who gave permission for Israel to be resettled and the Temple rebuilt.

R. YAAKOV ETTLINGER [6]: Chief Rabbi of Altona from 1836 until his death in 1871, and mentor of many outstanding German Rabbis including R. Samson Raphael Hirsch and R. Azriel Hildesheimer. An outstanding and original Halachist and prolific writer (his responsa are known as *Binyan Tzion*), he led his orthodox colleagues in protesting at reformist innovations.

EZRA HASOFER [1]: Ezra, the Scribe, one of the major leaders of the exiles who returned to Israel c. 350 B.C.E. Extremely active on the religious front, he renewed the spiritual life of the people by confirming their acceptance of the Torah and by reorganizing the religious institutions, as reported in the Scriptural books of the later Hagiographa.

R. MOSHE FEINSTEIN [6]: (1895-1986) Acknowledged Halachic authority of the twentieth century. Born in Minsk, he settled in

New York prior to the outbreak of World War II and became a leading influence on Orthodox American Jewry, who addressed many contemporary Halachic problems to him.

R. MOSHE FRESCO [6]: Originally of Salonika where his *Yadav shel Moshe* was published, he became Chief Rabbi of the Ottoman Empire c. 1835.

RABBAN GAMLIEL (THE ELDER) **[2]:** A grandson of Hillel I, he was a first-generation *Tanna* (c. 50 C.E.). The title Rabban was bestowed upon him as President of the Sanhedrin, a post he inherited from his father and passed on to his son.

RABBAN GAMLIEL II (OF YAVNEH) **[2]:** Grandson of the first Rabban Gamliel, his life was spared by the Roman conquerors at the request of R. Yochanan b. Zakkai. He presided over the reestablished Yeshivah and Sanhedrin at Yavneh, but at one stage angered his colleagues who temporarily deposed him. On his reinstatement he was obliged to share the Presidency with R. Elazar b. Azaryah.

R. SHLOMO GANZFRIED [6]: Hungarian Rabbi (d. 1866). Although associated with a number of publications, it was his *Kitzur Shulchan Aruch* (Abbreviated Code of Jewish Law) which spread his fame; immensely popular, it is to be found in most orthodox Jewish homes as a standard reference.

R. GERSHOM MEOR HAGOLAH [5]: The title of *Meor Hagolah* ("Light of the Diaspora") indicates the esteem in which R. Gershom was held by eleventh-century European Jewry. His Yeshivah in Mainz, which eclipsed those in Babylonia, laid the foundation of advanced Talmudic study in Ashkenazic lands. He himself is best remembered for his leadership of the Synod of Mainz, which enacted a number of decrees aimed at improving the quality of the religious and social life of the Ashkenazic Jew, inter alia a ban on polygamy and a prohibition on divorcing one's wife against her will.

R. GIDAL [3]: Second-generation Babylonian *Amora* often mentioned in the Gemara as quoting Rav, his teacher.

GOLIATH [1]: Powerful Philistine giant and warrior in the time of King Saul, defeated by young David (see DAVID HAMELECH).

R. NACHMAN SHLOMO GREENSPAN [6]: Outstanding Talmudic scholar. Of Polish origin, he studied under and with such luminaries as the Sochatchover Rebbe, R. Chaim Soloveitchik, the Rogatchover Ilui, R. Meir Simcha HaKohen and R. Aaron Kotler. Rabbi Greenspan immigrated to Britain just before the outbreak of World War I and became Rosh Yeshivah in Glasgow, subsequently moving to Leeds and then to the Yeshivas Etz Chaim, London, where he remained until his death in 1963.

R. REUVEN GROZOVSKY [6]: Son-in-law of R. Baruch Dov Liebovitz and lecturer at his Yeshivah at Kamenitz. He left Lithuania for New York before the outbreak of the Second World War and became Rosh Yeshivah of Mesivta Torah Vodaath in that city.

RABBI A. GURWICZ [6]: Currently Rosh Yeshivah, Gateshead Yeshivah.

R. HAI GAON [4]: Son of R. Sherira Gaon, he succeeded his father as Gaon of Pumbedita, when R. Sherira voluntarily abdicated in his favor. He and his Yeshivah were the preeminent Torah authorities of his time, but after his death in 1038 at the age of ninety-nine, the ancient Babylonian seats of learning went into sharp decline. Ravad, in his *Sefer Hakabbalah*, writes of him that he was the last and greatest of all the *Geonim*, and such was his status that his official seal bore the image of the Lion of Judah as befits a descendant of the Royal House of David.

R. RAFAEL HAKOHEN [6]: Much-respected Rabbi of the "Three Communities" of Altona, Hamburg, and Wandsbeck from

1766 until his retirement in 1799. Author of *Torat Yekutiel* on Code *Yoreh De'ah*.

RESPONSA HAMEYUCHAS LEHARAMBAN: Responsa of Rashba erroneously attributed to Ramban.

R. HAMNUNA [3]: Second-generation Babylonian *Amora*, disciple of Rav. (Several scholars of that name are mentioned in the Talmud.)

HAR HACARMEL [6]: Responsa of R. Eliyahu of Bilgoray.

HEISHIV MOSHE [6]: Responsa of R. Moshe Teitelbaum (1759-1841) of Ughely. A disciple of the Seer of Lublin, he was the leading Chassidic Rabbi in Hungary and established a dynasty which includes the Rabbis of Sighet and present-day Satmar.

HEROD [2]: An Idumean of non-Jewish origin, he rose to the throne of Judea, which he ruled with the support of Rome from 37-4 B.C.E.

RABBI DR. YITZCHAK HERZOG [6]: Born 1888 in Lomza, Poland, Rabbi Herzog grew up in Leeds, England, where his father was Rabbi. He accepted Rabbinical posts in Ireland, becoming first Chief Rabbi of the Irish Free State. In 1936 he was appointed Chief Rabbi of Palestine, then under the British Mandate, subsequently becoming the first Ashkenazic Chief Rabbi of the newly created State of Israel, a post he held until his death in 1959.

HILLEL (THE ELDER) [2]: Also known as "the Babylonian" on account of his birth and early life there. Descended from the House of David on his maternal side, he was appointed President of the Sanhedrin c. 30 B.C.E., establishing a dynasty which held office for some five hundred years. He and his colleague Shammai, who were the last of the *Zugot*, both established schools of learning, which were often in dispute. Apart from his great scholarship, Hillel was renowned for his humility and patience.

HILLEL II [3]: Thirteenth-generation descendant of Hillel the Elder, he was the last President of a formally convened Sanhedrin. C. 400 C.E., he and his colleagues fixed the Jewish Calendar and it has been operative ever since.

R. SAMSON RAPHAEL HIRSCH [6]: Born in Hamburg in 1808, he gained his Talmudic knowledge from his father and the eminent Rabbis of that city. For a short period he also studied in Bonn University, developing a friendship with Abraham Geiger, who was later to become one of his major opponents as Rabbi Hirsch became the foremost exponent of Orthodoxy in Germany. After holding a number of prestigious Rabbinical posts, he accepted the call to be Rabbi of the relatively small, independent Orthodox congregation of Frankfurt. He held this post for thirty-seven years until his death in 1888, during which period he developed it into a prototype and paradigm for newly emerging Orthodox congregations.

HOSHEA [1]: Hosea, the prophet whose prophecy is the subject of the first of the twelve smaller books of Prophecy. He was a contemporary of Yeshayahu, Amos and Micha (8th century B.C.E.), and considered by the Talmud as the greatest among them, for he not only induced the people to repent, but also taught them how to pray (*Pesachim* 87a).

R. HUNA [3]: Babylonian *Amora* of the second generation. In the main a disciple of Rav in Sura, but to a lesser degree also a pupil of Shmuel in Neharde'a. After Shmuel's death, R. Huna moved the Yeshivah of Sura to Masa Mechesia, remaining at its head until his death in 297 C.E.

R. HUNA berai de R. YEHOSHUA [3]: Fifth-generation Babylonian *Amora*, disciple first of Abbaye at Pumbedita and later of Rava at Mechuza. All his life a close friend of R. Pappa, he became his deputy at the Yeshivah in Naresh which R. Pappa founded.

R. SHLOMO HYMAN [6]: Alumnus of several renowned Lithuanian Yeshivahs. He lectured in Baranowicz under R. Elchonon Wasserman until 1926, at which time he was appointed to head a Yeshivah in Vilna. In 1935 he received a call to be Rosh Yeshivah of Mesivta Torah Vodaath in New York, a post he held until his death in 1945.

ITTUR SOFRIM [5]: Halachic compendium by R. Yitzchak b. R. Abba Mori (of Marseilles). The work is divided into three parts: (i) Mercantile Law, (ii) Laws demanding abstinence, and (iii) Laws concerning the Festivals. The author was a contemporary of Rabbenu Tam and Ravad III. According to Jerusalem legend, his book contains many mysteries and attempts to publish explanations are doomed—either the work is lost or the author dies before completion.

IYYOV [1]: Job, the main character in the Hagiographic book of that name which describes the drama of the human soul. Whether he actually existed, and if so, when, is the subject of Talmudic debate (*Bava Batra* 14b et seq; Talmud Yerushalmi, *Sotah* 5:6).

JOSEPHUS [2]: Historian of Judea and its Roman conquerors of the first century C.E. Of noble Jewish birth, he first fought against the Romans but later changed his allegiance, ultimately settling and dying in Rome.

R. KAHANA [3]: At least five *Amoraim* bearing this name are mentioned in the Gemara. The first was a contemporary of Rav; the second was his disciple. The third appears two generations later as a pupil of Rabbah. All three left Bavel to settle in Eretz Yisrael. The fourth R. Kahana was head of the Yeshivah at Pumbedita (c. 400 C.E.) and was the teacher of R. Ashi, while the fifth R. Kahana was a friend and colleague of R. Ashi.

R. YAAKOV KANIEWSKY [6]: Known throughout the Orthodox community as "the Steipler," he was a leading academic scholar of the mid-twentieth century (d. 1985). Like his brother-in-law the Chazon Ish, he had no official position but was accepted by the many who visited his home in Bnei Brak as their spiritual leader.

RABBI C. D. KAPLIN [6]: Currently Dayan of the London Beth Din.

R. YOSEF KARO [6]: (1488-1575) Author (inter alia) of the *Beit Yosef*, a monumental commentary on the *Tur* of R. Yaakov b. Asher, from which he extracted a digest which became known as the *Shulchan Aruch*, the Codes. Augmented by the glosses of Remah, this was accepted as the Code of Law by all sections of Orthodox Jewry. The *Mechaber* ("Author") as he is known, was born in Toledo and on the expulsion from Spain settled with his family in Portugal. After the expulsion from that country he spent forty years in Turkey, leaving in 1536 for Safed by way of Egypt. In Safed he was appointed head of the Beit Din in succession to his own mentor, R. Yaakov Berab. He also wrote the *Kesef Mishneh*.

KEREN ORAH [6]: Novellae of R. Yitzchak of Karlin (b. Minsk 1784). Reluctant to accept a Rabbinical appointment, nevertheless he succeeded his brother R. Yaakov as Rabbi of Karlin, a post he held until his death in 1848.

KESEF MISHNEH: See R. YOSEF KARO.

KESEF NIVCHAR [6]: Anthology of one hundred and sixty Talmudic themes collated by R. Baruch Benedict Goitein (c. 1770-1842), Rabbi of Hogyesz in Hungary.

KETZOT HACHOSHEN [6]: Novellae on Code *Choshen Mishpat* by R. Arieh Leib HaKohen Heller (c. 1745-1813), a descendant of the Tosafot Yom Tov. As Rabbi of Rozhyator, a small Galician town, he experienced extreme poverty, but as his fame spread he was appointed Rabbi of Stry where he established a large Yeshivah. Although opposed to Chassidism, of which Stry was a center, the Chassidic Rabbis recognized him as a "Prince of the Torah." The *Ketzot* and his two other works, the *Avnei Miluim* and the *Shev Sh'mateta*, gained immediate recognition and are today among the basic books of Yeshivah study.

KIRYAT SEFER: See MABIT.

KLI YAKAR [6]: Best-known work of R. Shlomo Efraim of Luntchitz, Rabbi of Prague from 1604 until his death in 1619. A renowned preacher who specialized in Biblical homily and interpretation, this work of commentary and explanation is often reprinted in the Chumash itself.

KNESSET HAGEDOLAH [6]: Halachic work based on the Codes by R. Chaim Benveniste (1603-1673), Rabbi of Izmir (Smyrna) Turkey from 1658.

KOLBO [5]: Halachic work by an unknown author, assumed by the Chida to have been a contemporary of R. Yaakov (author of the Turim, c. 1300) and of Spanish origin.

KOVETZ HE'AROT: See R. ELCHONON WASSERMAN.

KOVETZ SHIURIM: See R. ELCHONON WASSERMAN.

LECHEM MISHNEH [6]: Classic commentary on Rambam's *Yad Hachazakah* by R. Avraham di Boton of Salonika (1545-1588) (v. his comment on receiving a copy of the Kesef Mishneh by R. Yosef Karo: Hilchot Tefillah 11:15).

RABBI Y. LEVENBERG [6]: Currently Director of Jewish Studies, Menorah Grammar School, London.

R. LEVI BAR CHAMA [3]: Third-generation Eretz Yisrael *Amora* (sometimes quoted as R. Levi bar Lachmo) who specialized in homiletic discourses.

LIKUTEI SICHOT: See TANYA.

LOT [1]: Nephew of the Patriarch Avraham and progenitor of the biblical races of Ammon and Moab.

MABIT [6]: Acronym of the name of R. Moshe b. Yosef of Trani. After the Spanish expulsion his family settled temporarily in Salonika, where he was born in the year 1500 C.E. At age eighteen, he immigrated to Safed, Israel, where he became a friend and colleague of R. Yosef Karo, with whom he sat on the Beit Din of that town. He died in 1580.

MACHANEI EFRAIM [6]: Halachic work of R. Efraim Navon (1677-1735), Rabbi of Constantinople. The work follows the order of Rambam's *Yad* but in the main concentrates on civil and mercantile law.

MAGEN AVRAHAM [6]: Classic commentary on Code *Orach Chaim*, by R. Avraham Gumbiner (1637-1683). For many years his great scholarship went unrecognized in the town of Kalish, where he lived in great poverty serving as a schoolteacher. However, as a result of a visit by the Shach, he received the recognition he deserved and was eventually appointed a Dayan of that town.

MAGGID MISHNEH [5]: Title of one of the classical and indispensable commentaries on Rambam's *Mishneh Torah* (or *Yad Hachazakah*) by R. Vidal Yom Tov of Tolosa, a Spanish Rabbi of the second half of the fourteenth century, often referred to as *Harav Hamaggid*. Little is known about his life, but because of the designation *Hakadosh* ascribed to him by R. Yosef Karo, it has been suggested that he died a martyr's death.

MAHARAL OF PRAGUE [6]: Acronym of R. Yehudah Leow of Prague (1512 or 1526-1609). Of Polish origin, he served as Rabbi of Nikolsburg, Posen, and ultimately of Prague. His best-known works are his philosophical treatises on the Jewish past and on its future hopes, in which he explains many difficult Talmudic homilies. The Maharal of Prague holds an honored place in Jewish folklore as the creator of the Golem, which he used to defend his people against the notorious "blood libels" which abounded in his time.

MAHARAM OF ROTHENBURG: See R. MEIR OF ROTHENBURG.

MAHARIK [5]: Acronym of Our Teacher and Rabbi, R. Yosef Kolon. Of French birth (1410), he became the leading Halachic authority of the German communities which were established in northern Italy. Ultimately he was recognized by all Italian Jewry and held the Rabbinate of Pavia until his death (c. 1480).

MAHARIT [6]: Acronym of Our Teacher and Rabbi, R. Yosef of Trani, son of the Mabit. Born in Safed in 1568, he was chosen by the leaders of that town to travel abroad to obtain much-needed aid after the famine of 1599. After completing his errand, he was prevailed upon by the community of Constantinople to remain there, subsequently becoming Chief Rabbi of Turkey until his death in 1639.

MAHARSHA [6]: Acronym of R. Shmuel Eliezer Eidels (1555-1631). His novellae are classical commentaries on the Talmud, with special emphasis on *Tosafot*, written with an economy of language often making them difficult to follow. Loathe to accept a Rabbinical post, he was maintained by his mother-in-law Eidel, whose name became his surname. After her death he was forced to take up Rabbinical positions, first in Chelm, then in Lublin and ultimately in Ostrowa.

MAHARSHAL [6]: Initials by which R. Shlomo Luria (c. 1510-1574) is known. Rabbi and Rosh Yeshivah in several towns in Poland and Lithuania, including Brisk (Brest-Litovsk) and Lublin, he was mentor to many of the leaders of the next generation. Independent in his Halachic approach, he seems to have ignored the *Shulchan Aruch* of R. Yosef Karo, since its rulings were not primarily based on the decisions of the Tosafists and later Franco-German scholars. He authored the *Yam shel Shlomo*.

MALBIM [6]: Acronym from the name of R. Meir Leib b. Yechiel

Mechil (1809-1879), whose works of Biblical exegesis have become classic. He himself, after occupying several pulpits, became Rabbi of Bucharest and ultimately Chief Rabbi of Rumania, a position he held for only six years. His uncompromising stand against Reform Jewry made him many enemies who brought about his imprisonment and eventual banishment from Rumania. During the last fifteen years of his life he lived in various towns, holding Rabbinical positions only intermittently. He suffered persecution and calumny from both the Reform and the Chassidic Movements.

MECHILTA [2]: Tannaic commentary on the Book of *Shemot* consisting of both Halachic and Aggadic exegesis. Although there is no certainty as to its author, most scholars are of the view that it is the *Tanna* R. Yishmael (b. Elisha II, possibly the grandson of the martyred High Priest of the same name).

R. MEIR [2]: Distinguished pupil of R. Akiva and considered by the Talmud as the greatest of the fourth generation of *Tannaim*. Too profound for his colleagues, they could not always follow his reasoning and therefore did not always accept his views as Halachah. He had a lucid and concise method of explaining the law, and his texts form the basis of Rabi's *Mishnayot*, so much so that there is the Halachic rule, "A nameless mishnah is R. Meir's."

R. MEIR OF ROTHENBURG [5]: Talmudist, Halachist, and liturgist, greatest of the German Rabbis of the thirteenth century. On being imprisoned by the Emperor Rudolph I, he forbade the Jewish Community to pay the exorbitant ransom demanded so that the government should not be encouraged to imprison other communal leaders in the same way. He languished in prison for seven years, during which time he taught those disciples permitted to visit him and wrote to others, until his death in 1293. Even then his remains were not released for burial for a further fourteen years.

MEIRI [5]: R. Menachem b. Shlomo, born to the Meiri family (1249) possibly in Perpignan. There he lived most of his life, often engaging in Halachic controversies with disciples of the Ramban; twenty-four of these disputes he reports in his responsa, *Magen Avot*. His major literary work is the *Beit Habechirah* on the Talmud, which both explains the *sugyah* and summarizes the Halachah derived from it. This and most of Meiri's other works remained unpublished until comparatively recently and therefore did not influence the ultimate Halachah. As a student of philosophy and a secular savant, Meiri played an important role in resisting a Rabbinic ban on non-Torah study.

R. MENACHEM OF MERSEBURG [5]: German Halachist who flourished in the first half of the fifteenth century. Although his rulings formed the basis of the customs of Saxony, only fragments of his work have reached us.

MESHECH CHOCHMAH: See OR SAMEACH.

MIDRASH RABBAH [3-5]: Collection of Aggadic and homiletic essays on each of the five books of the Torah and *Megillot*. The earliest section is the Amoraic *Bereshit Rabbah* of the sixth century.

RABBI M. MILLER [6]: Currently vice principal, Gateshead Jewish Seminary.

MISHNEH LEMELECH [6]: Novellae and disquisitions on the *Yad* now normally found alongside Rambam's own text, by R. Yehudah Rosanes (1657-1727), a leading Turkish Rabbi. A staunch anti-Shabbetaian, he showed leniency to those who recanted, thereby angering the more zealous, some of whom broke into his house and destroyed many of his writings. His other popular work is the *Parashat Derachim*, which consists of twenty-six Halachic and Aggadic sermons. This is normally printed with his *Derech Mitzvotcho*, dealing with the 613 precepts of the Torah as enumerated by Rambam.

MORDECHAI [1]: Scriptural figure, hero of the Purim story recounted in the Book of Esther. He returned to Israel as a member of the Great Assembly.

MORDECHAI [5]: Halachic compendium of R. Mordechai b. Hillel arranged according to the order of the Talmudic Tractates and normally printed as an appendix to the Rif. This work is of special importance to the Ashkenazic Authorities. He and his family suffered martyrs' deaths in 1298 during the Rindfleish massacres.

MOSHE RABBENU [1]: Moses, our teacher, first leader of Israel. He led his people from slavery in Egypt and brought them to Sinai to receive the Torah by Divine Revelation. He himself is the first link in the chain of Torah transmission, and indeed the Pentateuch is known as the Five Books of Moshe.

R. NACHMAN [3]: Second-generation Babylonian *Amora* who flourished in Mechuza c. 300 C.E. Related to the Exilarch by marriage, he was appointed communal judge and because of his experience became accepted as the leading judicial authority of his time.

R. NATAN [2]: Fourth-generation *Tanna* (c. 150 C.E.). Son of the Exilarch in Babylonia, he traveled to *Eretz Yisrael* to join the Sanhedrin, at that time in Usha under the presidency of R. Shimon b. Gamliel II, where, because of his high birth and judicial prowess, he was quickly elected Chief Justice.

NECHEMIAH [1]: Lay leader, possibly Babylonian Exilarch, during the reign of Darius II, son of Queen Esther. A senior courtier to the King, he obtained permission for the rebuilding of Jerusalem and the Temple, which he accomplished together with Ezra, the then spiritual leader, as reported in the Scriptural Books of both Ezra and Nechemiah.

R. NECHEMIAH [2]: Fourth-generation Eretz Yisrael *Tanna* (c.

130 C.E.). A pupil of R. Akiva, his notes formed the basis of the *Tosefta* which elaborate the more sparsely constructed Mishnah of Rabi.

R. NECHUNIA b. HAKANAH [2]: Second-generation Judean *Tanna*. Renowned for his piety, he lived to an exceptionally old age.

NETIVOT HAMISHPAT [6]: Commentary on Codes, *Choshen Mishpat* by R. Yaakov Lorbeerbaum of Lisa (d. 1832). This work, together with its contemporary *Ketzot Hachoshen*, which are often in dispute, are classics much studied in the Lithuanian-type Yeshivahs. R. Yaakov MeLissa's other much-studied works are *Chavat Da'at on Code Yorah De'ah*, *Beit Yaakov on Code Even Ha'ezer*, *Torat Gittin*, and *Derech Hachaim*, an anthology of liturgical and ritual laws covering the whole year, now often printed in prayer books.

NETZIV [6]: Initials of R. Naftali Tzvi Yehudah Berlin (1817-1893), Rosh Yeshivah of Volozhin for forty years during which time, because of the caliber of the students he attracted, it became the spiritual and academic center for the whole of Russian Jewry.

NIMUKEI YOSEF [5]: Commentary on the Rif by R. Yosef Chaviva (c. 1450), Spanish Halachist of whom little is known.

R. NISSIM GAON [5]: An early *Rishon* (d. Kairouan, Tunisia, 1050), contemporaneous with R. Hai Gaon, whose opinions he continuously sought on many Talmudic and Halachic matters.

NODA B'YEHUDAH [6]: Title of the collected responsa of R. Yechezkel Landau (1713-1793), Rabbi of Prague, which has become one of the classics of responsa literature. Active in Prague as Rabbi, teacher and judge, he also, in his capacity of Chief Rabbi of Bohemia, represented the Jews before the Austrian Government. He vigorously opposed those groups which developed anti-Rabbinic attitudes, as he did both the old Shabbetaian movement and the newer Chassidic one.

ONEG YOM TOV [6]: Collected responsa and novellae of R. Rafael Yom Tov Heilpern (1816-1879), Rabbi of Mehzrich and then of Bialystok.

OR HACHAIM [6]: Commentary on the Pentateuch by R. Chaim ibn Attar (born in Sali, Morocco, 1696). A renowned Halachist and Kabbalist, his journeys through Morocco, Italy, and ultimately Eretz Yisrael on his way to Jerusalem, and his achievements in those places have become part of Jewish folklore. He died after only a short period in Jerusalem in 1743.

OR SAME'ACH [6]: Novellae on Rambam's *Yad* by R. Meir Simcha HaKohen (b. 1843) who also wrote the Torah commentary *Meshech Chochmah*. In 1888 he was appointed to the important post of Rabbi of Dvinsk, where, despite being called to the Rabbinate of Jerusalem in 1903, he remained until his death in 1926.

OTZAR CHAIM [6]: Collection of novellae, comments, and aphorisms arranged in Biblical order by Rabbi Chaim Yaakov Zuckerman (d. 1972), who also edited a similar work on Festivals called *Birkat Chaim*.

OTZAR HAGEONIM [4]: Contemporary collection of Geonic literature including commentaries, rulings, and responsa, many of which were found in the Cairo Geniza. The collection is arranged in order of Tractate.

OVADIAH [1]: Obadiah, author of the shortest Biblical book of prophecy. A contemporary of Elijah, he flourished during the reign of Ahab and Jezebel (c. 870-850 B.C.E.).

R. OVADIAH OF BERTINORO: See BERTINORO.

RABBI H. B. PADWA [6]: Currently *Av Beit Din* of the Union of Orthodox Hebrew Congregations of London.

R. PAPPA [3]: Leading Babylonian *Amora* of the fifth generation. A disciple of Rava at Mechuza, he was principal of the Yeshivah at Naresh, which succeeded Mechuza, from 352-371 C.E.

R. PERETZ HAKOHEN [5]: (c. 1300-1370) Rabbi of Barcelona, a leading Halachist of his time, much quoted by his contemporaries and successors.

PNEI YEHOSHUA [6]: Talmudic novellae of R. Yaakov Yehoshua Falk (1680-1756). Born in Krakow, he lived his early married life in Hamburg, home of his first wife. Together with his then only daughter and other members of his family, his wife was killed in an explosion in 1702 from which he miraculously escaped. He held several Rabbinical positions, the final one being that of Frankfurt.

RABBAH (b. NACHMEINI) [3]: Leading third-generation Babylonian *Amora*. Known for his profound scholarship, he was appointed Rosh Yeshivah of Pumbedita in 299 C.E. So successful was he that the Yeshivah, which had 400 full-time students, played host to 12,000 who came twice a year to hear his lectures during each of the two *Kallah* months. This angered the civil authorities, who believed the calumny that he caused 12,000 families to stop paying taxes, and he was forced to flee Pumbedita to avoid persecution. He died soon after, having held office for 22 years.

RABBAH bar b. CHANA [3]: Born in Babylon (c. 300 C.E.), he traveled to Eretz Yisrael and is numbered among the third-generation Eretz Yisrael *Amoraim*. He traveled extensively before returning to his native land, and the Talmud contains a number of reports of his (others say of his grandson's of the same name) esoteric sightings.

RABBAH b. R. HUNA [3]: Third-generation Babylonian *Amora* (c. 300 C.E.). After the death of R. Chisda he gave the lectures in the Yeshivah of Sura but was never formally installed as

Rosh Yeshivah. His chief teacher was his father, R. Huna, but he also studied under R. Huna's mentor, Rav.

RABBENU HAKADOSH: See R. YEHUDAH HANASI.

RABI: See R. YEHUDAH HANASI.

RACH [5]: Acronym of Rabbenu Chananel (b. Chushiel). One of the first *Rishonim*, he was virtually contemporaneous with R. Hai Gaon. His Talmud commentary, where available, is usually printed alongside the main text. He was principal of the Yeshivah of Kairouan, Tunisia, until his death c. 1055.

RACHEL [1]: Favorite wife of Yaakov the Patriarch, she is numbered as one of the four Matriarchs. Yirmeyahu's description of Rachel weeping for her exiled children has always been of special significance to exiled Jewry.

RADVAZ [6]: Acronym of R. David b. Avi Zimra (1479-1573), early *Acharon*. Born in Spain but educated in Safed, he immigrated to Egypt in 1512 where he remained for 40 years. There he became Chief Rabbi and exercised great influence not only on his own people, but on non-Jews too. He returned to Eretz Yisrael and attempted to settle in Jerusalem, but soon moved to Safed where he remained until his death.

R. RAFAEL YAAKOV b. AVRAHAM MENASHE:
See *Be'er Hamayim.*

RAMBAM [5]: Acronym of R. Moshe b. Maimon (Maimonides). Born in Cordova in 1135. He and his family wandered for thirty years through Spain, Morocco, and Crusade-ravaged Eretz Yisrael, finding refuge in Egypt, where eventually he became Court physician and *Naggid* (Prince) of Egyptian Jewry. His major work, *Mishneh Torah* or *Yad Hachazakah*, was the first significant Halachic Codification, covering the entire Halachah. Written in concise and lucid Hebrew, it is one of the pillars of Halachah. Rambam's other writings were in Arabic and include *Sefer Hamitzvot*, a prologue to the *Yad*, a commentary on the Mishnah, and two philosophical treatises—*Shemoneh Perakim* and *Moreh Nevuchim* (*Guide to the Perplexed*).

RAMBAN [5]: Acronym of R. Moshe b. Nachman (Nachmanides). Born in Gerona, Spain, in 1194, he spent most of his life there practicing medicine as a profession and teaching Torah to his disciples. In 1263 he was the Jewish representative in a religious disputation in the presence of King James of Aragon. Although successful, he was soon expelled from that country and at the age of 72 he arrived in Jerusalem, where he established a synagogue and revived the almost non-existent Jewish community. He eventually settled in Acco where he completed his monumental commentary on the Torah and where he died in 1270.

RAN [5]: Acronym of R. Nissim b. Reuven, also known as Ranbar (c.1270-1375), Rabbi of Barcelona. The foremost Rabbinical authority of his time, he replied to queries from France, Italy, Africa, and even Eretz Yisrael (although only 77 of his responsa have reached us). His commentaries on the Tractate of *Nedarim* and on the Rif are universally studied, as is his collection of homilies known as *Derashot HaRan*.

RANBAR (R. NISSIM b. REUVEN): See RAN.

RASHBA [5]: Acronym of R. Shlomo ibn Aderet of Barcelona (1235-1310). A disciple of R. Yonah of Gerondi and Ramban, he was accepted by virtually every Jewish community as the ultimate Halachic Authority of his time, and the collection of some three thousand responsa under his name is the most extensive of the early *Rishonim*. His reported decisions have weighed heavily in deciding the final Halachah.

RASHBAM [5]: Acronym of R. Shmuel b. Meir (c. 1085-1174), grandson and disciple of Rashi. In a number of Tractates on which Rashi apparently did not complete his Talmudic commentary, that of Rashbam is printed alongside the main text. His commentary on the Torah is often to be found in popular editions of the Pentateuch.

RASHBASH [5]: Acronym of R. Shlomo b. Shimon (Duran). He succeeded his father, Tashbatz, as Rabbi of Algiers, a post he held until his death in 1477. Like his father, he wrote many responsa in answer to queries addressed to him from Spain and North Africa.

RASHI [5]: Acronym of R. Shlomo Yitzchaki (1040-1105). Author of the most widely studied commentaries on the Torah and the Talmud, commentaries which are basic to the understanding of, and inseparable from, the main texts of both. Rashi studied in German Yeshivahs led by the disciples of R. Gershom *Meor Hagolah*, but he refused Rabbinical office and returned to his native Troyes, where he earned his livelihood as a wine merchant, all the while studying with his own disciples and working on his commentaries. His influence as a Halachist can be gauged from the many contemporary works which quote his decisions. Legends concerning his birth and later incidents in his life have passed into Jewish folklore.

RAV [2-3]: Title accorded by the Talmud to R. Abba Aricha b. Aivu. A native of Babylonia, he traveled to Eretz Yisrael to study with, and under, Rabi and is therefore recognized as a *Tanna*, with competence to disagree with other *Tannaim*. He returned to Babylonia and in 219 C.E. founded the great Yeshivah of Sura, which he headed for 28 years until his death. His influence on the later Babylonian *Amoraim* was such that he is often referred to in the Babylonian Talmud merely as "our great teacher" and not by name.

RAVA [3]: Fourth-generation Babylonian *Amora*, disciple of Rabbah and R. Yosef at Pumbedita. After R. Yosef's death Rava moved to Mechuza and founded a small Yeshivah, while his colleague Abbaye headed the major one at Pumbedita. After Abbaye's death in 338, Rava was appointed to succeed him, and the two Yeshivahs merged, Pumbedita moving to Mechuza, where Rava remained as Principal until his death in 352 C.E. Many Halachic debates between Abbaye and Rava are reported in the Talmud, which cites them as masterpieces of analytical reasoning.

RAVAD I [5]: Acronym of R. Avraham Ibn Daud, best known for his *Sefer Hakabbalah*, a historical work detailing the unbroken chain of Torah transmission from Moshe to his own time. Ravad was martyred c. 1180 by the King of Toledo, for refusing to renounce his faith.

RAVAD II [5]: Acronym of R. Avraham *Av Beit Din*, a title signifying the office he held as Chief Rabbinical Justice of Narbonne in Provence until his death in 1179. His influence can be seen in the Halachic and Talmudic work of later scholars who quote his (unpublished) commentaries and responsa.

RAVAD III [5]: Acronym of R. Avraham b. David of Posquieres (Provence), son-in-law of Ravad II. Best known for his commentaries on Rambam's *Yad*, which he held in great esteem despite his seemingly harsh critical tone, Ravad also wrote Talmudic commentaries, commentaries on Rif, works of Halachah and Kabbalah. Indeed, a famed mystic, there are a number of legends concerning his instruction by the prophet Eliyahu. An extremely wealthy man, Ravad eschewed luxuries all his earthly life, which ended c. 1197.

REMAH [6]: Acronym of R. Moshe Isserles of Krakow (1525 or 1530-1572). A recognized Halachic authority, he corresponded with the greatest scholars of his time, including R. Yosef Karo, whose commentary on the *Tur* was published just as Remah had begun writing his own. This work was later published as *Darchei Moshe* and formed the basis of his commentaries—the *Mappah* ("Tablecloth") on the *Shulchan Aruch* ("Prepared Table") or Codes of R. Yosef Karo. In these he quotes Ashkenazic Authorities and customs ignored by the Sephardi R. Karo. By spreading his "tablecloth" on the "prepared table," Remah ensured the universal acceptance of the Codes.

RIF [5]: Acronym of R. Yitzchak Alfasi of Fez, Morocco (1013-1103), where he spent most of his life. His magnum opus, *Sefer Hahalachot*, is in the form of an abridged version of the Talmud, often assembling material from scattered discourses and incorporating the work of the *Geonim* of the earlier period, so as to give a clear picture of the practical Halachah. In the main, both the *Yad* of Rambam and the Codes follow Rif's rulings.

RI MIGASH [5]: Acronym of R. Yosef (ben Meir Halevi) ibn Migash. Born in Seville in 1077, at the age of 12 he entered the Yeshivah of Rif at Lucena. Fourteen years later, Rif, prior to his death, nominated him as his successor, passing over his own son, himself a renowned scholar. Ri Migash held the post of Rosh Yeshivah at Lucena until his own death in 1141. Although Rambam claims him as his mentor, his pupilage was not a direct one, but presumably through his father, who did indeed study under Ri Migash.

RITVA [5]: Acronym of R. Yom Tov ben Avraham Eshvili of Seville (c. 1300), best known for his comprehensive novellae and commentaries on most Tractates of the Talmud.

RIVAM [5]: Acronym of R. Yitzchak b. Meir of Ramerupt, France (c. 1090-1130). Tosafist, brother of Rashbam and Rabbenu Tam and grandson of Rashi.

RIVASH [5]: Acronym of R. Yitzchak b. Sheshet (Perfet). Born in Barcelona in 1326, he became Rabbi of Saragossa and other communities. In 1391 he fled to Algiers where eventually he was appointed Chief Rabbi until his death in 1407.

ROSH [5]: R. Osher (b. Yechiel). A native of Germany (b. 1250), he fled that land after the imprisonment of his mentor, Maharam of Rothenburg. He arrived in Spain in 1306, where he was eventually appointed Rabbi of Toledo. The father of R. Yaakov, author of the *Turim*, who traveled with him, he was recognized as a leading Halachic Authority for both Ashkenazic and Sephardic Jewry.

RABBI S. RUBIN [6]: Currently Rabbi of Beth Hamedrash Sassow, London.

RUTH [1]: Heroine of the Scriptural book which bears her name and ancestress of King David, her conversion to Judaism created a legal furor because she was from Moab.

RUZHINER REBBE [6]: R. Yisrael Friedman (1797-1850), eminent Chassidic leader in the Ukraine, first at Ruzhin and subsequently, after imprisonment by the Russian authorities, at Sadegora in Bukovina. His six sons and three sons-in-law were also Chassidic leaders, establishing important dynasties, some of which are still extant.

R. SA'ADIAH GAON [4]: Born in 882 in Egypt. At the age of 40, he settled in Babylonia and was immediately appointed to high office in the then flourishing Yeshivah of Pumbedita. When the Gaonate of the declining Yeshivah of Sura became vacant, he was appointed in the hope that his eminence could help revive it. As a result of a dispute with the Exilarch, he was deposed in 932 and forced to flee Baghdad. During his enforced exile he wrote his important philosophical work, *Beliefs and Opinions*. In 937 he was restored to his office, which he held until his death in 942.

R. CHAIM SANZ: See DIVREI CHAIM.

R. AARON SASSOON [6]: Talmudist and Halachic Authority in the Ottoman Empire. His main activity was teaching, first in Salonika and subsequently, from 1600 until his death in 1626, in Constantinople.

RABBI E. SCHLESSINGER [6]: Currently Rosh Yeshivah, Yeshivah Horomoh, London.

SEFAT EMET [6]: (1847-1905) Title of works on *Chumash* and Talmud by R. Yehudah Aryeh Leib of Ger. Grandson of R. Yitzchak Meir, founder of the Gerer dynasty, he was proclaimed Rebbe at the age of 23, a position he held for 35 years until his death, wielding great influence on the Jews of Poland.

SEFER HACHINNUCH [5]: Rishonic compilation which explains both background and detail of every precept and prohibition expressly mentioned in the Torah, following the same sequence in which they appear in the Torah. Of uncertain authorship, the popular ascription to R. Aharon Halevi of Barcelona (c.1230-1300 C.E.), a contemporary and colleague of Rashba, has been refuted by bibliographers.

SEFER HAITTUR: See ITTUR SOFRIM.

SHA'AREI YOSHER: See R. SHIMON SHKOP.

SHACH [6]: Acronym of *Siftei Kohen*, a classic commentary on Codes *Yoreh De'ah* and *Choshen Mishpat* by R. Shabbtai HaKohen (1621-1662). Together with the contemporaneous work of the Taz and S'ma, with whom Shach is often in dispute, it is usually printed alongside the main text of the Codes. The Shach lived most of his adult life in Vilna, but in 1655, to escape persecution, he fled to Moravia where he was appointed Rabbi of Holesor; there he died and is buried.

SHAMMAI [2]: Scholar of the second era of this period, and with his colleague, Hillel, the last of the *Zugot*. A jealous defender of the independence and authority of the Sanhedrin of which he was the senior member, Josephus reports that Shammai had the courage to defy the tyrannical King Herod. Like his colleague Hillel, Shammai founded an important Torah academy which in later generations was often in dispute with that of Hillel.

RABBI MEIR SHAPIRA [6]: Known today as the "Lubliner Rav" (although very influential in Lublin, he was never actually its Rav). Born in 1887, he received *semichah* at the age of 15 and rapidly became one of the communal leaders of Polish Jewry. To encourage Talmud study he devised the *Daf Hayomi* ("daily page") program and established a major Yeshivah, *Chachmei Lublin*, in that town. In 1933 he was called to the prestigious post of Rabbi of Lodz, which he accepted only after securing that community's agreement that it would shoulder the debts of the Yeshivah. Rabbi Shapira died in 1934 before taking up his appointment in Lodz.

SHAUL [1]: Saul, first King of Israel, anointed by the prophet Samuel. Saul was of the tribe of Benjamin. The monarchy was transferred from his family to David of the tribe of Judah.

SHEMAYAH [2]: Scholar of the second era of this period, who, together with his colleague Avtalyon, made up the penultimate *Zug*—c. 40 B.C.E.

SHEMOT RABBAH: See MIDRASH RABBAH.

R. SHERIRA GAON [4]: Appointed *Gaon* of the declining Yeshivah of Pumbedita in 968 at the age of 70, he restored it to its former role as the supreme source of Halachic authority for world Jewry. A prolific respondent, his best-known work is the classic *Epistle of R. Sherira Gaon*, a concise Jewish and Talmudic historiography. Two years before he died at the age of 100, he appointed his son and close collaborator, R. Hai, as his successor.

R. SHESHET [3]: Second-generation Babylonian *Amora* (c.290 C.E.), famed for his retentive memory and knowledge of *Mishnayot* and *Baraitot*. Although he was blind, he had keen insight and perception, and his use of these gifts is the subject of a number of Talmudic reports.

SHEV SHEMATETA: See KETZOT HACHOSHEN.

SHEVUT YAAKOV [6]: Responsa of Rabbi Yaakov Reischer (c. 1670-1733). He served as Rabbi of Metz from 1718 and was the author of *Iyun Yaakov* on *Ein Yaakov*, and the self-defending work *Lo Hibit Aven b'Yaakov*.

RABBAN SHIMON b. GAMLIEL I [2]: Of the first generation of *Tannaim*, he was the fourth Nasi of the House of Hillel and presided over the Sanhedrin at the time of the destruction of Jerusalem by the Romans. He was martyred together with his colleague, R. Yishmael the High Priest, in the year 68 C.E.

RABBAN SHIMON b. GAMLIEL II [2]: Of the fourth generation of *Tannaim*, he was the sixth Nasi of the House of Hillel and presided over the Sanhedrin, at that time exiled to Usha in the Galilee. Disciple of R. Akiva, colleague of R. Meir, and father and mentor of Rabbi, he greatly influenced the later redactors of the Mishnah.

R. SHIMON BAR YOCHAI [2]: Eminent *Tanna* of the fourth generation. A disciple of R. Akiva, he openly defied the Roman tyranny and was forced to hide in the Judean desert for thirteen years, accompanied only by his son R. Elazar, during which time they devoted themselves exclusively to their studies. As the author of the *Zohar* (mystical commentary on the Pentateuch), he laid the foundation for future study of the Kabbalah. The grave in Meron where he and his son are buried is a venerated place of pilgrimage.

R. SHIMON b. ELAZAR [2]: Of the fifth and final generation of *Tannaim* (c. 170 C.E.). A disciple of R. Meir and contemporary of Rabbi, he was not only an eminent Halachist, but also a successful preacher often quoted in the Talmud.

R. SHIMON b. LAKISH [3]: Also known as *Resh Lakish*. An Eretz Yisrael *Amora* of the second generation, he was brother-in-law, disciple-cum-colleague, and disputant of R. Yochanan, the Rosh Yeshivah of Eretz Yisrael, and so played an important role in the development of the Jerusalem Talmud.

R. SHIMON b. YEHOTZADAK [2]: Of the last of the *Tannaim*, he was in fact of the transitionary period between *Tannaim* and *Amoraim* in Eretz Yisrael.

SHIMON HATZADDIK [2]: Considered to be the last of the *Anshei Knesset Hagedolah* (Men of the Great Assembly) he is the first scholar of the post-Scriptural period to be named in the Talmud. Of exemplary piety, he served as High Priest for 40 years and was venerated by Alexander the Great, who protected the Temple in Jerusalem for his sake.

SHITAH MEKUBETZET [6]: Collocation of Rishonic novellae and interpretations, many of which were not otherwise preserved, by R. Betzalel Ashkenazi (1520-1594). R. Ashkenazi was first, Chief Rabbi of Egypt (to which post he succeeded his mentor, the Radvaz) and subsequently, chief Rabbi of Jerusalem.

R. SHIMON SHKOP [6]: (1860-1940) Eminent Lithuanian Rosh Yeshivah, first at Telz where he lectured for eighteen years, and from 1920 until his death, at Grodno, where he was the Principal. He disbanded his Yeshivah and died just as the German forces were about to enter Grodno. His lectures were renowned for their logical analysis of the point in debate.

SHLOMO HAMELECH [1]: King Solomon, son and successor of King David, his name became synonymous with wisdom. He presided over the largest-ever Jewish Empire, during which time he built the First Temple (1032 B.C.E.) in Jerusalem.

SHMUEL [1]: The prophet Samuel, last of the Judges, whose life and work are the subjects of the first part of the Scriptural book which bears his name.

SHMUEL [3]: Leading first-generation Babylonian *Amora* and contemporary of Rav. Head of the great Yeshivah in Neharde'a which rivaled that of Rav at Sura, Shmuel was also the senior judge of Babylonia, an accomplished astronomer, and a renowned doctor. For reasons which remain obscure, Rabi, whom Shmuel healed, never ordained him with *semichah*, and therefore he is known as Mar (master) Shmuel.

SHOFTIM [1]: Judges, Scriptural book covering a period which began with the death of Yehoshua and ended with the rise of the Prophet Shmuel, during which time Israel was governed by successive Judges.

SHULCHAN ARUCH: The Codes; see R. YOSEF KARO.

R. CHAIM SHMULEVITCH [6]: Also known as R. Chaim Stutziner. A pupil of Mir Yeshivah in Lithuania, he became one of its leaders, guiding it through the Second World War, during which time it was exiled to Shanghai. After the war, he helped the Yeshivah resettle in Jerusalem, ultimately becoming its Rosh Yeshivah until his death in 1979.

RABBI Y. SILBER [6]: Currently head of Kolel Rabinow, London.

S'MA [6]: Acronym of *Sefer Meirat Einaim*, commentary on the Code *Choshen Mishpat* by R. Yehoshua Falk HaKohen (c. 1555-1614), disciple of Remah and Maharshal. Although he refused Rabbinical office, preferring to teach in his Yeshivah, nevertheless he was accepted as a leading Halachic Authority of his time, presiding on occasion over "The Council of the Four Lands." His *S'ma* is invariably printed alongside the main text of the Code.

RABBI MOSHE SOFER: See CHATAM SOFER.

SOLOVEITCHIK [6]: Family name of the Rabbis of Brisk (Brest-Litovsk). R. Chaim Soloveitchik (1853-1918) evolved a novel approach to Talmudic analysis. To describe different concepts, he invented a new terminology which has become basic idiom in contemporary Yeshivahs.

STEIPLER: See R. YAAKOV KANIEWSKY.

SUMCHUS [2]: Fifth-generation *Tanna*, pupil of R. Meir (c. 200 C.E.).

TANA D'VEI ELIYAHU [3]: Record of the lessons given by Eliyahu Hanavi to the second-generation Babylonian *Amora*, R. Annan.

TANYA [6]: Homiletic work of R. Shneur Zalman of Ladi (1754-1813), founder of the Chabad Chassidic movement. A disciple of the Maggid of Mehzrich, he was one of the eminent Chassidic leaders of the third generation. An outstanding Talmudic scholar, he has been described as the "Rambam of Chassidism."

TASHBATZ [5]: Acronym of *Teshuvot Shimon ben Tzemach*, the responsa (approx. 800) of R. Shimon Duran. Born in Majorca in 1361, he was forced to flee with his family to Algiers to escape massacre. In 1407, on the death of Rivash, he was appointed spiritual leader of the Algerian Jewish Community, to which post he was succeeded, on his own death in 1444, by his son R. Shlomo (Rashbash).

TAZ [6]: The initials of the work *Turei Zahav*, a commentary on *Shulchan Aruch* (now normally printed alongside the main text), by R. David b. Shmuel Halevi (1586-1667), son-in-law of the Bach.

TERUMAT HADESHEN [5]: Halachic essays by R. Yisrael Isserlein (1390-1460) of Lenstadt in the form of questions posed by the author himself (many based on actual inquiries) and his rulings. The work is often cited by later Ashkenazic authorities, and many of his rulings are quoted by Remah in his glosses on the *Shulchan Aruch*.

TIFERET YISRAEL [6]: Concise commentary on the Mishnah by R. Israel Lipschutz, Rabbi of Cologne and subsequently

Danzig until his death in 1860. The work, which quotes the author's son R. Baruch Isaac as well as R. Akiva Eger and the Vilna Gaon, is now included in all comprehensive editions of the Mishnah.

TORAH TEMIMAH [6]: Collocation of Talmudic and Midrashic quotations arranged according to the Scriptural verses to which they refer and annotated by R. Baruch Halevi Epstein (1860-1942), son of the Aruch Hashulchan. Widely recognized for his scholarship, R. Epstein refused prestigious Rabbinical posts in Pinsk, Moscow, and Petrograd, preferring to work in a bank and devote all his spare time to his studies. This work became a classic in his own lifetime.

TORAT KOHANIM [2]: Tannaic exegetical Midrash which interprets the Book of *Vayikra* verse by verse. As much of *Vayikra* is concerned with sacrificial ritual, its original name *Sifra* gave way to the contemporary one meaning "Priestly Law."

TOSAFOT [5]: Literally, "additions"; these are a collection of analytical and comparative comments on the Talmud (many now printed alongside the main Talmudic text) by Rashi's pupils and their successors. Originally written as additions to Rashi's commentary, they developed over a period of some 140 years into an independent body of interpretations.

TOSAFOT YOM TOV [6]: Commentary on the Mishnah by R. Yom Tov Lipman Heller (1579-1654), written as an "addition" to the already existing commentary of R. Ovadiah of Bertinoro. His autobiography, *Megillat Eivah*, tells of his troubled life, of the death sentence (subsequently commuted) passed on him for defending the Talmud, of the decree of expulsion from Vladimir (subsequently rescinded) and of "those who hate without cause." His last years were spent as *Av Beit Din* of Krakow, where he died (as described by a contemporary) "not leaving the wherewithal to purchase shrouds, because he never took dishonest money."

TUR [5]: More fully, *Arba'ah Turim* ("four rows"—reflecting the four sections of which it consists), a Halachic compendium and the magnum opus of R. Yaakov, son of the Rosh. Ordered by topic, it covers only laws relevant to the exile period and forms the basis of R. Yosef Karo's *Shulchan Aruch*. R. Yaakov fled Germany together with his father, living first in Barcelona and subsequently in Toledo, where his father and later his younger brother, who was to become his son-in-law, served as Rabbis. He himself accepted a position on the Beit Din, but preferred writing to the responsibilities of the Rabbinate.

TZADOK [2]: Pupil of Antigonus of Socho (c. 240 B.C.E.). Misunderstanding his teacher's maxims, he denied the Rabbinical tradition and formed an opposition sect known by his name—*Tzadokim* (Sadduees), a sect succeeded by the later Karaites.

TZEMACH TZEDEK [6]: Responsa of R. Menachem Mendel Krochmal. Born in Krakow c.1600, he studied together with his contemporary the Taz, under the Bach. To avoid the upheavals suffered by Polish Jewry at that time, he settled in Moravia, ultimately being appointed Rabbi of Nickolsburg and Chief Rabbi of the province, posts he held until his death in 1661.

ULLA [3]: Third-generation Eretz Yisrael *Amora* (c. 300 C.E.). He made several trips to Babylonia, reporting the views of the Eretz Yisrael scholars to the Babylonians and vice versa.

R. ELCHONON WASSERMAN [6]: (1875-1941) Eminent Rosh Yeshivah of Baranowicz, Lithuania, he was regarded as the spiritual successor to the Chafetz Chaim, emerging as one of the outstanding leaders of Orthodox Jewry. In addition to his academic activities and authorship of *Kovetz He'arot* and *Kovetz Shiurim*, he contributed extensively to the Jewish press and was an influential member of Agudat Yisrael. He was murdered by the Nazis, meeting his death with faith and nobility.

RABBI YITZCHAK WASSERMAN [6]: For ten years Rabbi in London, currently Rosh Yeshivah, Ohel Yaakov, Bnei Brak.

YAAKOV AVINU [1]: Yaakov our father, the third Patriarch, who was given the name Yisrael.

R. YAAKOV HECHASSID [5]: Flourished in Marvege, France, c. 1200. Later Authorities cite his "Responsa from Heaven," which report the Halachic answers he received in dreams. Chida, in his book of biographies, *Shem Hagedolim*, discusses the propriety of this method of arriving at the Halachah, in his essay on the author.

YAD HACHAZAKAH: See RAMBAM.

YADAV SHEL MOSHE: See R. MOSHE FRESCO OF SALONIKA.

YAM SHEL SHLOMO: See MAHARSHAL.

YECHEZKEL [1]: Ezekiel, one of the later prophets, whose prophecy spanned the destruction of the First Temple. His prophecies, which are reported in the Scriptural book of Yechezkel, are at times extremely vivid and at others obscure. He prophesied the resurrection of the nation with the famous vision of "the dry bones." Yechezkel died and was buried in Babylonia (Iraq), where his tomb is a destination of pilgrims.

YEHOSHAFAT [1]: Jehoshafat, King of Judea (reigned c. 870-846 B.C.E.). Mentioned in *Tanach* in both books of *Melachim* and in the second book of *Divrei Hayamim*.

YEHOSHUA [1]: Joshua, disciple and successor of Moses, he led the Israelites from the wilderness into Canaan, conquering and dividing the Land as reported in the Scriptural book which bears his name.

R. YEHOSHUA (b. CHANANIAH) [2]: second-generation *Tanna* (prominent c. 100-80 B.C.E.), who, together with the Nasi Rabban Gamliel II and R. Eliezer b. Hurkanos, was an acknowledged leader of the generation following the *Churban*, during which the Sanhedrin was finally established in Yavneh. Popular with the Emperor and Senators of Rome, he acted as a spokesman for the conquered Jewish nation.

R. YEHUDAH [2]: Normally "R. Yehudah" in the Mishnah refers to R. Yehudah b. Ilai, the disciple of R. Akiva. He was one of the fourth generation of *Tannaim* active during the difficult years following the Roman conquest.

R. YEHUDAH [3]: Normally "R. Yehudah" in the Gemara is identified as R. Yehudah b. Yechezkel. Born in Babylonia on the day Rabi died in Eretz Yisrael, he became an outstanding disciple of both Rav and Shmuel. R. Yehudah reestablished the dispersed Yeshivah of Neharde'a in Pumbedita in the year 257 C.E. and headed it until his death in 299, during which time it was regarded as the major academy of the Jewish world.

R. YEHUDAH b. BETEIRA [2]: There were in fact two Babylonian *Tannaim* of this name, one belonging to the first generation active before the destruction of the Second Temple and the other of the third generation (prominent c. 110-135 C.E.). Both headed distinguished Yeshivahs in Netzivim, Babylonia, which, having a well-developed community outside the jurisdiction of Rome, provided a haven for a number of persecuted Eretz Yisrael *Tannaim*.

R. YEHUDAH HANASI [2]: Undisputed leader of the fifth and final generation of *Tannaim* (prominent c. 170-200 C.E.). Venerated by his coreligionists and esteemed by the occupying Roman authorities, he was able to gather around him the most accomplished scholars of his time, and with their help redacted the vast accumulation of Oral Law into the concise, but comprehensive, order of *Mishnayot* which forms the basis of the Talmud—both Jerusalem and Babylonian. The title by which he is normally known—Rabi—signifies his unique role, as the "Teacher" of Israel, in preserving the Oral Law for posterity.

R. YEMAR b. SHELEMIAH [3]: Sixth-generation Babylonian *Amora* (c. 380-440 C.E.), colleague of R. Ashi and his successor as head of the academy at Sura.

YESHAYAHU [1]: Isaiah, the author of the Scriptural book of prophecy which bears his name. He was active c. 740-700 B.C.E. in the declining years of the first Judean Kingdom. Father-in-law of King Hezekiah, he was the grandfather of King Menashe who ultimately had him murdered.

YIRMEYAHU HANAVI [1]: Jeremiah the Prophet, active before and after the destruction of the First Temple, whose prophecies are the subject of the Scriptural book bearing his name. He suffered at the hands of those who mocked his rebukes, and when, sadly, his prophecies were fulfilled and he saw the ruins of Jerusalem he wrote his *Eichah*, now part of the Hagiographa.

R. YISHMAEL (b. ELISHA I) [2]: Served as one of the last High Priests before the Roman destruction of the Temple (70 C.E.). A *Tanna* of the first generation which succeeded Hillel and Shammai, the last of the *Zugot*, he shared a martyr's death with his friend and colleague Rabban Shimon b. Gamliel at the hands of the Romans, his own being contrived in a particularly cruel and capricious manner.

R. YISHMAEL (b. ELISHA II) [2]: Third-generation *Tanna*, grandson of the High Priest of the same name. A prisoner in Rome in his childhood, he was ransomed by R. Yehoshua and became one of the eminent *Tannaim* of the Usha, and subsequently Yavneh, periods. He compiled the *Mechilta* and the famous *Baraita* bearing his name which enumerates thirteen hermeneutical principles.

R. YISHMAEL (b. R. YOCHANAN b. BEROKA) **[2]:** A fourth-generation *Tanna* (prominent c. 135-170 C.E.). A student during the Yavneh period, he became an eminent member of the Sanhedrin during its second Usha period.

YITRO [1]: Jethro, biblical figure (Exodus); father-in-law of Moses. A priest of Midian who came to recognize the One God, he is credited by Scripture with the systematic organization of jurisprudence in the Wilderness.

R. YITZCHAK [3]: Numerous scholars of this name are mentioned in the Talmud, usually identified by the names of their fathers. Normally the *Amora* quoted merely as "R. Yitzchak" is identified as R. Yitzchak b. Acha. He was a third-generation Eretz Yisrael *Amora* who also spent time in Babylonia.

R. YITZCHAK (5): Tosafist normally quoted as "Ri." A nephew of Rabbenu Tam and Rashbam, his full name was R. Yitzchak b. Shmuel of Dampierre, and apart from Rabbenu Tam is the scholar most quoted in *Tosafot*.

R. YOCHANAN [3]: Leading Eretz Yisrael *Amora* of the second generation and head of the Yeshivah in Tiberias from 228-288 C.E., during which time it became recognized as the central Yeshivah for the communities of both Eretz Yisrael and Babylonia. Together with his brother-in-law and colleague R. Shimon b. Lakish, he laid the foundation for the Jerusalem Talmud, which was redacted in its final form some sixty years after his death.

R. YOCHANAN b. GUDGADA [2]: Second-generation *Tanna*. A Levite, he was among those responsible for the Gates of the Temple.

RABBI YOEL SIRKES: See BACH.

R. YONAH GERONDI [5]: Halachist and moralist; born in Gerona c. 1180. One of the most active critics of Rambam's philosophical works, he later relented and set out to travel to Rambam's tomb in Tiberias with the object of asking for forgiveness. En route he stopped in Barcelona for three years, lecturing to the scholars of that city among whom was Rashba. Setting out from Barcelona to continue his journey, he was detained by the community of Toledo which asked him to stay and give it Talmudic instruction. He never completed his pilgrimage, dying suddenly in Toledo in 1263.

· **R. YOSEF (FIEMER) OF SLUTZK [6]:** Born in Sokod, Lithuania, 1796, he was for a short period Rabbi of Zamutis, where among his pupils was R. Yisrael Lipkin (known as R. Yisrael Salanter). At the age of 33 he was appointed to the prestigious post of Rabbi of Slutzk, which he held until his death in 1864.

R. YOSEF b. RAVA [3]: Fifth-generation Babylonian *Amora*, son of Rava who was head of the academy at Mechuza.

R. YOSEI b. CHALAFTA [2]: Fourth-generation *Tanna*, disciple of R. Akiva and colleague of R. Meir. Head of the Yeshivah in Sepphoris, he witnessed the martyrdom of mentors, colleagues, and students. It may have been these experiences which moved him to write the historical *Baraita, Seder Olam.*

R. YOSEI b. CHANINA [3]: Second-generation Eretz Yisrael *Amora*, one of the earliest disciples of R. Yochanan. Not only a renowned Halachist, he was also a popular preacher.

R. YOSEI HAGELILI [2]: Galilean *Tanna* of the third generation. He remained in Galilee during the Roman persecution of Judea, thereby escaping the worst of the terror. However, once the Sanhedrin was established in Yavneh, he joined his colleagues there to become an important member of it.

ZECHARIAH [1]: One of the last of the prophets (c.520 B.C.E.), author of the Scriptural book which bears his name.

R. SHMUEL YOSEF ZEVIN [6]: Born in Belorussia in 1890, he held several Rabbinical posts in Russia before emigrating to Eretz Yisrael in 1934. A lucid writer with an original style, his works, among which is the contemporary classic *Hamo'adim B'Halachah*, are immensely popular. As editor of the *Encyclopedia Talmudit from its foundation in 1942 until his death in 1978, he set its pattern of concise and informed treatment of complex Talmudic literature.*

ZICHRON YEHUDAH [5]: Ninety responsa of R. Yehudah b. Harosh, younger brother and son-in-law of the Tur. Born in Cologne in 1270, he fled with his father to Spain to escape the horrors of the Crusades. In 1321 his father appointed him to be his deputy as Rabbi of Toledo, to which post he succeeded on his father's death in 1327, becoming recognized by the Government as Chief Rabbi of Castille. His Beit Din carried great authority, being able to inflict both capital and corporal punishment. R. Yehudah died in 1349.

R. ZUTRA b. TOVIAH [3]: Second-generation Babylonian *Amora*, disciple of Rav.

Glossary

Aramaic words are indicated by (A.).

ACHARONIM: the Latter Authorities, those scholars who have flourished since the sixteenth century.

ADAR: the Hebrew month corresponding to February-March; in a leap year, an additional month is added, making an Adar I and an Adar II.

AGGADAH: homiletic passages in Rabbinic literature; Jewish legends and folk tales.

AGUNAH: a wife whose husband has deserted her or disappeared, without divorcing her, making it impossible for her to remarry.

AMALEK: a Biblical nation descended from Esau; the first to attack the fledgling nation of Israel, and its most implacable enemy.

AMIDAH: the thrice-daily silent prayer, recited standing. On a weekday it consists of nineteen (originally eighteen) benedictions, thirteen of which are supplications.

AMMON: a Biblical nation descended from Lot, nephew of the Patriarch Abraham. No longer identifiable.

AMORA (AMORAIM): (A.) the Sages whose opinions comprise the GEMARA.

ARACHIN: lit., values; the Talmudic tractate which deals with valuations and other matters concerning consecrated persons and property.

ASHKENAZI: of European origin, guided by or based on the original German tradition.

ASMACHTA: (A.) lit., support or backing; a Scriptural word or phrase relied upon by the Rabbis to support their legislation; promises of intent which are not legally binding.

AV BEIT DIN: the Chief Justice, or presiding judge, second to the Nasi.

AVODAH: worship or service; labor. The *Avodah* refers to the Temple service and ritual.

AVODAH ZARAH: idol worship; the Talmudic tractate which in the main deals with this subject.

BAR METZRA: (A.) a neighbor who has the right of preemption.

BARAITA: (A.) a Tannaic compilation, normally expanding on subjects dealt with in the MISHNAH, to which it is secondary.

BAT KOL: a Heavenly Voice, regarded as a lower grade of prophecy.

BAVA BATRA: (A.) lit., final gate; the third tractate of the Order of NEZIKIN.

BAVA KAMA: (A.) lit., first gate; the first tractate of the Order of NEZIKIN.

BAVA METZIA: (A.) lit., middle gate; the second tractate of the Order of NEZIKIN.

BECHOROT: lit., firstborn (pl.); firstborn male sons are to be "redeemed" and appropriate animals to be sacrificed; the Talmudic Tractate which in the main deals with this subject.

BEIN HAZEMANIM: a semester break.

BEIT DIN (BATTEI DIN): Jewish Courts of Law.

BEIT HAMIDRASH (BATTEI MIDRASHIM): house(s) of study.

BEIT HILLEL: the School of Hillel.

BEIT SHAMMAI: the School of Shammai.

BEMIDBAR: the fourth of the Five Books of the Pentateuch.

BEN: son (of).

BERACHOT: benedictions; the Talmudic Tractate which deals in the main with that subject.

BERESHIT: Genesis, the first of the Five Books of the Pentateuch.

BIKKURIM: the first fully developed fruits (of the Seven Species) of each year, which were taken to Jerusalem and given to the KOHANIM as an offering.

BINYAN AV: a basic law used as a precedent.

CHALIFIN: lit., an exchange; an act of transfer by way of a nominal exchange.

CHALITZAH: the ceremony by which one releases his deceased childless brother's widow from all matrimonial obligation to her late husband's family.

CHAMETZ: leavened foods that are prohibited on PESACH.

CHATZER: a courtyard.

CHAZAKAH: status; presumption; possession (of land).

CHAZAL: a Hebrew acronym for "Our Sages of Blessed Memory."

CHEZKAT MAMON: the status or presumption of possession.

CHOSHEN MISHPAT: the title of the fourth part of the TUR and SHULCHAN ARUCH, which deals with Civil and Mercantile Law.

CHULLIN: lit., unconsecrated; the Talmudic tractate which deals, in the main, with the laws surrounding the eating of meat, including the laws of SHECHITAH.

CHUMASH: the Pentateuch.

DA'AT: knowledge, intention or consent.

DAVAR SHEBAMAMON: a monetary matter.

DAVAR SHELO BA LE'OLAM: something not yet in existence, although anticipated, e.g. next year's crop.

DAYAN: a judge.

DERASHAH: a discourse.

DEVARIM: Deuteronomy, the last of the Five Books of the Pentateuch.

DIN TORAH: lit., Torah law; a dispute judged by a Rabbinical court in accordance with the HALACHAH.

DINA D'GARMI: (A.) laws of indirect or consequential damages.

DINA DEMALCHUTA: (A.) The principle that State Laws are laws.

DIVREI HAYAMIM: Chronicles, part of the Hagiographa; a Scriptural history from Creation through the Babylonian exile, written by Ezra the Scribe.

EFAH and HIN: ancient measures.

EDUYOT: lit., testimonies; the tractate of the MISHNAH which quotes Tannaic testimony as to the ultimate ruling on a number of unrelated matters.

ERETZ YISRAEL: the Land of Israel.

ERUV CHATZEROT: a Halachic arrangement for Sabbath observance whereby a symbolic uniting of separate households enables items to be carried from one household to the other; and to and from, as well as through, a common courtyard.

ERUV TAVSHILIN: a Halachic arrangement when a Festival falls on the eve of the Sabbath, in which some food is set aside before the Festival, to be eaten on the Sabbath, thereby enabling preparations of food on the Festival for the Sabbath.

ERUV TECHUMIM: a Halachic arrangement whereby some food is set down, before Shabbat or a Festival, thus establishing a Halachic dwelling from which are measured the boundaries within which one is permitted to move about.

ERUVIN: the Talmudic tractate which deals with ERUV CHATZ-EROT and ERUV TECHUMIM.

EVEN HA'EZER: the title of the third part of the TUR and SHULCHAN ARUCH, which deals with marriage, divorce and related topics.

EXILARCH: (resh galuta [A.]) the political leader of the Jewish People in Babylonia during and after the first Exile.

GAON (GEONIM): genius(es); title of the head of Babylonian yeshivahs.

GEMIRAT HADA'AT: firm resolve; finality of intention.

GEMARA: (A.) a commentary on the MISHNAH (together they comprise the Talmud).

GET: a Halachic bill of divorce.

GEZERAH: a decree, religious, political or social.

GEZERAH SHAVAH: an analogy of syllogism, one of the hermeneutical principles.

GITTIN: (A.) the Talmudic tractate which deals in the main with divorce and related topics.

HALACHAH: lit., the way; the Law as finally decided; the legal parts of Jewish traditional literature.

HALACHAH LEMOSHE MISINAI: those laws given to Moses on Mt. Sinai, which have no source in Scripture.

HEFKER: ownerless or unclaimed property; denotes lawlessness and licentiousness.

HEKDESH: property consecrated for sacrifice or other Temple use.

HETER ISKA: (A.) a legal method of avoiding the prohibition of interest.

HORAYOT: lit., rulings; the Talmudic tractate which deals with erroneous decisions.

KALLAH MONTHS: the two months (Elul and Adar) during which a large assembly of scholars gathered at the great Yeshivahs of Babylonia to hear Torah lectures from the ROSHEI YESHIVOT.

KELIM: lit., vessels; the Tractate which deals with the TUMAH of vessels and their possible purification.

KERITOT: lit., cut off; Divine punishment by premature death, often coupled with exclusion from the afterlife; the Talmudic tractate which deals in the main with the sacrificial atonement demanded of an accidental transgressor.

KETUBAH (KETUBOT): statutory marriage contract which every husband must give his bride; the Talmudic tractate which deals with this and related topics.

KIDDUSHIN: the act of betrothal; the Talmudic tractate which deals with this and related topics.

KINYAN: a formal act of acquisition.

KINYAN CHATZER: a formal act of acquisition by means of one's personal domain.

KLAL UPRAT: a hermeneutic principle, *klal* being a generalization and *prat* a detailed specification.

KOHEN (KOHANIM): member(s) of the priestly caste, descended from Aaron, the first High Priest.

KAM LEIH BIDERABBAH MINEIH: (A.) the major (penalty) is sufficient, a Jewish legal maxim.

KORBAN PESACH: the animal sacrificially slaughtered on the eve of PESACH and eaten roasted after nightfall.

KORBAN TAMID: the twice daily (morning and afternoon) burnt offering paid for out of communal funds.

LULAV: a palm branch, one of the Four Species taken on the Festival of SUKKOT; it is bound with two others—the myrtle and the willow branches—while the fourth, the *etrog*, is held independently.

MA'AMAD SHLOSHTAN: lit., "in the presence of the three of them"; a Rabbinical method of transferring a debt from one creditor to another, which can only be employed when the debtor, the original creditor, and the subsequent creditor are all present together.

MA'ASEH: an act, action or occurrence.

MAKKOT: lit., blows; corporal punishment; the Talmudic tractate which deals, among other things, with this subject.

MATZAH: unleavened bread.

MEGILLAH: a scroll; the Talmudic tractate which concentrates on the reading of the Scroll of Esther on PURIM.

MENACHOT: lit., offerings; the Talmudic tractate which deals with the laws and rituals of the meal offering.

MASECHTA: (A.) tractate.

MESHICHAH: lit., drawing; an act of acquisition by drawing the article concerned into one's possession.

MEYA'ESH: one who despairs; one who abandons hope for the return of a lost or stolen object.

MIDIVREI SOFRIM: from the words of the Scribes or Scholars.

MI-D'ORAITA: (A.) from the Torah; a Scriptural precept, as opposed to a Rabbinic one.

MI-D'RABBANAN: (A.) from an enactment of the Sages; a Rabbinic precept.

MIDRASH: a collection of non-literal interpretations and homiletic teachings of the Sages.

MIGGO: (A.) lit., "From the content of"; an indication that a statement is true because, had the litigant been prepared to make an untrue statement, there is a stronger one available to him without fear of contradiction.

MIKVEH: a ritual bath.

MINCHAH: the afternoon prayer service; the meal offering in the Temple.

MINHAG: custom, both social and ritual.

MITASEK: preoccupied; intending to do one thing (e.g., to pick up already cut flowers) and unintentionally doing another (e.g., picking still growing flowers).

MISHNAH (MISHNAYOT): an orderly redaction and summary by R. Yehudah Hanasi of the accumulated Oral Law, which forms the basis of the Talmud.

MITZVAH (MITZVOT): Divine precept(s); used colloquially to mean "good deed(s)."

MOAB: the Biblical nation descended from Lot, the nephew of the Patriarch Abraham. No longer identifiable.

MASHIACH: lit., the anointed one; the Messiah.

MUKTZEH: lit., set aside; that which may not be used or handled on the Sabbath or Festivals, although its use does not constitute prohibited work.

MUSAF: additional offerings in the Temple on Holy Days. Today the word signifies the additional prayers recited on those days.

NASI: President (of the SANHEDRIN).

NEDARIM: oaths, whereby a person obligates himself in some way; the Talmudic tractate which concentrates on this subject.

NEVELAH: the flesh of an animal not ritually slaughtered.

NEZIKIN: lit., damages; the Talmudic order of tractates which in the main deals with Jewish Civil Law.

OMER: a dry measure, particularly that of the offering of barley on the 16th of Nissan, before which the new crops of that year are forbidden; also, the 49 days which are counted between PESACH and SHAVUOT.

ONA'AH fraud; deceit.

ORACH CHAIM: the title of the first part of the TUR and SHULCHAN ARUCH, which deals with daily ritual including the Sabbath and Festivals.

ORLAH: lit., uncircumcised; not ready. The concept is applied to newly planted trees, the fruits of which are entirely prohibited for a period of three years. The name of the Talmudic Tractate concentrating on this subject.

PARAH ADUMAH: a red heifer, whose ashes can purify those who have become Levitically Unclean.

PESACH: the Festival of Passover.

PIGUL: lit., abhorred; a sacrificial offering rendered unfit as a result of the officiant's intention, e.g., that it be eaten at an improper time.

PIRKEI AVOT: *Chapters of the Fathers,* a Talmudic tractate which deals with ethics and moral behavior.

PROZBOL: a legal innovation of Hillel, whereby registration of a loan in court exempts it from automatic cancellation during the Sabbatical year.

PURIM: a minor Festival which commemorates the salvation of the Jewish people as reported in the Book of Esther.

RABBAN: (A.) our teacher.

RABBENU: our teacher.

RABBANAN SAVORAI: (A.) the generation of Scholars who flourished immediately after the closing of the Babylonian Talmud.

RISHONIM: the Early Authorities, those scholars who flourished between the eleventh and sixteenth centuries.

ROSH HASHANAH: the New Year; the Talmudic tractate which deals in the main with this subject and the related subject of the new moon.

ROSH YESHIVAH (ROSHEI YESHIVAH OR YESHIVOT): the principal of a Talmudic Academy.

ROV: a majority.

SIFRA: (A.) Tannaic compilation of BARAITOT, based on VAYIKRA.

SANHEDRIN: the highest court in Israel; the Talmudic tractate dealing with the demonstration of justice and penology.

SEMICHAH: (1) Rabbinical ordination; (2) the laying on of hands on a sacrificial animal.

SEMICHUT HADA'AT: confident reliance that the partner in a transaction will adhere to the bargain.

SEPHARADI: of Spanish origin or tradition.

SEVARAH: logic; reasoning.

SHA'ATNEZ: a garment which contains a mixture of wool and linen, the wearing of which is prohibited by the Torah.

SHAVUOT: the festival celebrated seven weeks after PESACH which commemorates the giving of the Torah at Mount Sinai.

SHECHITAH: ritual slaughter.

SHEMA: "Hear O Israel..." (*Devarim* 6:5), the opening words of the fundamental Jewish prayer which proclaims the Unity of God.

SHEMITTAH: the seventh, Sabbatical, year, during which there are prohibitions on agricultural work in Israel, and there is a remission of debts.

SHEMOT: the second of the Five Books of the Pentateuch.

SHEVI'IT: lit., seventh; another name for SHEMITTAH; the Talmudic tractate which deals with this subject.

SHEVUAH (SHEVUOT): oath(s) made in support of a statement, or prohibiting or mandating a course of action; the name of the Talmudic tractate which discusses these oaths.

SHEYIBADEL L'CHAIM: an expression when mentioning a living person together with the dead, meaning "may he be set apart (from the dead person mentioned), for life"

SHOCHET: a ritual slaughterer.

SHALIACH TZIBBUR: lit., a representative of the congregation; the cantor, who leads the congregation in prayer.

SHEMOT: Exodus, the second of the Five Books of the Pentateuch.

SHIUR(-IM): lecture(s) on a Torah topic.

SHOMER: a guardian, bailee, or keeper. There are four types in Jewish Law: unpaid, paid, hirer (who pays for the use) and borrower.

SHULCHAN ARUCH: lit., prepared table; Code of Law.

SIDDUR: the prayer book, which contains the prayers in a proper order.

SIFREI: a Tannaic compilation of BARAITOT, based on the Biblical books of Numbers and Deuteronomy.

SINAI: the mountain in the wilderness upon which God gave the Torah to Moses.

SOTAH: a wife suspected or convicted of infidelity; the Talmudic tractate which deals with the laws and ritual concerning a *sotah*.

SUKKAH: lit., booth; the ritual booth which is dwelt in during the Festival of SUKKOT; the Talmudic tractate which deals with both the laws of the Sukkah and the ritual of the Festival.

SUKKOT: the Festival of Tabernacles.

TAKKANAH: a regulation; a remedy.

TAKKANOT HASHAVIM: a remedy for assisting penitents.

TANACH: Hebrew acronym for *Torah* (Pentateuch), *Nevi'im* (Prophets) and *Ketuvim* (Hagiographa).

TANNA (TANNAIM): (A.) scholars of the Mishnah and earlier periods, often mentioned in MISHNAYOT and BARAITOT.

TEFILLIN: phylacteries; worn on the forehead and on the (left) arm each day (except Sabbaths and Festivals), during morning prayer, they contain Scriptural verses basic to faith and submission to God's will.

TEREFAH: lit., a torn animal; the word is commonly used to denote any non-kosher food.

TERUMAH: the first levy on the annual harvest, to be given to a KOHEN.

TORAH SHEBE'AL PEH: the Oral Law.

TORAH SHEBICHTAV: the Written Law.

TORAT KOHANIM: the Biblical book of Leviticus and related Tannaic BARAITOT.

TOSEFTA: (A.) a Tannaic compilation similar to the BARAITA, which supports and expands the MISHNAH.

TUMAH: the state of ritual impurity as defined in the Book of Leviticus, caused by contact with death, impure objects and creatures or by bodily emission.

VAYIKRA: the third of the Five Books of the Pentateuch.

YAVAM: one whose brother has died childless, and who is thereby legally obliged to marry the widow. If, however, he does not wish to do so he must release her by the ceremony of CHALITZAH, before a Beit Din. Currently CHALITZAH is considered preferable.

YECHEZKEL: the Scriptural Book of Ezekiel.

YEHOSHUA: the Scriptural Book of Joshua.

YESHIVAH: a Talmudical academy.

YEVAMOT: a Talmudic tractate dealing with widowhood, levirate marriage, and related topics (see YAVAM).

YOM KIPPUR: the Day of Atonement.

YOMA: (A.) lit., the day; a Talmudic tractate dealing with the laws and ritual of Yom Kippur.

YOREH DE'AH: the title of the second part of the *Arb'ah Turim* and SHULCHAN ARUCH, it deals in the main with objects and actions which are prohibited.

ZAKEN MAMRE: a "rebellious scholar," defying the Great Sanhedrin and ruling against the majority, instructing people to follow his ruling.

TZADOKIM: the Sadducees, followers of Tzadok (third century B.C.E.), who denied the authenticity of the Oral Law.

ZEVACHIM: a Talmudic tractate which deals in the main with the Temple ritual involved in animal sacrifices.

ZUGOT: pairs; for five generations (beginning about 150 years after the rebuilding of the Second Temple) the Spiritual leadership of Israel was shared by the NASI and the AV BEIT DIN.

ZUZIM: medium-denomination coins in Talmudic times.

Index

Page number followed by "n" refers to footnote on that page.